LITERACY AT THE CROSSROADS

CROSSROADS

Crucial Talk About Reading,
Writing, and Other Teaching Dilemmas

REGIE ROUTMAN

HEINEMANN
PORTSMOUTH, NH

Heinemann

A Division of Reed Elsevier Inc.

361 Hanover Street

Portsmouth, NH 03801-3912

Offices and agents throughout the world

The author and publisher thank those who generously gave permission to reprint borrowed material.

The views of Anne P. Sweet, expressed on pages 103–4, do not necessarily represent the views of the U. S. Department of Education.

Library of Congress Cataloging-in-Publication Data

Routman, Regie

    Literacy at the crossroads : crucial talk about reading, writing, and other teaching dilemmas / Regie Routman.

       p.   cm.

    Includes bibliographical references and index.

    ISBN 0-435-07210-2

    1. Language arts--United States. 2. Politics and education--United States. 3. Literacy--United States. 4. Reading--United States. 5. English language--Composition and exercises--Study and teaching--United States.   I. Title.

LB1576.R758 1996

302.2'044--dc20   96-12254

                                              CIP

Editor: Toby Gordon

Copy Editor: Alan Huisman

Production: Renée Le Verrier and Melissa L. Inglis

Cover design: Jenny Jensen Greenleaf and Michael Leary

Cover image by Tony King

Manufacturing: Louise Richardson

Printed in the United States of America on acid-free paper

99 98 97   RRD   4 5 6 7 8 9

Contents

A Note About Notes *ix*
Dedication *x*
Acknowledgments *xi*
Introduction: A Teacher Speaks Out *xv*

PART I

Dealing with the Politics of Education

1 *Understanding the Backlash:* What's Going on in Reading and Writing? *3*

School Bashing: Do We Deserve the "Hits"? 3

Are Kids Poorer Readers Today? 4

Raising Our Goals for Teaching Reading 5

Are Kids Poorer Spellers Today? 6

The Controversy Over Phonics and Whole Language 8

Messages Parents Receive 9

Media Hype 10

Television's Prescriptive Point of View 11

Learning to Deal with the Media 13

What We Can Do to Get Our Messages Out 15

Final Perspectives 16

2 *Lessons and Legacies from the Nineties:* Learning from California and Other Places 18

    California: Complex Issues Without Simple Solutions 18

    Looking at the Big Picture 20

    Lessons from California 22

    Alief, Texas: Educators and Parents Learning to Work Together 23

    Lessons from Alief 25

    Littleton, Colorado: A Conflict in Values and Beliefs 25

    Lessons from Littleton 27

    Fairfax County, Virginia: Innovation with Community Support 30

    Successful Practices 31

    Final Perspectives 33

3 *Whole Language:* Rhetoric and Realities 35

    Whole Language Hasn't Failed: We Have Failed Whole Language 35

    What's Gone Wrong? Misinterpreting Whole Language 36

    I'm Whole Language—I Don't Teach Phonics 37

    Whole Language Teaching Requires More Support and Time to Evolve 38

    Making Parents Part of the Process 40

    What Does Whole Language Really Mean? 41

    Defining Whole Language 41

    Beliefs About Whole Language 42

    Some Misconceptions of Whole Language 42

    Some Key Principles and Practices of Whole Language 45

    Whole Language at the University: An Excellent Model in Practice 49

    Dissenting Voices in the Ranks 51

Reading Recovery Does Fit Under the Whole Language Umbrella 52

It's Not Necessary to Have Total Agreement to Have Unity 53

4 **Becoming Political in Our Schools:** *The Need to Be Articulate, Astute, and Active* 54

The Politics of Change 54

The Only One Who Welcomes Change Is a Wet Baby 54

A Genuine Committee Process: Not Business as Usual 55

Creating Ownership for Teachers 56

It Is Possible to Be Too Democratic 57

Forging a New Vision for the Language Arts 57

In-House Resistance 58

Perspectives from Our Committee Process 59

Lessons from Our Process of Change 61

Necessary Partnerships 62

What We Can Do to Foster Parent Support 64

Final Perspectives 72

PART II

Back to Basics and Other Teaching Dilemmas

5 **Back to Basics:** *What Does It Mean?* 77

Those Were the Good Old Days 77

Using Real Books and Paper and Pencil 79

Reviewing the Language-Learning Research of the Seventies 80

Understanding Language Learning by Looking at Ourselves 81

What We Can Do to Provide Good, Solid Reading Instruction 82

What We Can Do to Provide Good, Solid Writing Instruction 86

Reenvisioning "Back to Basics" 88

6 *Phonics Phobia* **91**

    Beyond "Sounding It Out" **91**

    What Does the Research Say About Phonics? **92**

    Commonsense Views About Phonics **93**

    The Push for Intensive Systematic Phonics: Why and How? **96**

    A Workshop in Intensive Systematic Phonics 96

    *A Few Disabled Readers Benefit from Intensive
      Systematic Phonics 99*

    What We Can Do to Keep Phonics in Perspective **100**

    Final Perspectives **103**

7 *Spelling, Grammar, Handwriting, and
Other "Questionable" Practices* **105**

    Teaching the Skills **105**

    We Need to Do More Teaching 107

    Sometimes, It's Okay to Tell Them 107

    What's Happened to the Teaching of Spelling? **109**

    Putting Invented Spelling in Perspective 109

    So, How Should I Teach Spelling? **111**

    What We Can Do to Communicate How We Teach Spelling 117

    Where Does Grammar Fit In? **119**

    What We Can Do About Grammar 120

    We Still Need to Teach and Value Handwriting **121**

    What We Can Do About Handwriting 122

8 *Other Dilemmas* **124**

    Using a Published Series: Pros and Cons **124**

    The Good News 125

    The Not-So-Good News 125

    What We Can Do About Basals 126

We Must Preserve Our Libraries 127

What We Can Do to Promote Quality Libraries 128

Teacher Education: Not Just the Job of the University 130

We Need to Encourage Smart Students to Become Teachers 131

New Teachers Need Lots of Support 132

How One School District Supported a New Teacher 134

More Help for Novice Teachers: What We Can Do 137

Changing Demographics 138

What Do Changing Demographics Mean for Us as Teachers? 139

Standardized Testing and How to Deal with It 140

Putting Standardized Testing in Perspective for Parents 142

Still More Dilemmas 143

PART III

Empowerment for Life

9 *What Happens When We Empower Students and Teachers* 147

Choice with Intention 148

Seeing Evaluation Through a New Lens 149

Moving to Student-Led Conferences 153

Students Writing Their Own Narrative Report Cards 159

What Makes a Good Teacher? 163

10 *Leading the Literacy Life We Want Our Students to Lead* 166

Inquiry and Change: Become a Teacher-Researcher 167

Cultivate Your Interests 169

Take Charge of Your Own Professional Development and Learning 171

*Make Time for Professional and Personal
Reading and Reflection 172*

Be More Collegial 173

Share Knowledge and Materials 175

Collaborate as Learners: Start a Support Group 176

Using Our Literate Selves as Models for Teaching 177

Looking at Ourselves as Readers to Inform Our Teaching 177

Envisioning Ourselves as Writers 182

Why We Must Write 183

Enter the Public Debate 184

Make Time for Reflection, Writing, and Action 184

APPENDICES *186*

  **Appendix A: On Grammar Exercises to Teach
  Speaking and Writing 187**

  Appendix B: Encourage Independent Reading at Home 188

  **Appendix C: Discourage Heavy Use of Television
  and Electronic Media 189**

  Appendix D: Blank Weekly Review 190

  Appendix E: Weekly Review 192

  Appendix F: FACTS: On the Teaching of Phonics 194

  **Appendix G: Reading Strategies for Unknown Words
  Beyond "Sound It Out" 198**

  Appendix H: FACTS: On Teaching Skills in Context 199

  Appendix I: Explanation of Spelling Program 203

NOTES *204*

INDEX *216*

A Note About Notes

In order to keep the text clean and unencumbered, which seems important in a passionate argument like this, I've used neither numbered footnotes/endnotes nor parenthetical author-date citations.

However, at the end of the book is a notes section, divided by chapter and sequenced consecutively by page number. Sources and/or elaboration, including bibliographic information to help you find the referenced material easily, are presented after a brief identifying phrase or statement linked to the text.

Also, many of the people I quote made their comments to me in private conversations (face to face or on the telephone) or in personal notes and letters. Rather than stating this each time, I would like to alert you here that if a quoted statement is not otherwise acknowledged it was made in this personal context.

I hope you find this approach allows you to read more deeply and easily and still acknowledges my sources and lets you consult them yourself if you wish.

Dedication

To my colleagues
in the Shaker Heights, Ohio City School District
for their commitment to excellence,
ongoing support and friendship,
and for all I have been privileged to learn with them and from them

Acknowledgments

I am proud and privileged to have had so many voices help shape this book, and I am much in their debt. My heartfelt thanks to everyone who gave so generously of their time and knowledge.

First, this book would not exist at all were it not for the gentle persuasion of Toby Gordon, Heinemann's publisher, who suggested its urgent need and then supported me throughout the process of writing it. Toby is the best kind of editor; she trusts the author's voice but steps in when necessary with excellent suggestions. I have been and continue to be greatly enriched by her wisdom and friendship.

Others at Heinemann worked long and hard to publish this book in record time, and I am grateful to them all. Bill Varner supplied me with research articles and books and responded to my continuing queries with good humor, persistence, and timely action. Victoria Merecki, who assisted Bill, also made fine contributions. I was blessed to have Alan Huisman as my gifted copy editor. His meticulous editing, his intelligent suggestions, his praise, criticism, and great care, all contributed to a more understandable text. Melissa Inglis coordinated production and paged the book with patience, grace, and precision. Production manager Renée Le Verrier arranged for the lively cover design by Jenny Greenleaf and Michael Leary and wielded her skillful hand throughout the production process. Roberta Lew dealt deftly with permissions, and Renée Nicholls was a diligent proofreader. John Brotzman created the index with skill and intelligence. Manufacturing supervisor Louise Richardson carefully oversaw the printing of the book.

To Mike Gibbons, marketing director, I owe much. Mike worked—and continues to work—tirelessly, supporting me and orchestrating the marketing process with great care and attention to detail. His assistant Sheila Peters provided important administrative support, and Ray Coutu contributed his invaluable marketing efforts. Scott Mahler, editorial director, gave a welcome vote of confidence. Karen Hiller, Susie Stroud, Cherie Lebel, and Lori Lampert continue to make my work easier and more manageable.

Many people assisted me by finding and verifying information, supplying relevant resources and facts, responding to portions of the text, and/or supporting me with their friendship. I am grateful to Richard Abrahamson, Gwen Art, Leslie Bakkila, Patsy Bannon, Julie Beers, Barbara Berlin, Marcia Bliss, Jane Braunger, Carol Brown, Betty J. Bush, Andrea Butler, Janet Butler, Hallie Butze, George Cannon, Bonnie Chambers, Harriet Cooper, Linda Cooper, Susan Egging, Alan Farstrup, Gay Fawcett, Robyn Feinstein, Elizabeth Franklin, Yvonne Freeman, Susan Gardner, Margaret Genisio, Richard Gentry, Chris Hayward, Pat Heilbron, Jim Henry, Rebecca Kimberly, Dick Koblitz, Barbara Kohm, Karen McNally, Jeff McQuillan, Susan Mears, Carlton Moody, Becky Mulzer, Kathy O'Neal, Jim Paces, Janet Parrack, John Philbrook, Gay Su Pinnell, Sandy Redman, John Ridley, Tena Rosner, Norris Ross, Richard Routman, Joan Schaefer, Jim Servis, Karen Sher, Karen Ann Smith, Barbara Speer, Ellen Stepanian, Dorothy Strickland, Ali Sullo, Larry Svec, Anne P. Sweet, Jerry Treadway, B. J. Wagner, Carol Weinstock, Yair Weinstock, Marlo Welshons, Cathy Whitehouse, Betsy Woodring, and Danny Young.

As a writer, I depend on feedback from trusted colleagues, and I have incorporated many of their suggestions into this book. The following exemplary educators read and gave thoughtful responses to the entire text:

- Karen Anderson, exceptional first-grade teacher, read and responded with care and affirmation.
- Holly Burgess, talented and impassioned high school English teacher, read with a discerning eye and offered many valuable suggestions and perspectives. Her keen insights and her warm friendship were a sustaining force throughout the writing, and I am especially indebted to her.
- Ann Mc Callum, language arts coordinator and consultant, graciously shared her considerable expertise and experiences from a large school district. Her input and advice were invaluable.
- It continues to be a privilege to work with and learn from superior second-grade teacher and friend Loretta Martin. I applaud all she has accomplished and generously shared with me.
- Peg Rimedio's honesty extended my thinking. I admire her dedication and ability as a kindergarten teacher and teacher-researcher.

- Third-grade teacher Lee Sattelemeyer had thoughtful conversations with me in the margins of the manuscript. His comments reflected his caring friendship, generosity, and wealth of good ideas.

- Innovative fourth-grade teacher Joan Servis is a teacher and friend I hold in highest esteem. For her collegiality, intellectual curiosity, cheerleading, and common sense, I am thankful.

- Judie Thelen, university professor and dear friend, constantly strived (and continues to strive) to learn more, share everything, and respond frankly with grace and humor.

- Judy Wallis, language arts/social studies coordinator, unstintingly shared her extraordinary knowledge and her materials and took much of her valuable time to talk through some rough spots in the text.

- Rosemary Weltman, principal of a K–4 building, caused me to stretch my thinking and my vision and offered her honesty, leadership, and continuing friendship.

Other talented, respected educators read and responded to one or more chapters, and I also appreciate their thoughtful comments. Marlene Cohn applied her excellent skill as a reading teacher. Linda Cooper was insightful and supportive (she always is). Her continuing friendship and collegiality mean so much to me. Liz Crider offered me the gift of her friendship along with her kind and perceptive remarks. Jackie Douglass responded with helpful forthrightness. Mark Freeman, superintendent of schools, read parts of the book and responded with enthusiasm and pertinent comments. Karen Sher shared her thoughts with passion and much perception. Barbara Speer, teacher of children with learning disabilities, generously shared her perspectives. Bernice Stokes, director of elementary education, responded sensitively with relevant suggestions.

Special thanks to Connie Weaver for sharing her excellent literacy "Facts" and to Sandra Wilde for generously sharing research and practice related to spelling.

Several other outstanding educators gave generously of their time and expertise in lengthy interviews, either in person or by phone. For the generosity and wisdom of my friend Don Graves, I am indebted. To Don Murray, who took lots of time to talk with me and caused me to ponder and rethink, thank you. Thanks, too, to Jack Driscoll for his wise thoughts and common sense. Cile Chavez's comments broadened my horizons and greatly enriched this text. Sincere thanks to Mary Jo Lynch for her insights and information about libraries. At the Department of Education in California,

Diane Levin, Barbara Jeffus, and Dennis Parker generously shared information, responded to multiple drafts, and gave encouragement. To Lori Oczkus, who continued to send me ideas, materials, and affirmation, my warmest thanks.

Finally, I have debts of gratitude closer to home. My son Peter offered terrific support by reading and responding thoughtfully to the entire manuscript. His insightful conversations with me on paper and in person pushed me to think more deeply. For his love and clear thinking, I am always grateful. To his wife Claudine Chamberlain, who read and responded to part of an early draft with much support and enthusiasm, I am most appreciative. Loving thanks to my father, Manny Leventhal, who proudly read and commented on many chapter drafts.

Most important, in order to ensure that I had uninterrupted time to write, my husband Frank kept our home organized, clean, and peaceful and kept me nourished with home-cooked meals, lots of love, and steady encouragement. For that most wonderful gift—and for his perceptive contributions to the text as well—I am most fortunate and deeply thankful.

March 1996

Introduction

A Teacher Speaks Out

I've never thought of myself as a political person. Sure, I voted, wrote an occasional letter of protest, and spoke out for what I believed. But more often than not, I expressed my discontent or outrage privately or with friends. I relied on someone else to make the public statements. Like you, I didn't have time. I was too busy teaching and trying to have a life.

But these are different times. Today, unreasonable voices outside our profession are clamoring to tell us how and what to teach. People who have little idea how children learn to read and write are speaking out loudly, bombarding the media with simplistic "quick fixes" and loud criticism of sound educational practices. And we are letting them do it. While we have been quietly focusing on our students and our teaching and learning, forces outside our schools have been working diligently to move the clock back. The cry of "back to basics," for a return to skills-based, phonics-based teaching, threatens much of what we know about the complexities of teaching and learning. We seem to be heading down the literacy track at higher and higher speeds with a derailment guaranteed unless we can take charge of steering the course.

We teachers are not used to speaking out and being political. While some of us chose this profession because of long-held beliefs that teaching was the only job worth having, many others of us became teachers because it was safe and noncontroversial. We could be nurturers and caregivers in our classrooms, and we did not have to be "out there." We could close our doors and do "our thing." We depended on others to write the curriculum, plan staff development, allocate the budget, make policy decisions. "Just let us teach and concentrate on our students." Historically, teachers have only mobilized and spoken out when there's been the threat of a strike. Otherwise, we've been mostly silent while the media and others constantly criticize the institutions in which we teach and spread misinformation about our schools. We rarely speak up, seldom write letters of concern or protest, hesitate to write about our teaching. We've been silent partly because we've felt we didn't have the time or didn't know enough but also because we've been unaware of the political climate. And, traditionally, the public has not expected ideas or major reform to come from practicing teachers. Even in our own school districts, our ideas have not always been taken seriously. Often, when we did get involved in district committees and made suggestions, they went unheeded. Nothing changed, and we became discouraged. Indeed, some of us felt that we were not expected to come up with ideas outside the classroom.

But we can no longer keep our doors closed and be passive. We can no longer be naive or silent. We must speak out because our silence speaks volumes. Today, the political climate is against us in many places. Make no mistake. There is a backlash in education that demands our attention. We need to get smart, vocal, and politically savvy, and we need to do it now.

Organized groups outside our schools are working diligently to destroy much of what we know and believe about language learning and what we have fought hard for—more democratic classrooms, more meaning-focused approaches, students in charge of their own learning, teachers as respected decision makers and evaluators, and learning that is relevant to students' lives. The public debate about what children should learn and how they should learn it cannot be left to chance and faith in "others." We are the others. Our reasonable and knowledgeable voices must become part of the conversation.

We need to know what the critics are saying about students' literacy and our schools so we can evaluate and deal with the information. Of course, it's a given that we need to do better and keep critiquing ourselves and our schools and strive to improve. That will always be the case. But we also need to celebrate and publicize our successes, our constant striving to do our best for our students. If we don't tell our "good news," no one is going to do it for us.

Taking a Political Stand

Education is political, and it's time we teachers got political in dealing with it. It's taken me a while to figure out what that means. I believe becoming political means actively and thoughtfully entering the educational conversation in order to make a positive difference for children, their families, and ourselves.

It means having the language and the knowledge to move beyond our classrooms and schools into the wider public arena to state our case. It means carefully listening with an open mind and being responsive to the public's concerns and questions. It means knowing how and when to communicate and who to seek out for support. Getting political means using research and reason instead of emotion and extremist views. It means being professional in the highest sense, so that our voices are listened to and respected. Becoming political means honoring diversity and using conflict as an opportunity for thoughtful dialogue, not confrontation. And it means all of us as educators, not just a few brave souls, raising our voices and our pens with integrity, to make sure that what we know, value, and believe about teaching and learning and democratic principles is taken seriously and acted upon.

The idea for this book came about quickly and unexpectedly. On a late October afternoon, my editor Toby Gordon and I were having a telephone conversation about literacy. I was talking about the signs I was seeing that scared me. The widely watched television program *20/20* had just done a segment recommending "direct instruction" and slamming "whole language." The reporting seemed biased and unfair since only "direct instruction" was examined. But to an uninformed public, it sounded convincing. Some parents in our school district were already coming in and asking teachers for "more phonics."

The very next week, Ted Koppel did an hour-long *Nightline* featuring Hooked on Phonics. While the reporting was more balanced, the implication up front was clear: parents are buying this program because we're not doing our jobs. At the start of the segment, Ted Koppel stated: "A lot of our schools are not teaching a lot of our children how to read."

I found it terribly disconcerting that prime-time television, viewed by millions, was focusing on reading so one-dimensionally by presenting a phonics program as mainstream practice. I had also been reading and hearing other news reports from around the country that indicated that curriculums and teachers were under fire and that changes were already occurring because of a "backlash."

"You know, Regie," Toby suggested, "maybe you should set aside the new book for teachers and write a political book. Teachers trust your rational voice." The idea both terrified and excited me. How could I write a political book? Like many of my colleagues, I avoided confrontation, poured hours into my teaching, and hoped that "others" would speak out and take care of "the problem." But that night I had difficulty sleeping. All the things I might say to teachers about the current literacy climate went through my head, along with all my doubts about being able to say them clearly and intelligently.

Several days later, after testing the waters by talking with some educators in different parts of the country, I told Toby, "I don't know if I can do this, but I'd like to try." And so the gestation of this book began.

Literacy at the Crossroads is an attempt to bring critical issues to light, to clarify these teaching issues and dilemmas that affect all of us, and to give specific suggestions on actions we must take so that we can continue to do what's right and best for children. It is written as an act of faith, out of a belief in democratic principles and the ability of informed citizens to change practices, out of my conviction that we teachers can and must speak out. We can no longer sit on the sidelines and hope for the best.

Part I

Dealing with the Politics of Education

1

Understanding the Backlash

Are schools better or worse than in years past? Are we doing a poorer job teaching reading and writing? Yes, no, and maybe. It all depends on what research you use, what you read and how you interpret it, what your experiences have been, and who and what you decide to believe.

School Bashing: Do We Deserve the "Hits"?

Bashing our public schools is a national pastime that dates back to before the turn of the century. Whether or not the bashing springs from a public right to speak out against institutions we support or from a deep-seated dissatisfaction of past and present experiences is unclear. Because we in society pay for public schools and most of us send our children to them, schools are constantly being scrutinized. When it's perceived that things have gone wrong— and they inevitably appear to go wrong—groups and individuals look for a scapegoat rather than work together toward a solution.

Criticizing our schools remains as popular as ever. School bashing followed the space race, the cold war, and the period of social protest in the sixties and seventies. In the 1980s, the U.S. Department of Education released *A Nation at Risk*, a brutal criticism of American education. Now, in the nineties, schools are once again being attacked vehemently with a cry of "back to basics." Today, the criticism seems to focus particularly on reading and writing and how they should be taught. As usual, the public wants quick solutions to complex issues.

While no one denies that there are some terrible schools in America, this is "largely true because those schools lack resources and must contend with some of society's worst social problems." Most of us, it seems, are pretty satisfied with our local schools. In fact, the large majority of parents who send their children to public schools believe the schools are doing a pretty good job.

Nonetheless, good news about public education is rarely reported. There is hard evidence that the United States government suppressed "good news" about our public schools during the Reagan and Bush eras. *The Sandia Report,* a comprehensive study that carefully documented the performance of our public schools, contradicted the education critics by finding no system-wide failure in education. The report, which was commissioned by the U.S. government and drafted in late 1990, was suppressed until Bush, our "education president," left office. Even when the report finally circulated, few people saw it.

Bad news in education captures the public's interest and sells newspapers. People seem to be drawn to the notion of intellectual decline and things getting worse. When attention is directed away from the local level, support dwindles and criticism grows. The cover of *Business Week* on April 17, 1995, asks, "Will Our Schools Ever Get Better?" The lead paragraph of the cover story begins, "Americans are fed up with their public schools." Even Ann Landers joins the brouhaha. In answer to the question "What are they teaching in our schools these days?" (at the end of a letter decrying our citizenry's lack of general knowledge), she replies, "They are teaching drivers ed., computer science, personal hygiene and Japanese wood-block carving. Not as much readin', writin' and 'rithmetic as when I was in school."

So what are we to believe? We need to look beyond the rhetoric and the hype and carefully examine the research and our own teaching experiences. Then, as knowledgeable and responsible practitioners, we can and must add our reasonable voices to the escalating debate and criticism. And we must do more. A backlash in education doesn't change our jobs as teachers of language arts, which is to make our students the best readers, writers, and thinkers possible.

Are Kids Poorer Readers Today?

Whether or not students are viewed as poorer readers today depends a lot on how you define reading, what you measure and value, and how test scores are interpreted. Generally speaking, if we look only at the "basics"—decoding the words on a literal level—reading achievement in the United States is actually quite good. However, when we look at how well students understand and apply what they read, they need to do a lot better.

Let's take a look at some of the research and get some perspective:

- A 1995 literacy study claims, "One thing is sure: unqualified statements proclaiming that today's students are less literate than past students are flat-out wrong."
- In a study of reading achievement in thirty-two countries, the United States outscored all countries except Finland.
- Evidence from three "then and now" studies indicates that students today are reading and writing at least as well—and often better—than in the past: today's students outperform earlier students in almost all study areas; overall, scores have increased slightly on standardized achievement tests; and reading scores among thirteen- and seventeen-year-olds have continued to increase (based on the National Assessment of Educational Progress).

The National Council of Teachers of English and the International Reading Association summarize their recent findings this way: "Thus, evidence suggests that students today read better and write better than at any other time in the history of the country."

Raising Our Goals for Teaching Reading

However, when we look beyond decoding and literal comprehension to reading as a complex, thinking process, we get different results. The same data that say our students are better readers today also point to four critical instructional needs:

- more reading instruction for all students
- more difficult texts, especially for average and better readers
- more critical analysis and synthesis of information from multiple texts
- more emphasis on meaningful vocabulary throughout the grades.

Overall, the research shows that U.S. students do not do well when asked to apply knowledge. No doubt, this is because teachers and textbooks have failed to emphasize a higher level of thinking. Research indicates that for the past fifty years, we have overfocused on "asking students for simple responses to unimportant questions."

The largest national assessment of reading confirms that U.S. students are competent at literal levels and incompetent at critical and analytical levels. The federally funded National Assessment of Educational Progress (NAEP) is mandated by the U.S. Congress and reported through the U.S. Department of Education. The assessment includes 60 to 70 percent performance-based tasks and 30 to 40 percent multiple-choice items. *No state scored an average of "proficient" or better on the 1992 and 1994 NAEPs.*

In California, which has recently taken a lot of heat for its low test scores, the statewide CLAS test revealed that about 80 percent of fourth graders can decode and comprehend literally (consistent with the NAEP). These same 80 percent, however, scored below the "proficient" benchmark, meaning they cannot think and make knowledge from the information they've read. In 1994, the difference between California, the lowest-scoring state, and the highest-scoring state was only about 15 percent on the NAEP scale. Dennis Parker, administrator for the State Department of Education, clarifies the issues:

> We've "raised the bar" in reading in California and at the national level. Reading now means *reading, understanding, and thinking.* If we just get better at teaching kids *how to read* without giving at least equal attention to teaching them *how to think*, we will see few if any gains over the next five years, and the public will be more disenchanted with us than ever.

There are signs that, as a society, we are beginning to move toward a more critical literacy while redefining what it means to be literate. The new literacy requires "an active, meaning-making self," teachers that "model the roles and operations of thinkers and learners," and a collaborative work setting that provides a "network of tools" for acquiring new skills and solving problems. Traditionally, when we move to new literacy practices, old practices remain, and resistance is common. "Resistance to a form of literacy is one way to protect local and family practices from intervention and possible elimination by other literacies."

Our task is clear. Despite the public outcry that we are not teaching the basics, the irony is that we are overfocusing on discrete skills and superficial learning at the expense of not teaching our students how to interpret, evaluate, analyze, and apply knowledge for Information Age learning. As demands for literacy in our society continue to increase, we will need more students who can read, analyze, and use complex texts, including those available on computers and electronic media.

Are Kids Poorer Spellers Today?

The answer depends on what we look at and how we define spelling. Performance on standardized tests usually involves selecting the correct written spelling from a number of choices (which is a proofreading task, not spelling). In today's classrooms, where students are writing more and taking more risks, it sometimes looks as if they are poorer spellers than those of years ago, but they're probably not.

Students who are encouraged to use invented spellings write more than students in a traditional spelling program. Spelling expert Sandra Wilde reports that if you compare these two groups and look only at the percentage of words that are correct, students in a traditional group score a higher percentage. But when you compare the number of words students write, the students using invented spelling actually have more words spelled correctly because they have written so many more words altogether.

This is not surprising. Many of us who teach in the primary grades have had a new student come into our classroom who spells every word correctly. After rejoicing in what on the surface appears to be a competent speller, we quickly find out that these students will only write the words they can spell. Their writing is typically brief, lackluster, and without voice. When correctness is valued above all else in writing, we get students who write correctly but who refuse to take risks or accept challenges.

Then too, when all writing is assigned and children do not see the writing process as functional and useful, spelling suffers. I have seen spelling improve dramatically when students are writing for real purposes and audiences: spelling matters because students want their message to be understood.

However, there are classrooms where students are writing for authentic reasons and standard spelling is not valued enough or being taught well. Spelling researcher Richard Gentry, author of several books on spelling for teachers and parents, says,

> I believe kids really *are* poorer spellers today. The problem with spelling is too many teachers stopped teaching it. For many kids, expert spelling is not *caught* (from reading and writing), it must be *taught*! The proof is in the classroom.

Part of the problem is that philosophies are not articulated and agreed on across the grades. A parent in one school district who was very pleased with the way her children learned to read and gained vocabulary through a literature/whole language approach in the early grades was dissatisfied with the teaching of spelling. She says, "I was given the message of 'hands off' and told not to help my child with spelling at home, that it would interfere with creativity. Then, when my child entered the upper elementary grades and the middle school, he was marked down for spelling."

Finally, while there's no question we need to be doing a better job teaching spelling and clearly articulating our beliefs and expectations, our kids are probably not poorer spellers than they used to be. According to the NAEP, students in grades 4 and 11 show no change in the percentage of misspellings in their writing between 1984 and 1992.

> Students in grade 4 misspelled an average of 9 percent of the words they used, and even the better spellers (the 25 percent whose papers had the fewest misspellings) misspelled up to 3 percent of their words in 1992. At grade 11, students averaged only 2 percent misspellings overall, and the best spellers had essentially no spelling errors.

Not only must we become more knowledgeable about how spelling is learned and taught, we must become vocal. Otherwise, the backlash will continue. In Texas, the state legislature recently appropriated twenty-seven million dollars for published spelling series for grades 1 through 5. Going back to a prescribed spelling program greatly affects Texas's art program, because the funds for spelling texts came out of the total state art budget of sixty-five million. Opposition to the move was organized but unsuccessful.

The Controversy Over Phonics and Whole Language

I find it interesting that the people who rail against invented spelling are the very same people who want more phonics. The irony is that invented spelling relies on phonics. Children have to match and apply their sound and letter knowledge in order to compose texts. Because children's invented spellings demonstrate what they know about sound sequences, visual patterns, graphophonic relationships, and meaning, we use children's invented spellings to inform and guide our teaching of phonics. Sandra Wilde jokingly suggests we should call invented spelling "phonics-based spelling," so that parents understand what it really is.

There are those who would ordain phonics as the eleventh commandment: *Thou shalt teach phonics.* Phonics has become such a highly charged issue that much of the backlash over how reading should be taught centers strictly around phonics. Today the controversy rages over whole language and phonics, especially at the beginning reading levels. Critics of whole language proclaim phonics isn't being taught. Phonics-first advocates believe phonics teaching needs to be systematic and intense and that phonics knowledge precedes reading. Whole language advocates place phonics in the context of reading whole and predictable texts, as one of the cueing systems, along with the meaning and structure of the text, that readers use. Sorting out the rhetoric from the realities can be daunting. I attempt to do just that in Chapters 3 and 6.

We are an either-or society, pigeonholing ourselves and others into black or white positions—Republican or Democrat, moderate or liberal, pro-abortion or anti-abortion, whole language or phonics. In reality, however, our viewpoints usually do not fit so neatly into a pre-chosen label and all the label represents. Lots of people who talk against whole language pit it against phonics, as if the two were mutually exclusive. They are not, nor have they ever been. It is, however, the position on phonics—and all the misperceptions and practices about phonics—that most fuels the debate for and against whole language. *The reality is and has always been that phonics is part of whole language.*

In California, this debate has thrown the entire educational system into an uproar.

> California's 1987 English–language arts framework did *not* call for a "whole language only—no skills" language arts curriculum. (It deliberately does not even contain the words "whole language"; those who conceived the framework did not want to imply whole language at the expense of skills—unfortunately, that's the message that was heard anyway.) What the framework *did* call for was an integrated literature-based approach in which skills are taught in meaningful contexts. Yes, perhaps it deemphasized skills, but the framework certainly did not call for their abandonment.

The problem seems to lie in the skills emphasis. Who decides how much phonics and skills are enough? What should an exemplary phonics program look like?

> Specifically, current research indicates that the most effective way to teach reading is to emphasize the holistic process of reading as suggested by the whole language advocates, but also to ensure that students have a strong grounding in phonics as emphasized by the skills proponents.

Good teachers that I work with do just that, but we don't always communicate effectively enough with our parents and communities. A "strong" grounding in phonics can be interpreted and misinterpreted in many ways.

Messages Parents Receive

The message that parents receive about the primary importance of phonics in learning to read is contrary to the wide body of research that puts meaningful encounters with print in social contexts as most critical to emerging literacy. Yet parents are continually bombarded with information that puts phonics first.

When the literacy lessons presented on the highly popular and long-running *Sesame Street* were analyzed, the major emphasis was found to be on letters and their sounds. Focus on meaning, reading, and writing as part of everyday life and on the usefulness and importance of written language was sorely lacking. No wonder that parents of young children believe that phonics is the most critical element in learning to read.

Although Gateway Educational Products Ltd., the company that sells the controversial Hooked on Phonics program, recently filed for bankruptcy (no doubt because the Federal Trade Commission had insisted Gateway drop certain advertising claims), parents received and bought the message that kids learn to read through heavy phonics drills. In 1994, Hooked on Phonics sales worldwide were equal to about 130 million dollars.

Media Hype

In many cases, the news media fuel the whole language versus phonics controversy as well as misinform and excite the public. The polarization forces people to take sides and ultimately shuts down the conversation, as each side spends all its time defending its position.

Typical of the kind of distortion the media promotes is an excerpt from an article published in *USA Today*. The author claims that the whole language approach to teaching "is based on the philosophy that the best way for children to learn to read is for them to listen to reading, to read aloud and to write—not 'stunt' them with rules like punctuation and spelling. Phonics were banned." Phonics may not have been emphasized enough, but the teaching of phonics was never "banned."

Also typical is the following statement from a recent article in *The Boston Globe*:

> A major battle brews in Massachusetts between those who say that learning to read is about the acquisition of skills—being able to "decode" written language by understanding phonics—and new-thinking educators who say reading comes more naturally if young pupils are immersed in interesting materials, the whole-language approach.

A statement like this does a lot of damage. It's simplistic, a half-truth. It provides ammunition for the battle and guarantees casualties. Read on for more examples of media hype and misinformation:

- "What whole language does not teach are the skills or components of the reading process."
- "Many of the more glossy educational innovations . . . like whole language, in which students learn reading by grasping whole words rather than by sounding them out phonetically, have been subjected to withering rebukes by many parents and educators."
- "More and more schools refuse, on the basis of various political and ethical and intellectual theories, to teach writing."

Diane Levin, language arts consultant for the California Department of Education, says of the continuing misrepresentation:

> To "buy" what has been reported in the news media, one would have to believe that every teacher in California is using something called "whole language" in their classrooms and that it has failed miserably. You'd have to believe further that no one is teaching skills, like phonics or spelling. To carry this media myth further, you'd have to believe that the California Reading Task Force has demanded a "back to basic" curriculum for all language arts programs in the state. None of these beliefs reflect reality.

Since the above media statements are unsubstantiated ("Unfortunately, many school critics do not seem to care whether what they say can be backed up with data"), we need to know what the media are saying and correct the misimpressions for our parents and communities.

Television's Prescriptive Point of View

The enormous power of television adds to the controversy. In October 1995, ABC's *20/20* ran a segment on Zig Englemann and his thirty-year-old teaching approach, acknowledged to be used by only one percent of educators. The segment began with Hugh Downs saying,

> What if somebody could come up with a method of teaching children how to read that was simple and worked every time? That sounds like the impossible dream to many frustrated parents and school kids. But we found such a method, and you may be shocked to find out that most school systems refuse to try it. Why can't Johnny read? John Stossel went back to school to find out and as you'll learn, the answer may be as simple as A, B, C.

The rhetoric is appealing, effectively playing to the public's desire for a panacea. The program segment continues by advocating for "direct instruction" and against "whole language," with claims made that I found to be irresponsible journalism. Calling "direct instruction" a method that "outperforms other techniques" and that "works every time" is simplistic and misleading. Reading is far too complex a process to be reduced to a formula. And to say one method outperforms another without more specific information tells an incomplete story.

While ABC chose to highlight an outdated, little-used technique and present it as a desirable, successful program, the ramifications of such emphasis reverberate nationally and internationally; *20/20* is a respected news program, viewed on average by 20.5 million people a week. That's a staggering number of people, many if not most of whom believe what they see and hear. There should have been a bombardment of letters from us educators protesting, but there wasn't. The segment generated several hundred letters, about equally divided pro and con. Senior producer of the segment, Shelly Lewis, said, "We definitely shook up some educators, but we haven't had a ton of letters." And letters violently opposed to what was presented were definitely in the minority.

So why wasn't there a huge response from the public and an outcry from educators? Unfortunately, because these statements are made on a well-known television program, most viewers believe them—even though research fails to support the claims. As for us educators, we failed to consider—or didn't realize the ramifications—of the segment. Furthermore, most of us are not in the habit of taking a political stance even though we need to be.

Many statements made on the program serve to further misinform and fuel the whole language/phonics-skills debate.

"Every year, the schools spend more, yet things get worse."

"Today most American kids are taught to read through something called whole language instruction."

"Here in California, for example, most of the kids can't read at grade level."

"Mechanical, repetitive drills. You learn the old-fashioned way, by memorizing letters and sounding out words."

"No, teachers do what they're told to do or what they're permitted to do. ... The culprits are your administrators."

I found it interesting that books were never mentioned in the twenty-minute *20/20* report on teaching reading. The "direct instruction" technique (also known as the Distar program)—repetitive, military-like, whole-class drills with scripted teacher materials—that was advocated focuses on sounds and words in isolation. Spending the recommended thirty to forty minutes a day on a "skill and drill" method would leave little time for actual reading. This fact was never brought up. Not to mention that "direct instruction" is a totally prescriptive, packaged program without any inquiry focus or the teacher as decision maker. It's certainly not reading as a thinking, problem-solving process.

As best I could ascertain by talking to the producer and senior producer of the program, the segment ran because a senior executive read an article about Englemann and found him "charismatic." The reason for doing the segment seemed to be a combination of an "interesting guy" and an "interesting method." Through the profile of Englemann, I was told, parents would become aware of a method that "seems to work very well." Maeve Kenny, the free-lance producer for the segment, viewed the approach as an enormous success because "the kids were all reading." Essentially, the television program was free advertising for an old teaching program that hardly anyone uses.

Part of the problem, here and elsewhere, is that people reporting on education are often not educators. Reading, as presented on *20/20*, was decoding the words, not a meaning-seeking, problem-solving endeavor between a book and a reader. When I asked senior producer Shelly Lewis, "Didn't the drill and skill bother you?" she replied, "No. That's how many of us learned." I came away from my conversation with the *20/20* producers feeling that they had no idea of the implications and damage that such reporting could do.

All the more reason that our voices as educators must be clearly and loudly heard. We must do everything in our power to ensure that the media represent what is going on in education fairly and accurately. When they don't, they need to hear from us—lots of us.

Learning to Deal with the Media

Sometimes it feels like we in education are constantly under unfair attack by the media. It makes us wonder if we're a deliberate target. Jack Driscoll, former editor of the *Boston Globe*, where he worked for thirty-seven years, believes, "There is no inherent bias against public schools." Driscoll also believes that the level of substantive reporting has improved over the last thirty years and that in-depth education stories are more likely to appear in newspapers, as opposed to other media. Most reporters try to do a credible job and cover education as student learning as opposed to focusing on the bureaucracy of education.

Still, the end result of what gets reported seems to be overwhelmingly negative, with the media and other reports perpetuating the myth of declining student literacy. It seems to me that as long as we remain a society obsessed by test scores—scores used to rate, rank, and sort our students—we will have media stories that focus on what's wrong in education. Test scores and testing programs continue to rank schools and school systems, drive school curriculums, determine our special education populations, and influence educational policy. The struggle over how to grade and how to measure achievement rages on. Although these issues are sometimes presented as black or white, like most complex issues, there are all shades of gray.

Perhaps it's because of time constraints, but television, especially, seems to lend itself to making issues appear black or white by using fragmented sound bites and simplistic reporting. Television images or messages can appear more substantial and convincing than written ones because sound, as well as sight, is involved. Unlike reading and holding a book or newspaper, where we can wrestle with the text's message and meaning for as long as we like, television reporting allows no opportunity for revisiting and rethinking the text. It's easy to "suspend belief" and become passive receptors of whatever sounds, messages, and dramatic stories the producers choose to convey. The result is we become less critical and evaluative in our thinking.

Journalists are generalists. Forced to filter complex information and put it at a level that the general public will understand, reported news can seem confusing. To try to remain objective, journalists may present opposing points of view so readers can make up their own minds. At times, a little known or supported point of view gets reported because journalists feel obliged to present a balanced picture. My son Peter, who has worked as a newspaper reporter for several years, says, "This is the journalist's dilemma: do you remain objective or do you promote advocacy journalism and write about what appears to be the truth?"

The bad news about our schools seems to surface automatically. What we need to do as educators is make sure that the good news reaches our public. We need to bombard the media with good-news stories because, as Jack Driscoll says, "so-called positive stories are not remembered while one critical story is always remembered." We need to keep in mind that conscientious reporters are always looking for current issues, trends, new ideas, and human interest stories and that local newspapers can have an enormous influence on local education.

Powerful special-interest groups seeking to influence education in this country know how to approach the media and get their stories covered. Don Murray, a veteran columnist and writer for the *Boston Globe*, says, "The attacker always has the first advantage in the press because it's news." We need to counteract these groups, critically review their messages and respond to them, and have the education stories start to come from the insiders—us. We have no time to lose.

What We Can Do to Get Our Messages Out

Here's how we can do it, either through district administrators and public relations people, or better still, directly:

• *Get to know the local education reporters.*
Even small newspapers tend to have education reporters, whose primary concern and interest is coverage of education issues. (Newspapers don't always identify these people under their by-lines.) We need to find out who these people are, try to develop a rapport with them. Call them up; seek them out at public functions; write to them; make an appointment to talk with them in person or by phone. Invite them into our classrooms. (Jack Driscoll: "Newspaper people are nosy and tend to read what comes across their desks. Anything in writing to a reporter or editor can be useful to them. When I was editor at the *Globe*, I wanted to see every piece of mail that came in.")

• *Invite the media (as well as parents and community members) into our classrooms.*
Call the local newspapers, and invite reporters in for "show and tell." Reporters are like the rest of us when it comes to kids; most of us are drawn to them. There is no one who can tell our classroom stories of what is really going on better than the children we teach.

• *Brag about the "good stuff" we are doing.*
Hard as it is for us to toot our own horns, it's not likely that the media are going to feature an outstanding teacher without our help. Journalists are interested in personalities and profiles of interesting people. We need to let reporters know what's unique and wonderful about our own or a colleague's teaching style, or write the profile ourselves. We should not assume what we're doing in our classroom is similar to what goes on in every other class-room. (Don Murray: "If you have ideas about curriculum, you have to pre-sent them in terms of personalities to dramatically show what's going on in

the schools. In Denmark, teacher stories get in the newspapers, and they are written by teachers.") We need to do much more of this and tell the stories of how kids have been changed by school.

• *Make videos and photos of our teaching.*
Share these with the local media as well as parent-teacher organizations. It's difficult to argue with a convincing demonstration by a group of children.

• *Invite school board members into our classrooms and schools.*
Plan a preconference visit to explain what we're doing and why we're doing it.

• *Write an editorial for the local newspaper.*
This is doable and important. Writing an editorial is one of the best ways to get our opinion in the newspaper.

• *Find out how to write a press release.*

• *Attend community meetings and board of education meetings when we can.*
We can no longer just have others inform us. We need to be there to get first-hand information and knowledge. Become an active participant in community groups—League of Women Voters, Association of American University Women (AAUW), the Rotary Club, etc. Work within the group to present positive images of schools. Go to Board of Education meetings. Find out what's going on and speak out.

Final Perspectives

We Americans like easy solutions to complex problems. Although the media and noneducators offer "quick fixes," there are none. Dealing with the backlash in education in a politically responsible way requires small and large gestures. It requires all of us to take a stand.

While writing this book, I caught myself by surprise, seeing opportunities to take a stand where before it hadn't occurred to me. For example, when a Reading Recovery teacher—who was taking a "wait and see what happens" approach—told me she was worried that the program might be cut in her district, we talked about how she might get together with the other teachers and become proactive. At first she looked surprised, but then she smiled and said, "Great idea. I'm going to do it." Another teacher and I had a conversation about the pressing need for social workers in our elementary grades. We talked about writing a letter to our superintendent asking him to think about using our big annual parent-sponsored fundraiser to buy more educators instead of the usual technology. Usually, we just talk. This time we're going to act.

2

Lessons and Legacies from the Nineties

LEARNING FROM CALIFORNIA AND OTHER PLACES

Who owns our schools? Who decides what the reading and writing programs should be and what constitutes "basic"? Who decides when and if change and innovation enhance or constrain? What happens when parents perceive that their needs and wants for their children are not being met? In California and elsewhere, the backlash in education has had sobering consequences.

California: Complex Issues Without Simple Solutions

Although the reasons are not clear, California has been increasingly looked to as a leader in education. Maybe it's because of California's reputation for innovation and change. Or perhaps it's because of the passage of Proposition 13 in 1978, which drastically changed the basis of school funding. Then again, it could be because of the excellent reputation of and wide choices offered by the public university system. Or perhaps it's the 1987 literature-based English-language arts framework, which caused publishers to change their product to fit a state framework (as opposed to the basal publisher's product driving instruction). Or the fact that the framework was taken so seriously by the rest of the country, being either adopted or used as a model by many other states. Perhaps it's the fact that California's textbook adoptions are now worth close to 300 million dollars in revenues for publishers. Or perhaps it's the allure, or the vision of our future, of a state with so much diversity that nearly one out of every four Americans is born outside the United States. In any case, much of what happens in California seems to be pivotal for many of us. So it's important that we take a look at the educational climate and happenings in this state and learn from them.

By the late 1980s, California—with its literature-based framework firmly in place—seemed to be a model for other states. The state prided itself on the use of quality literature in every classroom. Teachers were reading aloud wonderful books to students, and students were reading and responding to high-quality literature found in trade books and various state-adopted literature series. But many students were failing to learn to read, especially at the beginning levels.

Diane Levin, language arts consultant at the California Department of Education, acknowledges that lack of teacher know-how was a major issue:

> Part of the problem was this: the paradigm shift from a basic-skills emphasis to a print-rich, literature-based emphasis was a major one. For such a shift to be successful would require not only time and buy-in from the educational community but massive teacher training. Over time, there was buy-in (although we are fully aware of educators who refused to let go of their skill-based approaches and accompanying worksheets). There was also some teacher training but by all calculations, the number of teachers fully and effectively trained in a literature-based approach is proportionally low.

So while the California framework, as it came to be known, recommended the teaching of skills in context (as opposed to in isolation), in actuality, the teacher training to empower all teachers to do this successfully was insufficient. In addition, the framework was widely misinterpreted. Some teachers and districts mistakenly believed that specific phonics instruction was unwarranted. Further, many interpreted a literature-based classroom to mean that all students were to be reading from the same literature at the same time, in other words, whole-class instruction all the time. Added to that factor was the implementation of many of the state-adopted published series. While the anthologies being used were rich in quality literature, there was, perhaps, insufficient support for explicit teaching of some of the basic reading skills and strategies.

In 1994, when students in California scored close to rock bottom on the National Assessment of Educational Progress test, the finger pointing and blaming began in earnest. (It was not just LEP [limited English proficient] students and minorities who scored poorly. White students and children of college graduates also scored close to last place, as compared with other states in the nation.)

Delaine Eastin, California's Superintendent of Public Instruction, took action by forming a state task force of educators, community members, business persons, and parents. Their charge was to develop a set of recommendations to improve student achievement so that "every student might leave the third grade no longer learning to read, but reading to learn."

In September 1995, after the task force had reviewed vast amounts of research and heard testimony from reading and curriculum experts, the state of California released the nationally recognized task force report. One of the recommendations is that attention must be given to a "systematic skills instruction program." Critics have taken that to mean California is returning to a "skill and drill" mentality in teaching reading. Although "direct skills instruction" is recommended, that is only part of the "balanced and comprehensive approach." Notice, also, that a "strong literature, language, and comprehension" component is mentioned first.

Specifically the task force calls for:

(1) a strong literature, language, and comprehension program that includes a balance of oral and written language; (2) an organized, explicit skills program that includes phonemic awareness (sounds in words), phonics, and decoding skills to address the needs of the emergent reader; (3) ongoing diagnosis that informs teaching and assessment that ensures accountability; and (4) a powerful early intervention program that provides individual tutoring for children at risk of reading failure.

Another major recommendation of the task force is the redesign of teacher education and training "with a greater emphasis on beginning reading. The public schools and teacher training institutions need to increase their collaborative efforts to improve the preparation of teachers."

Some disagree with the task force report, saying the problem has been exaggerated and that kids really are reading. So who and what does one believe? It seems clear that California is part of a backlash against the claim that children will learn to read naturally as long as they are immersed in rich literature and language experiences. Of course, there are some children who do learn to read like that, especially if they come from homes where they have been read to from an early age and have had lots of rich experiences with language and books. They are the lucky ones. But we who actually teach reading know that most of our children need some explicit instruction along with immersion in wonderful literature.

Looking at the Big Picture

While California's bottom-of-the-barrel showing on a national reading test made for juicy headlines around the country, the media rarely included the whole story. Test scores in isolation tell us little that is helpful. California is a unique state with many circumstances that have contributed and continue to contribute major challenges to literacy achievement:

• *The highest class size in the nation.*
Twenty-nine or thirty students per class is the average. (While the 1996–1997 Budget Act provided funds to reduce K–3 class size to twenty students, 24 percent of the teachers hired for class size reduction lack teaching credentials. As well, insufficient funds are available for needed professional development and additional facilities for new classroom space.)

• *Exceedingly low funding for education.*
Per capita income has continued to decline steadily since 1988. Only ten states spend less than California does in per-pupil expenditure. Per-pupil spending in California is under $5,000, compared with a state like New Jersey, which spends more than $10,000.

• *Inadequate school and public libraries.*
California ranks near the bottom for all states in books per pupil in its elementary school libraries. High-quality library programs have fifteen to twenty-seven titles per student; in California, the average number of titles per student is thirteen. Book budgets for schools and public libraries have been cut despite California's increasing population. Additionally, the hours the public library is open have been cut by 30 percent since 1987, "giving California the distinction of having the worst public library access in the United States." According to Barbara Jeffus, school library consultant in the California Department of Education, California ranks fiftieth out of fifty states in overall school library services. (See page 127 for the research that connects the quality of library programs to reading achievement.)

• *A continually increasing percentage of LEP (limited English proficient) students.*
California has the highest population of ESL (English as a second language) students in the country. No state has been impacted more dramatically by immigration and a "demographic upheaval" in the last decade than California, where two-thirds of the nation's Hispanics now live. While the growing needs of these students demand specialized materials—as well as staff development—funding for materials continues to decline.

• *No uniform or mandatory staff development for teachers.*

Teaching language arts—especially beginning reading—is complicated by all these important factors that cannot be easily dismissed. If students do not have books to read, they are not likely to become readers. If the quality of school and public libraries—as well as their accessibility—is limited, then students, their families, and teachers have few resources for supporting the teaching of reading across the curriculum. If teachers do not learn how to teach reading, through professional development in the schools or at the university, then students—especially in a state as diverse as California—will continue to suffer. And if funding for education remains severely limited, those cutbacks may continue to result in lower achievement. The recent rise and fall of reading test scores in third grade and sixth grade can be directly correlated to the amount of per-pupil spending in California.

Nevertheless, educators in California—and in other places—must be equal to the challenging task before them. There have always been, and there will always be, "outside factors," to a greater or lesser degree. Without minimizing the real problems and issues we face in public school education today, we must, at the same time, not dwell on these factors excessively. If we do, we will render ourselves helpless. Instead, we must assume the noble job of public school education in a democracy—that is, we must successfully educate all the children who come to us, no ifs, ands, or buts.

What happened in California is being called the "failure of whole language." It was not whole language that failed. It was the implementation of a set of practices without adequate funding, staff development, community support, and understanding.

Diane Levin says, in retrospect, that the California framework's message probably wasn't as clear as it should have been. Additionally, the framework was not written with a parent audience in mind, so some parents didn't understand what was going on. Left out of the process, many parents began to have misgivings about some of the changes. Newspaper articles on the subject have served only to confuse them further.

Sometimes the pendulum swings too far, and that seems to have been the case in at least some parts of California. What we seem to be seeing now is a "correction phase," and once again, we need to be careful that we don't give up all the great literature, the discussions, and the writing surrounding the framework and return to an overemphasis on "skills" and "phonics." Even California officials seem to realize this, stating that the goal is to balance a "more structured phonics and basic skills approach" with the state's literature-based approach.

Lessons from California

• *Change without staff development does not work.*
Changing beliefs and materials without providing ongoing professional

development and support for educators is doomed to failure.

• *Teacher education at the state level must be more explicit in the teaching of reading.*
In California and elsewhere, teachers need to learn more about how to teach children to read using literature, not just how to use and appreciate quality literature for its own sake. One of the problems may be that some methods course instructors are former teachers who may be perpetuating misconceptions.

• *Parents need to be included at the ground level whenever we are making major changes in practice and policy.*
If changes—and the language of change—are not clear to parents, we risk losing their support.

• *We need to learn how to teach second-language learners more effectively.*
There is still much disagreement about bilingual education. However, a growing body of research favors long-term models that emphasize competency in both English and the child's native language.

• *The amount of money we spend on education does matter.*
Generally speaking, historically and presently, school districts that spend more per student—if they spend the money effectively—have higher achievement. In particular, when the money is used to reduce class size and hire experienced teachers, achievement levels rise.

Alief, Texas: Educators and Parents Learning to Work Together

The Alief Independent School District in Houston, Texas, prided itself on being a professionally alive community with sound educational practices. Changes in the instructional program were made slowly and thoughtfully and reflected current research in learning. Further, the district provided administrators and teachers with quality staff development presented by leaders in their fields. Alief enjoyed a wide reputation as an excellent school district. That notion was confirmed for me when I did a workshop there in 1993. I was extremely impressed with the knowledge of the staff.

During the 1980s, the demographics of the district had undergone significant change. The once white-collar, mostly young professional community became both ethnically and economically diverse. By 1995, the district's thirty-seven thousand students represented four fairly evenly divided groups: African American, Hispanic, Asian, and white. As the district became more diverse, the needs and concerns of the community also became more diverse.

For more than a decade, Alief had built its language arts program around the philosophy of whole language. Though the program seemed well received by most of the community, a few parents began to question teaching practices. These parents worried when they heard the staff talk about invented spelling, developmentally appropriate practices, and process stressed over product. As an outgrowth of their concern, the school board adopted a "back to basics" approach.

For more than a year parents, teachers, and administrators met and engaged in discussion aimed at clarifying parents' expectations and explaining program practices. The meetings were difficult for both teachers and parents, reflecting the divisions in the once cohesive community. Even though mutual respect and understanding began to emerge as the year drew to a close, parents did request that the district offer an alternative to the current language arts program. They selected a more traditional reading and spelling program to be used in four of the district's nineteen elementary schools. From the 1995–96 school year on, parents could request the program as an alternative to the district's whole language program.

The discussions revealed that parents feared the instructional program was no longer emphasizing spelling, phonics, and reading and writing skills—things parents believed essential for their children's success. Teachers and administrators learned that parents didn't always understand the terminology used by educators. They also learned the importance of constantly assessing and evaluating the quality and thoroughness of the instructional program, of allowing parents to participate in curricular discussions especially when there is change, and the need for care in parent communication to ensure understanding.

During the summer and fall of 1995, the district responded by providing additional staff development in phonics instruction. They created more materials and learning opportunities to assist the staff in teaching reading skills, and helped teachers plan spelling and writing instruction. In addition, the district created new ways to bring parents into schools and provided more opportunities for parents, teachers, and administrators to talk together.

Lessons from Alief

Judy Wallis, language arts/social studies coordinator for Alief since 1988, has the following lessons to share:

- Change may proceed successfully for a time, but unless the community understands curricular changes, questions will eventually arise.
- Educational language and terms confuse parents and often fail to communicate clearly.
- We must always look critically at ourselves and our practices in order to improve and refine them.
- Continuing staff development in the teaching of phonics, spelling, and reading skills is critical to the success of any language arts program.
- When questions arise, educators must listen carefully. Parents deserve to know that their concerns will always be taken seriously.

Littleton, Colorado: A Conflict in Values and Beliefs

Littletown, Colorado, was long known as a very progressive school district, so much so that educators from over one hundred school districts, representing more than thirty states, came to visit and learn in the early 1990s. An old, established community on the outskirts of metropolitan Denver, the district—approximately seventeen thousand K–12 students—seemed to lead the reform movement in education. From 1989 through 1994, under the leadership of Superintendent Cile Chavez, educators found Littleton a great place to work. Teachers and administrators were encouraged to learn as much as they could and to try out new ideas. The language arts curriculum allowed for flexibility. While there was an adopted, literature-based basal series, many trade books supplemented it. Although no phonics workbooks were used, skills teaching was embedded at every level and test scores were good. The parents in this mostly white middle- to upper-class community were highly supportive of their schools.

In the early 1990s, Littleton gained national recognition by instituting performance-based graduation requirements and other reforms. Specifically that meant, in some schools, portfolios and performance-based assessment would be used along with the standard high school credits and traditional grading system. Performance-based graduation meant that seniors would formally have to demonstrate and apply what they had learned in order to graduate. In other words, students would need to show a "real life" understanding of the curriculum.

> At that time, there was no organized opposition to the reform. The superintendent and board encouraged school-based restructuring and performance-based education, and the school sought the support and participation of parents through neighborhood meetings and frequent newsletters. Excitement was growing among the faculty.

However, while some students were rigorously working on more complex tasks and using more writing and technology across the curriculum, many of them were struggling with the demonstrations and believed they would not be able to graduate. Critics claimed less class time was being spent on cultural common knowledge.

In an effort to explain the importance of teaching children to be information seekers instead of information regurgitators, one high school principal said something to the effect of, "Kids don't need to know what the capital of Florida is. They need to know how to find it." Some parents interpreted that to mean that "the facts" were no longer being taught. Parents who did not understand the change or see the need for it believed that the school system was deserting any emphasis on facts and "the basics."

A small group of parents who perceived their concerns were not being addressed became vocal. Three of them ran for the school board on a "back to basics" platform, and in November 1993, they all got elected. In retrospect, some parents said that they voted for "back to basics" as "the answer" to various perceived problems but that they didn't really know what they were voting for. The newly elected board, with a three-to-two majority, ended the comprehensive local reform by quickly scrapping Littleton's performance-based high school graduation system and forcing the resignation of the nationally recognized superintendent, Cile Chavez. The "open" language arts curriculum, difficult for many to understand, was rewritten in a "scope and sequence" format.

Following those actions, more than half of the administrators chose to leave the district, as did a significant number of the teachers. With the departure of many strong curricular leaders, district cohesiveness disappeared. As Sandy Redman, a teacher with over twenty-five years teaching experience in Littleton, put it, "We lost the heart of our leadership."

However, in the November 1995 school board elections, the "back to basics" slate was defeated by a two-to-one margin, and three self-proclaimed "moderates" were elected. So, it looks like things may be on their way to changing, once again, in Littleton.

Lessons from Littleton

In December 1995, I spoke at length with Cile Chavez, the former superintendent of Littleton. A brilliant and insightful educator and speaker, she talks not only about Littleton but the bigger picture in education across the country. We can learn much from her experience and wisdom.

Can you talk about what your vision was for Littleton and how you attempted to carry it out?
First of all, I don't believe in mandates, and, of course, they don't work. Everything we did involved school-based decision making. The mission statement we wrote was one sentence: "Our actions will result in greater student self-esteem and performance." We adopted a strategic plan with four priorities to meet our mission statement.

The first was, *We will adapt and change resources and practices to meet the changing needs of kids.* People were magnificent. They believed in what we were doing. There was lots of self-sacrifice and commitment to kids. Every dollar we could show moving from management to instruction was critical. Here are some of the things we did:

- We subcontracted out custodial services in the central administration building. That saved sixty thousand dollars and bought us two assistant principals for two elementary schools.
- We reduced central administration and bought tremendous credit with our teachers. And that meant we had very few union issues. One thing we did was close down central administration over the holidays; that cut days off contracts and saved money. We also froze all employees' salaries for two years in a row. The result was we had two million dollars to spend. We then bought teachers in order to lower class size in the elementary grades, especially in kindergarten through second. Furthermore, we designated significant dollars for staff development in quality decision making and curriculum, and pay-for-performance plans for administrators and teachers.
- Three years in a row, our cafeteria workers took over the cafeteria and ran it. This turned the cafeteria into a self-supporting, profit-making venture, enabling us to give the board of education one hundred thousand dollars for indirect costs. Not one dollar of the general fund went

to cafeteria services. Savings as a result of the cafeteria workers' entre-preneurship all went to instruction.

• Visitors from all over the country came to learn. They purchased resource books that Littleton High School teachers wrote. The sixty thousand dollars profit from those sales went to teachers and teacher development. Teachers felt free to create.

Our second priority was, *We will move toward greater, school-centered decision making.* School-centered councils became the decision makers. My role moved from "queen of the buck" to working collaboratively with all levels. People purchased materials as they needed them as opposed to the traditional districtwide purchase of texts on a cycle basis.

Our third priority was, *We will explore and implement multiple assessments.* Beyond the districtwide administration of the Iowa Test of Basic Skills (ITBS), we didn't prescribe. We started off with the belief that you need quality data for quality assessment. Under the leadership of the principals, we had a year of study in the late 1980s in every school and the dialogue unfolded in each school. Ultimately, some schools moved into using portfolios, and we began restructuring around outcomes. Teachers kept moving forward. Some schools were more innovative than others.

Our final priority was, *We will explore restructuring.* In some schools that resulted in multiage classrooms, cooperative learning, conflict resolution, portfolio assessment. Conflict resolution and our early-morning discussion "circles" came to be highly criticized. Because self-esteem was mentioned first in our mission statement, our critics said we were too "touchy-feely" and not enough about academic rigor, which wasn't true.

In retrospect, what do you feel was the biggest cause of Littleton's problems that we all need to learn from?
For a long time, educators have felt isolated from the parents in the teaching-learning process. We've been saying for decades we need to get parents involved. But we were never thoughtful about what involvement meant. We have never really looked at parents as decision makers, which is important. In the absence of that voice, we made some assumptions about our expertise and authority and made decisions according to our best judgment.

Parent involvement needs to be a valued part of curriculum and decision making. This is a wake-up call for all of us: a lot of parents want to be significantly engaged in the learning processes of their children. For a long time we haven't heard parents' voices and sincerely didn't know how to blend these voices with professional voices.

How do you bring people along who don't understand our goals in education?
We have to help people move from opinion to considered judgment. Daniel Yankelovich says it's not just giving people more information or having good communication. That's not enough. You have to help people understand the consequences of doing something or not doing something.

In Littleton, when we moved to performance-based assessment, the parents who were later our biggest critics were not an active voice in the strategic plan and, especially, in the development of the goal of performance-based graduation. I've asked myself why. Is it simply because at that initial stage of implementation their children were in middle school? It certainly has implications for how wide our communication as educators needs to be. It's certainly not just for the customers at the door.

What do you say to teachers who work in a school district that does not support their beliefs about teaching and learning?
First of all, school doesn't belong to teachers but to the community. Clearly teachers are the predominant architects of the ethos in school. But when that ethos begins to change to the degree that teachers can't carry out their philosophy and there's no longer a match with the organization and their values, they have three choices. One, they can stay and try to shape opinions by seeking to understand, by listening and collaborating. Two, they can fight. Three, they can leave and find another arena that matches their values. Without that match, you can't get the parents' trust; you can't assume you have it.

I decided as superintendent that I didn't want to deliver what the new board wanted. I drew the line on the way they were treating people. They wanted a mandate for top-down management. I couldn't operate that way.

Why do you think there's such a backlash in education today? What's going on?
As educators, we need to look beyond the walls of schools to understand what's going on. People's tolerance level is low, and lots of people are just angry in general. And there's a huge fear factor in society today. Parents don't always feel that their kids are safe. Faith Popcorn, in her book *The Popcorn Report*, talks about "cocooning" and the need for people to feel safe. She defines cocooning as "the impulse to go *inside* when it just gets too tough and scary *outside*." People want safer neighborhoods. We're living in a period of more isolation. Here in Denver, as in other communities, walls are going up around whole neighborhoods. What is the real message of that?

Popcorn also talks about a specialization trend. People want customization. They act on, *I want it according to my prescription and needs. I don't care about the other thirty kids in the classroom.* This is one of the factors that has led to a call for charter schools.

Also, parents aren't interested in global competition and experts talking to experts. They don't want change and reform. The attitude of many is, *Prove to me that what you're doing is working.* They understand phonics and spelling from their own education. That's why they want to keep it just the way it's always been. Parents also want to influence their kids' values more. But we've always had some of that. That's why parents often select private or parochial schools for the children's education.

Is there anything else you learned from Littleton that the rest of us can learn from?
We need to understand that there are people with fundamentally different ideological frameworks, and that's America. People's ideologies are deep, and you can't always budge people. You can have a policy of school-centered decision making. But if a new board of education comes in and doesn't want that, they can shut down what's in place. In Littleton, in fact, the three board members that shut things down at Littleton High were actually parents from another high school.

What's your number one recommendation to us as educators to communicate more effectively with parents?
"Seek first to understand." Carve out meaningful dialogue, and what that means is not telling first, but rather, asking a lot of thoughtful questions and listening. Probe, probe, probe. But do it gently, as a caring spouse or friend would. Figure out what the parent concerns are. Ask effective questions that build trust. Arm yourself with facts. Have information that can help influence peoples' judgment. Listen with an open mind. Don't give the answers to your questions, even if you know them. If we do this for parents—offer options and get their feedback—with the majority of parents, we'll have greater support.

Fairfax County, Virginia: Innovation with Community Support

Let's move on now to a different setting, Fairfax County, Virginia. It's a district where innovative practice and community support have gone hand in hand, not an easy achievement. So how have they managed, for the most part, to avoid the "back to basics" push and media hype that has plagued some other districts? I spoke with Ann Mc Callum, language arts coordinator for the district from 1980–1995 and presently a language arts consultant to the district. "Of course, we have had our setbacks and detractors," she said, "but we did a lot of things right."

Since the mid 1980s, Fairfax County, Virginia—the tenth-largest school district in the United States—has managed to make and maintain innovative changes in the language arts without losing the support of the community. Despite the presence of strong conservative groups, support for home schooling, budget cuts, and the usual mix of potential for disaster in big school districts, educators in Fairfax County have managed to move forward without compromising their strongest beliefs about language learning. This county of 160,000 students (K–12) includes schools with affluent populations as well as Title I schools. While the population has become more diverse, high test scores have been maintained.

Successful Practices

Much of what Fairfax County has done well has implications for all of us educators. Some of the successful practices in place include:

• *Speaking clearly and without jargon.*
Fairfax County calls its program *language arts.* Sensitive to communicating in terms the public understands, the district has never used *whole language, scaffolding, activity-based math,* and others that might be misunderstood. *Invented spelling* has been replaced by *temporary spelling* to communicate the developmental aspects to parents. The present language arts program began to evolve in the 1980s with the implementation of the work of Donald Graves in elementary writing programs. By calling the official program *language arts,* all the good things teachers were already doing were included. Ann Mc Callum notes, "The myths sometimes associated with whole language didn't apply. Teachers continued to do explicit teaching and continued to teach phonics in grades 1 and 2."

• *Treating teachers as professionals.*
While most teachers have been encouraged to use trade books in the reading program, teachers have three basal series to choose from. (A small percentage of teachers pick and choose from one of these published series.) Additionally, many professional books have been purchased for all teachers at all elementary grade levels. Many teachers respond to their reading in Teachers as Readers groups. Prior to budget cuts, mini-sabbaticals were also offered to encourage teachers to continue their learning and sharing.

• *Reading Recovery.*
Fairfax County was the first district outside of Ohio to be involved in Reading Recovery, a successful early-intervention reading program for the lowest 15 to 20 percent of a beginning first-grade class. Three-quarters of all reading specialists and Title I specialists, as well as a small percentage of first-grade teachers, are Reading Recovery trained. Because of the program's high level of staff development, Reading Recovery teachers have been very articulate and taken leadership roles in talking with parents and the community. Also, thanks to Reading Recovery, many teachers have an understanding of the importance of having lots and lots of books in the classroom and having those books match up with kids' interests and abilities.

• *Reducing class size in grade one.*
In schools where lots of students were "at risk"—as determined by free lunch, test scores, economics, and large numbers of LEP (limited English proficient) students—class size was reduced to a ratio of fifteen students to one teacher. In 1992, when Superintendent Robert Spillane bravely urged this reduced teacher-student ratio for grade 1, thirty-two schools were able to benefit. In 1995–1996, forty-five schools had achieved a fifteen-to-one ratio in grade 1.

• *Focusing staff development in reading on the primary grades.*
With a move to more free-choice writing, trade books in the language arts, and more learner-centered teaching, the district realized that a new level of staff development was necessary. Hearing about a new practice would not be enough; teachers would have to see it. First-grade teachers received extensive staff development. Teachers doing a wonderful job showed their colleagues what they were doing in their classrooms. These teachers used slides, videos, and demonstration lessons and responded to questions about guided reading, management, and other issues.

• *Having "special" teachers come into the classroom and work hand in hand with teachers and students.*
Every school has a reading specialist. Title I schools have additional reading specialists.

• *Developing district assessment tools.*
The district developed its own standards and benchmarks for students so that parents could clearly understand expectations. Then assessments were developed for evaluating the instructional program.

• *Writing materials specifically for parents and teachers.*
Books and booklets (which included overhead transparencies) have been written to explain current approaches to language learning and teaching. For example, if parents were complaining about spelling, teachers could use the resource books to put together a workshop for parents. Three teachers—one each from grades 1, 3, and 6—were released from the classroom for two years so they could write these books and work on staff development.

• *Having release time for ongoing staff development.*
Early closings each Monday allow teachers to get to a central staff development meeting by 2 p.m. or to use a teleconferencing center. One Monday a month is saved for language arts. Other Mondays are used for other curriculum areas and faculty meetings. As an example of sensitivity to parent concerns, faculty meetings are sometimes used to role-play potentially difficult situations.

• *Involving students in parent-teacher conferences.*
Many schools are increasingly inviting students to play a major role in conferences.

• *Coordinating with Title I and the ESL program.*
To ensure that the language arts program is consistent for all students, Title I and ESL teachers work closely with all teachers.

Ann Mc Callum attributes most of the success in the school district to its teachers and says, "Any success we've enjoyed in Fairfax is due to good teaching by committed teachers." She also credits a core of knowledgeable and supportive administrators, many of whom were former reading specialists. She notes that when the Greater Washington Reading Council sponsors a Saturday conference, it's a sellout. Educators flock to after-school language arts programs that feature outstanding educators. The Teacher Research Conference doubles in attendance each year. Many teachers also belong to professional organizations, read professional journals and books, share ideas, and conduct classroom research.

Final Perspectives

What I learned from these stories and from talking to some of the people behind them is the absolute necessity of having clear and ongoing communication between us educators and the communities we serve. Without effective communication, especially with parents, trust inevitably breaks down. Once a problem becomes public, it seems to escalate and become an emotional issue, making it difficult to reason with people.

Furthermore, parents need to believe their concerns are being taken seriously. When parents are really listened to and respected, they support innovation that has included them in the process. If parents—even a small group—perceive they are not heard and respected, they lose trust in the schools and demand what they want until they get it.

Lastly, we educators must have more influence with our communities, school boards, state legislatures, and government *before* there is a problem. We must become leaders and spokespeople in the change process and bring other educators and community members along with us. We must influence district policy. If local and state boards and departments of education are writing curriculum, revising standards, and rewriting assessments, then teachers that have the necessary expertise must be represented.

Arm yourself with facts. Communicate clearly. Listen with an open mind. Speak wisely. Have information that can help influence people's judgment. As Cile Chavez said, "We have to help people move from opinion to considered judgment."

3

Whole Language

RHETORIC AND REALITIES

Whole Language Hasn't Failed: We Have Failed Whole Language

Whole language has become the scapegoat for everything wrong with education. Whole language is blamed for poor test scores, bad spelling, reading problems, illiteracy, you name it. The truth is, whole language hasn't been around long enough to accept responsibility for all the ills of education. More important, the principles on which whole language stands are research-based, sensible, and child-centered. Unfortunately, these principles have been misunderstood, maligned, and misused. *Whole language* has become a loaded, emotional term in some places.

To avoid tension and confrontation, in my own school district, we generally don't use the words *whole language* beyond the fourth grade. Some teachers in fifth and sixth grade and beyond complain about getting students who can't spell, write legibly, or "do grammar." In some cases, of course, our teaching hasn't been rigorous enough. However, I suspect, in most cases the blame game exists because of misunderstanding and differences in our philosophy of how kids learn.

It's easy, too, to blame the disillusionment with whole language in certain quarters to unfair press, the conservative movement, vocal parents, the Religious Right, or a host of other reasons that may or may not have contributed significantly to an erosion of public confidence We need first, however, to look to ourselves and our own beliefs and practices. We have not been publicly critical of ourselves, and we need to be. We have not acknowledged our growing pains or owned up to the fact that there is no way major change can occur without some warts showing up publicly.

35

Nevertheless, I believe that whole language and what it represents and accomplishes is too powerful to be lost. The move toward more democratic classrooms where students read and write for life purposes complements the characteristics and goals of "the good society." In these highly political times, whole language may be transformed, but it will not go away.

What's Gone Wrong?
Misinterpreting Whole Language

My best guess, based on working with teachers in my own district and talking with teachers around the country, is that only about 20 percent of us are truly grounded in whole language philosophy to the point where we can understand and apply it. Yet many teachers say they are "whole language." Then when things go wrong, whole language is blamed. That's partly what happened in California.

In many places, *whole language* has come to mean literature in the classroom with accompanying big books, journal writing, process writing, portfolios, and other artifacts. Teachers are said to be "doing" whole language, much the same way as one "does" an activity. There has been wholesale innovation without change. Many teachers have exchanged basals for trade books and worksheets for journals. Materials and methods have changed, but the old theories of learning are still in place. Instead of a scripted, packaged program, the teacher unilaterally decides what books and subjects will be studied, how children will be grouped, and what choices students can make. What is often missing is the constant self-monitoring and self-evaluating excellent teachers do, always asking themselves, *Why am I doing what I'm doing? Is this curriculum relevant and appropriate for children's interests and needs? Am I providing real choices for children?*

In the school district where I teach, and in many other places too, we've been "whole language" for many years. So what does that mean? We stopped using basals and worksheets, added lots of wonderful trade books to our language arts programs, and moved into a literature–writing process approach. We began experimenting with alternative assessment and portfolios. We negotiated the curriculum with our students. But has this happened in every classroom? Absolutely not. Some teachers have taken the new materials and continued teaching as they always have, in a question-and-answer, right-answer-in-the-teacher's-head format. Others have misinterpreted integrated teaching to mean cute themes. In some instances, every teacher writes his or her own curriculum, and parents have complained—rightfully so—that each year's curriculum and way of teaching is different, depending on what teacher their child happens to get.

In California, what had never been more than a literature-based reading program became equated with "whole language." As in other places, some educators misinterpreted whole language to mean whole-class teaching with literature. In many instances, small-group instruction all but disappeared along with attention to needed skills teaching.

I'm Whole Language—
I Don't Teach Phonics

Many teachers nationwide have grabbed onto the term *whole language* before understanding it. Some of us have made sweeping public statements that have been misunderstood. Naively unaware of the political fallout, we have told parents and community members:

"I'm whole language. I don't teach phonics."

"Spelling doesn't matter."

"We don't teach grammar."

"Just let the child write fluently. Don't worry about correctness."

These blatant misconceptions destroy the credibility of whole language teaching.

Those of us from a skills-oriented background kept what we knew worked. We could pick and choose. But other colleagues—some recent graduates and some veteran teachers too— never learned how to teach the cueing systems or integrate the skills into the curriculum. They didn't understand what teaching skills in context meant; they didn't know how to teach focus lessons when "things come up." Additionally, some teachers turned their district's message of *We're not using the phonics workbooks* to *They won't let me teach phonics.* Along with that misunderstanding, teachers who believed materials "teach" failed to realize that they could—or didn't know how to— teach phonics themselves, as part of daily reading and writing, without the workbooks.

Additionally, some educators have equated a child-centered, whole language classroom with not teaching explicitly. These educators believe if they set up the environment, establish a "community of learners," and do lots of reading and writing activities, learning will take place "naturally" and automatically. They immerse kids in wonderful literacy experiences but fail to provide adequate demonstrations and directed lessons and to hold students responsible for excellent work.

No wonder parents panic. Used to a structured, old-order way of teaching, they assume this new way is sloppy, careless, and without standards and expectations. On top of that, many have witnessed firsthand the illegible handwriting, abominable spelling, and lack of attention to conventions in writing in their children's work. Not in all places of course, but in enough arenas to cause concern and alarm. More and more parents have spoken out saying that we teachers aren't teaching, that we aren't doing our jobs.

Much of the criticism of whole language centers around skills and phonics. Leave out the emotion and bring in research and common sense, and then it becomes apparent that phonics and skills are part of whole language and always have been. That message has not gotten out, especially to parents.

It's interesting that if we can separate out the phonics/beginning reading quotient as it is related to whole language, proponents of explicit phonics instruction are able to recognize and credit the benefits and goals of whole language:

> The whole language movement is a valiant effort to remind us that effective instruction is accomplished not through prescription, censure, or regulations, but by teachers and children.
>
> Properly, then, the whole language movement should be a core component of a long-overdue and highly constructive educational revolution. It should be about restoring the confidence and authority of teachers. It should be an affirmation that education can only be as effective as it is sensitive to the strengths, interests, and needs of its students. The whole language movement should be about displacing compartmentalized instruction and rote facts and skills. And it should be about displacing such outmoded instructional regimens with highly integrated, meaningful, thoughtful, and self-engendering engagement with information and ideas.
>
> If, in fact, these are goals that drive the whole language movement, then they must be supported wholeheartedly by all concerned.

No argument here. Marilyn Adams and Maggie Bruck support what many of us do, once they disentangle the phonics issue.

Whole Language Teaching Requires More Support and Time to Evolve

Reform toward whole language has moved too quickly. We are an impatient society. Something new comes along, and we want it implemented instantly. Our attitude is like the slogan, "Just do it!" But when we are talking about a major philosophical and pedagogical shift, we need lots and lots of time, professional development, and continuous support and knowledge. Moving from a skills-based model to whole language is a profound shift. Deep, meaningful changes in thinking and practice take more time than teachers, administrators, parents, and communities have realized or acknowledged.

Professional development must be viewed as a necessity, not an option. District after district expects teachers to make massive changes without the necessary support. Just like our students, we teachers need excellent and repeated modeling by experts; time to practice and try out what we are learning without being evaluated; coaching by mentors and peers; and time for collegial collaboration, reflection, and sharing. Too often, this has not been the case.

My school district has many visitors who come to "see whole language" because their administrators expect "it" to be put in place within a year. They walk around with notebooks and cameras trying to permanently visualize lots of "ideas." It is not uncommon to see visitors copying down verbatim charts and products on bulletin boards and walls while ignoring the high-level conversation of a literature group in process. They ask for copies of forms (such as editing checklists) to be used in their own classrooms, not realizing that these forms have little value unless they are developed for and with the particular group of children in authentic literacy contexts. Somehow, massive change is supposed to happen as if by magic, just by saying the right buzz words. *Go forth and prosper as a whole language teacher.* One teacher likened it to "baptism by fire."

In the name of whole language, many of us have spent untold hours scrambling for activities, many of which are inauthentic and a waste of time—pulling vocabulary words from literature and designing exercises around those words, choosing weekly spelling words from literature, having students write answers to lots of factual questions. Teachers have exhausted themselves creating activities and had little energy left for reflection or time left to read and enjoy literature.

Loretta Martin, a talented whole language teacher, says, "After eight years, whole language is beginning to make sense to me. At first, I was expected to do the practice, but I didn't have the theory. Doing the how before I had the why in place was very difficult. A big change for me now is when I go to a conference, I spend all my time listening to speakers. Before, I spent hours at the exhibits, looking for activities. I can figure out the activities myself now." Kindergarten teacher Peg Rimedio concurs: "If you have the theory, the activities will come."

Then, too, you can't take away all of a teacher's supports and expect the teacher to do a good job. We have vastly underestimated—and even failed to consider—how difficult it is to create curriculum for every subject and teach without teachers' manuals or guides of some sort. Many teachers become exhausted to the point of burnout.

In a move that seemingly embraced whole language, one principal refused to let his teachers order the usual spelling workbooks. Most of the teachers, who were given nothing to replace the traditional spelling program, tried their best but floundered badly. Without professional development to gain the necessary knowledge to teach spelling in the context of writing, they taught spelling poorly or not at all.

Without sustained support and professional development, there will continue to be only pockets of whole language teachers doing well. Then, in the worst-case scenario, whole language will fail.

Making Parents Part of the Process

Unless we take the time to share the research on whole language and articulate our beliefs and practices to parents as their children enter our schools, we will be in for some rough going. Parents need to feel confident that what's going on in classrooms is right for their kids. We need to learn from the stories in Chapter 2. We need to help parents and community members understand that whole language is not a fad or a trend or an experiment but, rather, a theory of teaching, thinking, learning, and interacting with children that is based on research and reason and democratic principles. It has been my experience that when parents are part of the process and understand why we want and need change, they are mostly supportive of us and our practices.

When I conduct workshops for parents to explain what whole language is, I always connect what parents have naturally done well in teaching their children to what we are trying to do in the classroom. Parents quickly grasp the notion of invented spelling when it is compared to learning to walk and talk, developmental processes that all children go through in somewhat predictable stages. Emphasizing that researchers have learned about how young children acquire language from observing what parents and children do in the home sets the tone for recognizing "parents as experts" as opposed to the "we know best" attitude that alienates parents from the schools.

As I see it, we will continue to fail with parents, communities, and school boards until we:

- Give reassurance that the basic skills are receiving lots of attention.

- Make parents part of the process of change from the beginning, to include explaining the need for change.

- Invite parents into our classrooms to see what we are doing.

- Value parents as experts.

What Does Whole Language Really Mean?

Depending on who you talk to and what you read, whole language has been interpreted in many ways. As professional educators, we must clearly understand and articulate our beliefs and practices. Otherwise, we are at the mercy of noneducators and the media who make public statements that can set our teaching back. The following sections are not intended as dogma; they are prompts to get you to think about, reflect, and solidify your own thinking about whole language beliefs, misconceptions, principles, and practices.

Defining Whole Language

Lots of people, myself included, have said that they can't define whole language—that it's too complex and dynamic to do more than conceptualize it. Yet, we must try to define it if we use the term. Otherwise, our detractors will define it for us.

I agree with Yetta Goodman, who says we should keep using the term *whole language*. She urges, "Don't be afraid to label what we believe." Goodman believes that if we give up the term now, it won't be because the term isn't useful but because we're politically afraid. Whole language is being attacked even in places where the term was never used. What we must do is share our knowledge and reach out to the public.

So here's my definition. Is it right? I don't know. It's right for me today. No doubt, it will continue to evolve and change as I continue to grow as a learner and a teacher. What's important is that you have your own definition to articulate to parents, administrators, community members, and the media. Anyway, here goes:

> Whole language is a way of thinking, teaching, and learning in a social community where learners are continually supported to purposefully use language (reading, writing, speaking, listening, viewing, thinking, drawing, composing, making sense mathematically and scientifically, and so on) in order to inquire and to construct and evaluate their own understanding of texts and real-world issues.

My definition applies to us as teacher-learners as well as to students. Whole language is not just about child-centered learning; it is also about teacher professionalism.

Another way I define whole language, after I have introduced the language-learning activity described on page 81, is readily understood: "Whole language is nothing more or less than applying the conditions of language learning that we all use in the real world to the classroom, as authentically as we are able."

I also like Norma Mickelson's comprehensive definition:

> Whole language is a child-centered, holistic philosophy of learning and teaching which recognizes that language learning is both contextually and socially determined, and is constructive in nature. It provides children with a wide range of meaningful language and literary experiences across the entire curriculum, includes evaluation and parent involvement, and facilitates the development of responsible, cooperative, and caring individuals for whom language is a source of increasing empowerment.

Beliefs About Whole Language

Whole language, of course, is much more than a brief definition. It is a social, constructivist, democratic way of teaching, learning, evaluating, and being that values and builds on each student's language, culture, and strengths. Inquiry and language in authentic use are at the heart of the curriculum. Meaning and knowledge are constructed from the learner's experiences. Comprehension is always the objective. Skills and isolated facts are not relevant unless they take on a personal meaning. Whole language teachers believe that children learn best when curriculum is personally meaningful and relevant to their lives.

Any stated definition of whole language also implies risk taking, choice with intention, educational decisions based on the needs and interests of children, reading and writing quality literature in many genres, communicating for real-world purposes, collaboration, self-evaluation, and goal setting.

What do these beliefs look like in the classroom? In whole language classrooms students are talking, listening, reading, writing, collaborating, storytelling, responding to reading and writing, problem solving in all disciplines, and inquiring about topics of interest.

Some Misconceptions of Whole Language

Before we take a close look at what whole language is, let's look at what it isn't, so we can be clear to our many audiences and to ourselves. One major misconception is that you can require someone to become a whole language teacher. You can't. You can only support, encourage, and nurture their development. You can't mandate whole language any more than you can mandate thinking. Other misconceptions continue to contribute to the confusion experienced by educators, parents, community members, boards of education, publishers, and the media. Let's examine some of them.

• *Whole language doesn't work for children of color.*
I have heard many educators—of all cultures and colors—proclaim that whole language does not work for children of color. Dorothy Strickland, noted African American author and professor at Rutgers University, decries the need for separate practices for children of color.

> The need for a specialized curriculum, tailored to meet the needs of black and Hispanic children is, in my opinion, a big lie. Moreover, it is a lie that has the potential to do great harm. Like other children, black and Hispanic youngsters vary in ability, interest, motivation, background knowledge, and home experiences. What appeals to me about holistic practice is that it allows (no, requires) teachers to value and adapt what happens in the classroom to the great diversity among the students there, no matter who they are. Skills-based instruction, the type to which most children of color are subjected, tends to foster low-level uniformity and subvert academic potential.

Based on my own experiences teaching children of color for more than twenty years, I know that whole language works for all children (see pages 78–80). The same argument has been posed for students with special needs, and it is equally invalid for similar reasons.

• *Whole language is a method.*
It's not. It's a philosophy of literacy development that encompasses beliefs and principles about language learning. A corresponding teaching method and program evolves from the teacher's and children's thinking.

• *The basics are not taught.*
The cry of "back to basics" implies that we stopped teaching the basics; knowledgeable whole language teachers never left them. Phonics is a non-issue. Of course, it is taught (see Chapter 6). Conventions of language are important and are taught in context. The definition of what it means to be literate cannot be reduced to basic skills. As the research shows, we need to go much further than the basics to a higher literacy of thoughtfulness.

• *Whole language is a fad and trend whose time is past.*
Whole language, which supports and demands the making of meaning, is based on more than two decades of reading and writing research as well as on democratic principles. Whole language will not go away, nor should it.

• *There is no place for explicit instruction.*

Explicit instruction does not mean decontextualized drills. It does mean clearly teaching skills and strategies in a meaningful context so that the learner can continue to problem-solve and learn as independently as possible. Associated with the misconception about explicit instruction is the notion that the teacher never assigns. Nonsense. The difference is the teacher makes the expectations clear through explicit modeling. Explicit instruction—based on students' needs and interests as well as on curriculum requirements—takes place in a meaningful, literacy context.

• *Correctness doesn't matter.*

Absolutely false. Facts in a report, spelling, grammar, the format for a letter, are all expected to be correct for a real audience (not just the teacher). While teachers encourage invented spelling—approximations that match the child's developmental language level—spelling becomes conventional over time, with wide reading, writing, and explicit teaching.

• *Teaching is not rigorous.*

Just the opposite. Knowledgeable teachers have high expectations in all areas and those expectations are modeled. Spelling does matter; assignments are made; organization and accuracy count. My district's new K–12 language arts course of study includes benchmarks, rubrics, and writing exemplars to be sure our teaching is on target and rigorous. We, our students, and their families need to know what district expectations are.

Fourth-grade teacher Joan Servis agrees: "Having taught school for thirty-three years, I've been both a traditional skills-and-drill teacher and, for the past sixteen years, a whole language teacher. I can honestly say I have much higher expectations for my students now. I am asking them to think, not to parrot answers I've already given them."

• *You can buy whole language materials.*

You can't. Materials in themselves are not whole language; they are tools for learning. It's what the teacher does with the materials and how they are used that matter. Many publishers would have us believe otherwise. Sticking whole language labels on guides, books, and packaged materials, some marketing departments prey on teachers' weaknesses for easy solutions and "the answer." There are some wonderful commercial materials, but they are only as good as our own theory of literacy and language learning. We need to be choosy about what we buy and use.

• *The product isn't important; it's the process.*
Not true. The product *is* important, but how the student arrives at the product is at least equally important. The well-balanced portfolio has both—rough drafts, work in progress, and final products.

• *You have to have learning or literacy "centers."*
Some teachers successfully have writing centers, science centers, art centers. If they fit with whole language beliefs and practices, great. Often, however, teachers use "centers" as artifacts—prescribed activities they think need to be incorporated. The room may look whole language, but it's all on the surface unless the teacher is operating from a holistic philosophy.

• *You seldom group.*
Recent visitors to one of our K–4 buildings expressed surprise when they saw small-group reading. They said they had been given the message that grouping wasn't "allowed." They were teaching all reading whole class, using either shared reading or round-robin oral reading with follow-up questioning. They commented that they were "amazed" to see the high levels of reading and writing of our students.

There will always be times when we need to group students of like or similar abilities or interests. These groupings are not fixed; they are fluid. Unlike tracking (where the student is ability grouped for the entire course or year), grouping according to the strengths and needs of the students for a small part of the instructional program is what good teachers have always done. Teachers need to stop feeling guilty for grouping students to support one another, accomplish a specific goal, or do some explicit teaching.

Some Key Principles and Practices of Whole Language

It's too easy to just say, *I'm whole language.* Unless it embodies the accompanying principles and practices, *whole language* remains just a term without meaning—which is what has gotten a lot of us into trouble in the first place.

I used to think one became a whole language teacher after a period of years. I now realize that the journey of putting whole language theory into practice is lifelong. Whole language beliefs and practices have to fit together, which requires ongoing self-examination and learning. (While we're in process, we have to reassure parents that we're clear about our goals and objectives.)

The following key principles are true for me as an educator as well as for the students I teach. I believe these principles apply to students and teachers at all levels, kindergarten through university.

• *Responsibility for classroom community is shared.*

Classroom community is the umbrella under which all the other principles fit. Educator Ralph Peterson says, "*Community in itself is more important to learning than any method or technique.*" Without community—educators, students, and families taking responsibility to value, support, and be respectful of all people and cultures—a whole language classroom does not exist. The community functions on trust, respect, emotional and physical safety, distribution of knowledge. Implicitly understood is that threats of punishment and failure are missing; kids can assume power over their own learning.

So what does "community" look like in practice? For one thing, if the teacher is absent, learning and routines go on in the usual, orderly fashion. Since the teacher has not been the only authority in the classroom and since students understand why they are doing what they do, the old system of points and rewards isn't needed—it's been replaced by collaborative decision making. Being a collaborative community applies to such elements as discussing literature, creating charts and rules, gathering needed materials for a unit of study, caring for each other, problem-solving together. Of course, there are times when the teacher makes a unilateral decision, but this is not done to control but to further learning and getting along together. On the whole, teachers do less telling and explaining and more asking kids to tell and explain.

To support collaboration and socialization, the room is set up in a more homelike environment, with a comfortable reading area, areas (often carpeted) for group work and class gathering, and areas (often big tables instead of desks) where students can sit, read, write, and problem-solve together. Whole language communities are intellectually alive places.

• *Meaning making is collaborative as well as individual.*

Closely tied to community is the importance of collaborating with others in the learning process. Along with teachers and other adults (including parents), peers are used as mentors, sources of knowledge, decision makers, and collaborators. This concept of mentoring applies to us as teachers as well as to students, and recognizes that we cannot be expert at everything. At times, we all need "experts" to support our learning and problem-solving. Collaboration often leads to working more independently.

Competition in a whole language classroom is individual; it's for and within the self, for each of us to do her or his best job, meet individual challenges, set goals, evaluate herself or himself. Much of what is learned may be reflected through the portfolio process.

In whole language classrooms, collaboration and support may take the form of peer editing, partner reading, peer testing of spelling words, collaborative research and writing, small-group work, and more. There are times when kids can help each other in a way no one else can. Of the ongoing collaboration, fourth-grade teacher Leslie Bakkila says," Sometimes I think it's just noise and idle talk, but when I sit down with a group, they're always on task."

Collaboration is fair and necessary; it's what we do in the world. This ability to interact successfully with team members, to problem-solve, and to make new knowledge is one of the five competencies identified by the Secretary of Labor's Commission on Achieving Necessary Skills (SCANS) as necessary to lead a full and productive life.

• *The curriculum is negotiated.*
In whole language classrooms, students pursue their own inquiry questions and negotiate the curriculum with their teachers. That is, within the required state and district curriculum guides and courses of study, there are options to seek and make knowledge personally relevant.

Inquiry goes across the curriculum and depends on teacher knowledge as well as other "experts"—books and resources (including computer technology), classroom and school libraries (including a knowledgeable librarian), community members, parents. Teachers emphasize the "big ideas," not discrete facts and skills. Curriculum is concept-based, not skills-based, and builds on the needs and interests of children. Facts are important when they are connected to key concepts. Critical thinking is modeled and expected. There are no cute themes.

My favorite resource for understanding and applying the principles of curriculum negotiation is the outstanding text *Negotiating the Curriculum: Educating for the 21st Century*. The authors suggest that teachers and students should ask four questions about the content to be studied, and then negotiate the answers:

1. What do we know already?...

2. What do we want, and need, to find out?...

3. How will we go about finding out? . . .

4. How will we know, and show, that we've found out when we've finished? . . .

Curriculum is not about activities and materials. It is the theory of language learning that the teacher holds that drives instruction, learning, and evaluation.

• *Choice includes intention.*

It's not choice that's so significant; it's what students do with the choice. Choice is a big part of curriculum negotiation in which children have some control over their learning. However, choices are not superficial; that is, we are not simply talking about choosing from the teachers' required options. It took me a long time to figure that out. I always gave choices to students, but they couldn't choose not to do one of the choices I offered them.

Choices made by students (and teachers) are intentional and relevant to their purposes and interests. For example, writing for real and important reasons, reading books the learner chooses, researching a subject of interest within the nonnegotiable topic of study. For an example of significant choice with intention, see pages 148–49.

• *Assessment and instruction work together; self-evaluation, reflection, and goal setting are integral to daily instruction and practice.*

Students and teachers are constantly self-monitoring and reflecting: *Why am I doing this? What do I need to do/learn next?* Along with learner-directed inquiry, there is constant reexamination and reevaluation of our beliefs and practices. Students are viewed as learners, not test takers. Some part of assessment is often performance-based and part of a portfolio process. (See "Seeing Evaluation Through a New Lens," pages 149–61, for examples.)

• *The best fiction and nonfiction are used to teach and enjoy reading and writing.*

Students and teachers read, listen, and respond to stories, books, poems, essays, and other literary forms by award-winning authors and illustrators. To support the reading process, classroom and school libraries have a wealth of predictable, natural language texts as well as quality nonfiction, fiction, poetry, and other genres. Time each day for reading aloud by the teacher and for student self-selected sustained reading (often silent) is an integral part of every classroom. Wide reading supports writing, and authors are used as writing models. In literature conversations, the teacher's voice is only one voice, not the dominant authority. The meaning made from text is personal (and may be shared) and depends on the reader's prior experiences, interests, knowledge, and purposes.

• *Learners read and write to learn, across the curriculum, in and out of school.*

Reading and writing are integral to language arts and to the language arts as they are used in every discipline. There are many writing purposes, requiring a wide range of formats and audiences. Problem solving in math and science, reflecting while reading, retelling a story or experience, are all part of writing to learn, as is figuring out meaning through writing—as I am doing as I write this passage.

There are frequent opportunities to watch teachers and other models think and compose in front of students, to share and receive feedback, and to celebrate and publish. At times, reading and writing lessons require small and large groups as well as individual focus lessons and conferences.

• *Skills and strategies that are needed are taught.*

Teaching needed skills and strategies is not the same as fragmentation through drills and worksheets. Skills and strategies are taught in the literacy context. Judy Wallis, a language arts coordinator, notes that skills are definitional and that strategies are operational and depend on procedural knowledge.

And we don't always have to wait for a need to "come up" in the literature or writing. If we know students will need it, we can teach it through a focus lesson. Of course, it's a given that knowing what and when to teach depends on a highly knowledgeable and observant teacher.

Whole Language at the University: An Excellent Model in Practice

Like all professional teachers, Judie Thelen has struggled, changed, reflected, and grown in order to find her literate voice. Today, as a whole language teacher, she practices what she preaches. But I do not believe she is typical of college professors. Of her students, she says,

> I find that many of my students come to me with many misconceptions about what whole language is, and I believe it is because many of the faculty that have "taught" them do not have a clear grasp of what literature-based and whole language classrooms look like. What the students are getting are the strategies quite often associated with these philosophies—such as story maps, themes, invented spelling—all taught in isolation and not in the framework of a philosophy.

Judie (former president of the International Reading Association) runs her undergraduate and graduate classes at Frostburg (Maryland) State University as whole language classrooms. The exemplary way she teaches in the school of education is a model for all levels of teachers across all academic disciplines. Specifically, Judie

- *Sets up routines students can count on.*

    Presents syllabus the first day, with nonnegotiables (such as required reading and final exam) stated.

    Begins each class by reading aloud from various genres.

- *Sets up environment for small-group work and interaction.*

- *Negotiates the curriculum with her students.*

    Requires professional reading and response in reflection journals.

    Provides a structure by which students choose what to read.

    Lets students decide on how many professional articles to read and how to evaluate what they learn.

- *Demonstrates what she expects students to do.*

    Models everything she expects students to do (for example, professional reading, reflection journal).

- *Allows lots of choice.*

    Gives talks on professional books and articles, then lets students select which ones to read.

    Lets students determine the content and process of the final exam.

- *Teaches mini(focus)lessons based on students' needs and requests as they arise in class.*

    Discusses such topics as phonics, invented spelling, classroom management.

- *Promotes and expects social collaboration in learning.*

    Asks students to form discussion groups around same-title professional books.

- *Expects self-evaluation.*

    With students, establishes rubrics (specific criteria) for determining grades; students then grade themselves according to these rubrics.

• *Models herself as a learner.*

Reads constantly, takes risks, questions and talks constantly about her practice with colleagues, takes responsibility for her own learning.

What Judie Thelen does as a teacher-learner impacts her students greatly. Ann Mc Callum, who often interviews perspective new teachers for Fairfax County, Virginia, says that Frostburg teacher applicants show a high level of understanding and enthusiasm and that they carry impressive portfolios to illustrate their expertise. "The students I interviewed boggled my mind. They were extremely bright, articulate, and very well read professionally."

Dissenting Voices in the Ranks

One of the reasons for all the controversy surrounding whole language is that among those of us who say we are whole language, there are a wide range of views and beliefs. Some of our differences result because of our sophistication of thinking, our prior teaching and life experiences, our interpretation of the pedagogy, and our own uniqueness. That is as it should be in a democracy when we are talking about a complex philosophy and dynamic way of thinking about teaching and learning. Unfortunately, our tolerance level for each other's beliefs has not always been as high as it needs to be. That has cost us all dearly.

Here's what I'm talking about. Believing that "if it's theoretically inconsistent with whole language in any way, it's wrong," some of us have loudly proclaimed that any instruction of a "part" is not whole language. Some of us refuse to use the word *teach*, believing that any direction on the part of the teacher is inappropriate. *Phonics* has been seen as suspect, making many teachers afraid to use the word at all. Worse yet, our extreme positions have pitted whole language against a skills approach, fueling a debate that hardly needed additional fire to remain burning.

While publicly saying that we need to hear all the voices, some of us also say, by our actions, that all voices in the profession are not equally respected. While talking loudly about the respect we must show all students and how we need to build on students' strengths, we have not always shown that same respect to our colleagues by actively listening to what they have to say.

Reading Recovery Does Fit
Under the Whole Language Umbrella

One important example of rigid posturing that has hurt us is the critical stance some have taken with Reading Recovery. Rather than championing a highly researched and respected program that succeeds by helping struggling first graders become readers, we have picked the program to pieces. I have heard that the program is too directive, too costly, too pressured, and too rigid. In particular, the writing section of the Reading Recovery lesson is singled out as anti-whole language since the child is not allowed to use invented spelling.

I am a trained Reading Recovery teacher. I worked as a Reading Recovery teacher for four years. Then I spent the next six years working in second-grade classrooms daily, applying Reading Recovery strategies to small groups of struggling readers. Reading Recovery is not perfect. It is, however, the best early-intervention program I have ever seen. Students learn to read, and they learn quickly. Yes, they are "pulled out" of the classroom for thirty minutes a day, but this pullout lasts only twelve to fifteen weeks of their school career. By contrast, children pulled out for special programs such as Title I typically spend much of their school careers receiving support—a more costly endeavor in the long run.

As a Reading Recovery teacher, I initially had difficulty coming to terms with not using invented spelling. What made it acceptable to me was the realization that I was right there next to the child, and that I needed to maximize the brief teaching opportunity. Many of the words we were writing were basic words for reading. In a classroom of many students, the teacher is not available to each child. Children must be encouraged to use invented spellings so they can write freely and work out the rules of their language.

Perhaps most important, Reading Recovery was the best education I ever received on how to teach reading. The course was learner-centered, explicit, and used real books. Up until that time, my teaching of reading overrelied on phonics and skills in isolation, which was how I was instructed to teach reading when I was an undergraduate and graduate student. Reading Recovery enabled me to become a better reading teacher, not just with my Reading Recovery students, but with all students and teachers.

Let's keep all the good that Reading Recovery does for students and teachers primary. Gay Su Pinnell, President of the Reading Recovery Council of North America, puts the program in perspective:

> Reading Recovery was never intended to be or to mirror a comprehensive literacy classroom program. Reading Recovery provides "something extra"

for children, who in spite of good classroom teaching, need extra help. That help is focused on reading and writing that will help them develop the important concepts related to independence. This support comes at a critical time in their lives.

It's Not Necessary to Have
Total Agreement to Have Unity

We need to pull together and stop bashing each other. We talk loftily about the need for respect and community in our classrooms, but many of us do not live the model. We need to treat our colleagues and their differences with the same respect we have for our students. Democracy is not about getting others to do it our way but about educating our citizenry so they can make their own informed decisions. Why do we insist on total consensus with our fellow educators regarding whole language views yet welcome diversity of thinking and opinions with our students? While orthodoxy gives comfort by defining a set of principles, it also constrains by its rigidity.

We need to have the kind of community of learners we try to foster in our classrooms—caring, accepting, and supportive of our peers. We need to stop the in-fighting and put our energies into focusing on what's best for kids. What's best about whole language is the promise it holds that all children can and will learn. That same promise applies to us as educators too.

What we're about as teachers, after all, is not looking out for our own self-interests but for children's interests. We need to expand our whole language community to include, support, and welcome all who seek to be part of it. Then we'll be able to deal more effectively with our critics.

4

Becoming Political in Our Schools

THE NEED TO BE ARTICULATE, ASTUTE, AND ACTIVE

My first year teaching, I told my principal, "I'll never get involved in politics." She said, "Well then, you'll never be able to teach." I've had to live my teaching life by those words. There comes a time when you must speak out and take a stand.

Liz Crider, second-grade teacher

The Politics of Change

Most of us stay within our classrooms and schools; we shy away from becoming political and dealing with tough issues. Yet, being a responsible educator necessitates our astute and active participation and decision making in our school communities. In order for reform efforts to be successful, we must have collegial partnerships and ongoing communication with all the stakeholders. The committee process, teachers, administrators, teachers' unions, and parents all have a role in instrumenting change. Parents in particular are key to successful change. Because they are too often left out of the process, we need to pay particular attention to achieving more effective communication and better working relationships with parents, as well as with other community members.

The Only One Who Welcomes Change Is a Wet Baby

Whenever I make this statement to an audience of educators everyone laughs, because it's true. Resistance to change is as natural and common as

54

breathing. We all like comfort, safety, a predictable routine, and what has been successful in the past. We like what we know and what's familiar. Risk taking and change require energy, stamina, vision, patience, teamwork, and a willingness to be unsettled, at least for a time. Change can be messy and scary. Moreover, change is slow. Deep change happens in small steps, not giant leaps.

Most of us educators understand and support teaching processes and methods we have experienced and felt comfortable with ourselves. Without sufficient explanations and demonstrations, it is difficult for us to support new practices. Many of us (and our own children, depending on how old we are), as well as many of the parents of the children we teach, learned to read with lots of emphasis on phonics; we had spelling workbooks and weekly spelling tests; we had grammar exercises and math drills. Whether they worked or not, it's what many of us know and expect. It's what many call "the basics."

As a society, we are skeptical of fads, trends, and innovations—especially when they involve educating our children. As teachers, we must begin to share with parents and community members the reasons we seek reform and changes in our teaching practices. We cannot let the media and outside voices be the only ones heard. Otherwise, we are doomed to backlash and failure.

> The change process in contemporary American schooling is very fragile. Those who want to make schools fairer and more humane, more democratic and caring, face a very difficult battle. . . . The history of American schooling has been a history of struggle for control of what schools should be and for whom they should be.

A Genuine Committee Process:
Not Business as Usual

Because all of us must inevitably deal with change, and because change is so often problematic, I share the following story from my school district. I hope the possibilities, difficulties, and insights inherent to our change process can smooth the path of change for other educators.

Several years ago, we undertook to write a new language arts course of study as part of our state requirements. Two building principals and I were asked to co-chair the committee. It was only the second time that I know of that an elementary teacher in our district was co-chair of a district committee. (Later, Jon Bender, the head of the English department at the high school, joined me as a second teacher co-chair.) It was also the first time in my memory that a K–12 group of teachers were talking collaboratively about language arts curriculum. In the past, we had typically worked together at grade levels, as departments, or in our separate schools. It was easy and common to blame previous teachers and schools for what the kids couldn't do. Now face to face with each other, "culprits" eyed each other suspiciously. Many sat steely-eyed, arms crossed, ready for combat. I was plenty nervous opening that first meeting!

One of the first things I did was give everyone a copy of "Getting Reform Right: What Works and What Doesn't" and read several quotes from it: "'The implementation dip.' Even in cases where reform eventually succeeds, things will often go wrong before they go right" . . . "The absence of early difficulty in a reform effort was usually a sign that not much was being attempted". . . "Anxiety, difficulties, and uncertainty *are intrinsic to all successful change.*"

I wanted to say, up front, that we were in for rough going and uncertainty, that the change process would be rewarding, but also challenging and unsettling. I think most of us are more willing to undertake a difficult task if we are aware ahead of time of some of the challenges we'll be facing. There also has to be a belief or vision that the risk taking and all the mental/emotional discomfort associated with it will result in validation and support by other teachers and administrators.

Creating Ownership for Teachers

Many of us perceived that reform in our school district had typically been top-down. While we teachers had lots of opportunities to give input on district committees, inevitably some of us felt that our ideas did not prevail. From a teacher's viewpoint, it seemed like too many times we had spent hours, many of them after school, giving our best suggestions, only to be frustrated by a failure of action or a change of plan about which we were not consulted.

It was important to me that this time the process would be different. It would be impossible for this committee—of about thirty K–12 teachers (primarily) and administrators from across the district, along with one parent—to have a shared mission without a lot of time to talk about what we wanted students to know and be able to do. Our administration was very supportive, and for several years, we had two full, consecutive days of release time in which to meet and write a language arts curriculum.

It was a formidable task, so many different philosophies and beliefs about teaching and learning colliding, arguing, cajoling, convincing, evolving, changing. Looking back, I see that nothing could get written until we got to know one another, understood one another's biases, respected one another's beliefs, and listened really hard. It took months and months, but after a while we felt like a community. Our differences of opinion coexisted with common interests and goals for our students. A middle school teacher wisely said one day, "Curriculum is not a document; it's a dialogue." Although we finalized the one-page statement of our English language arts philosophy in one day, it was the months of prior discussion and at least a dozen drafts that made that final writing possible.

It Is Possible to Be Too Democratic

I've come to believe that the committee process can be too democratic. Not only did our K-12 committee meet during each school year, we met the week after school was out each June. In an effort to include more teachers from our middle school, who I felt were underrepresented, I personally called several of them and encouraged them to join our June meeting. I learned the hard way how difficult it can sometimes be to add new people once a trusting community has been formed.

Patiently, we listened to one middle school teacher for days as she explained her beliefs. Because she had not been part of our earlier curriculum rethinking process (and perhaps for other reasons as well), she was in a different place mentally, was out of sync with the rest of the group. We, in turn, became frustrated and impatient. In wanting to accommodate everyone, I think I and others were too patient.

We had accomplished little during that week, and the morale of the group was low. Some felt the week had been wasted; a few indicated they didn't want to stay with the process. I learned that as a leader, sometimes you have to take a stand and say, *Based on what most of you are saying, this is the way it's going to be.*

Forging a New Vision for the Language Arts

The goal of our committee was to create a language arts course of study that would be "user friendly" to students, parents, and teachers and that would also serve as an assessment tool. We did not want to separate instruction from assessment. We were also very conscious of not wanting to create the usual "shelf document," that is, the new curriculum in a shiny binder that gets a quick once-over before it's retired to the shelf. We were determined that our curricular change would not be in name only, that ongoing professional development would be part of the process.

A number of teachers on our committee pilot-tested the document for a year and found it too cumbersome, unwieldy, and time-consuming to be used for assessment. That is, the document did not work well as a "hard copy" to be shared with parents, students, and other teachers. It could, however, continue to be used to guide the assessments we did develop. In addition, we found that the language and terms we used, which we tried so hard to write in child-friendly terms, were not readily understood by our students. We eventually finalized a language arts course of study (to be reviewed and revised each year) that served as an explicit guide to what we needed to be teaching K-12 in reading and writing especially but also speaking and listening across the curriculum.

One of the benefits of our district committee work was the way many of us on the committee came to view teaching. Freed from the tunnel vision of our particular grade level, we learned that the process and goals for K-12 are remarkably similar. We began to use and understand the same language to talk about our teaching and learning processes. I believe our high school teachers also gained genuine respect for our talented kindergarten teachers and vice versa. Additionally, some of our high school teachers made changes in the way they conducted their classrooms, attempting to be more democratic and student-centered and incorporating the portfolios, negotiated curriculum, and other teaching strategies that some of us were attempting to implement at the elementary level.

Given the opportunity and time to work together, share ideas, and learn from each other, many of us reformed our teaching. It was our ongoing collaboration that pushed the change process forward.

In-House Resistance

Sometimes it's not just forces outside our classrooms that are resistant. Often we teachers fight hard to maintain the status quo. It seems a lot easier to be told what to do (by a teacher's manual) or to continue doing what we've always done than it is to reexamine our teaching and make changes.

It was not easy for the committee to come to consensus on our language art course of study. We tried hard to be democratic and inclusive. We wanted all teachers to have input in creating the K-12 language arts document we were writing. We didn't want ownership of the document to be perceived as belonging to an elite group. In a sincere effort to involve all teachers across the district, in small groups and over several days, all teachers were given a half day's release time to examine their language beliefs and take a look at our work in progress. Each small-group meeting began with the language-learning exercise described on pages 81–82. We wanted everyone to have a miniversion of the same opportunity we had had—time to meet across grade levels and talk with colleagues, time to explore beliefs about language learning and assessment, time to discuss and hash out differences, and time to look at the document and give input.

I was the facilitator for these workshops, and it was no easy task. While most teachers appreciated the opportunity to meet, a small number were openly hostile. One teacher spent the first half of the morning wandering the halls, refusing to come in. Others seemed just to be going through the motions of participation without making any genuine investment. At one point, we were talking about a balanced reading and writing program and looking at the "working explanations" our committee had written. I asked for contributions to our descriptions of such topics as shared reading, guided reading, independent writing. A teacher spoke at length about how no one was going to require him to read aloud to his students. It was unbelievable that a teacher could rally against reading aloud! What he was really saying was, *No one is going to tell me how and what to teach.* It was as if his academic freedom were being threatened.

Perspectives from Our Committee Process

We finished our language arts course of study about four years after we began. Painful as it is to admit, the process wasn't nearly as successful or rewarding as we'd expected it to be. Yes, we had a terrific document that we were proud of and that reflected our philosophy and thinking, but we no longer had the camaraderie we had when we began. With the exception of a few people, our enthusiasm was gone. By the time we were ready to introduce the completed document to our colleagues in every building, very few of our original committee members volunteered to help do it. We'd accomplished what we'd set out to do, but we had no closure or celebration for a job well done.

From the perspective that time allows, I see several overlapping factors that contributed to a loss of commitment and spirit:

1. We got tired. While we kept the adrenaline flowing for a while, the process went on too long, and we couldn't sustain the necessary energy and enthusiasm. Also, a levy failure made it impossible for us to have release days to work together the last year. Looking back, in some ways we never recovered from the disillusionment of that stressful summer week when we failed to move the process forward. After that we lost the

commitment of several key members and couldn't seem to regain the unity of purpose we had originally created.

2. We had too many people coming and going, and therefore lost the group cohesiveness and leadership that bound us together at the start. Our numbers began to dwindle. Some teachers and administrators retired, and new-to-the-process educators sporadically took their place. And we were never able to involve our middle school successfully; it remained underrepresented.

3. Based on perceived state timelines, there was ongoing administrative pressure to complete the document. Also, our director of elementary education—who was always very supportive and involved in the process—retired about six months before we finished. Knowing she was leaving and wanting to bring the project to a speedy close, she reorganized and consolidated it. While her intentions were the best, the end result of her efficiency was that the committee lost ownership of the process and never reinvested its energy in the same way. At that point, as one of the committee's leaders, I lost heart, along with a sense of excitement about our project.

It's difficult for me to end this story on a low note. In making myself remember the good times as we struggled together at the beginning, I can recall the heady excitement we felt in the possibility of making a real difference. I can fondly recall the stimulating conversation, the growing respect, as we learned to work together and learn from each other. We all looked forward to those early meetings.

Karen Sher, a kindergarten teacher, says, "I am convinced that the insight I've gained and the courage to take risks in my classroom were enhanced if not instigated by the power of collegial collaboration and support that arose in our language arts committee."

Holly Burgess, a high school teacher, says, "In short, I was excited by the ideas and words of the other teachers present, particularly the early elementary teachers. I learned so much from them, not just vocabulary and dedication, but I began to see much similarity in teaching style, approach, and beliefs about kids and learning between the entering school years and the early high school years. . . . I tried new ideas and talked more with my high school colleagues as we tried to maintain the excitement and energy of new ideas, whose nucleus was the committee and the opportunity it provided to meaningfully interact with colleagues."

Finally, Bernice Stokes, our new director of elementary education, pointed out to me that she noticed a gentle tone and genuine regard for staff members by the volunteer committee members. When they knowledgeably introduced the completed document to colleagues, there was no attitude of "we know best" or "take it or leave it." Rather, the attitude was one of colleagues sharing respectfully with valued colleagues. I guess that says a lot.

Lessons from Our
Process of Change

• To maintain group cohesiveness and spirit, a core group needs to stay together for the duration.
Without the continuity of a core group of committed educators working together, the change process gets compromised.

• The leadership needs to be clear, consistent, and strong.
At some point the leadership may need to take a stand and set democratic principles aside: *Look, here's how I think we should explain this to others. What do you think? Can you buy into this and support it?* Lee Sattelmeyer, a member of our committee, reflects, "The change process is more effective under the leadership of someone with a strong vision of what changes are needed. While that leadership has to be sensitive to 'angst' others are feeling, the leadership has to be willing to identify the crucial issues, point the group in the right direction, and cut the losses on nonessential issues that tend to sidetrack change and reform."

• Time needs to be limited.
Regular and frequent time to meet over one or two school years is far superior to infrequent meetings over many years.

• You can have too much input.
Although we wanted all teachers on our K-12 staff to have input and experiences similar to ours all through the process, that was unrealistic. It prolonged our decision making and complicated it. Representatives from grade levels and buildings can democratically represent the constituency.

• Include parents with diverse backgrounds and from all levels as part of the process.
While our intention was to involve parents, our effort to do so wasn't great enough. We had only one parent on our committee, for just one year. As a highly educated parent of elementary students, she did not know the

concerns of other parents and did not feel she could speak for them. Our intention was also to include students on our committee, but we never managed to do that.

• *Have more conversations across grade levels.*
When our K-12 committee first convened, we learned that we knew and understood very little about how and what our colleagues taught and thought. This was true even for grade levels that were close together. We need to do a better job in schools of talking, listening, meeting, working, and sharing with teachers of different grade levels.

Necessary Partnerships

If schools are to be the way we envision them, our definition of educators must include principals and other administrators. I'm as guilty as anyone of talking about teachers and administrators separately. Barbara Kohm, a principal of a diverse K–5 building in Clayton, a suburb of St. Louis, kindly pointed that out to me. After a workshop in which I had suggested some ways teachers might get their administrators to give them larger blocks of time, she reminded me that my statement "You can't make anyone do anything" applies to administrators too.

Barbara Kohm described how teachers in her building needed "more time" to work with their students on a deeper level once they had moved toward whole language and a more constructivist philosophy of teaching. A committee made up of the principal, one representative from each grade level, and interested specialists looked at the issue of time and decided that their primary goal was to create big blocks of time for reading and writing workshop. With the principal as one voice on the committee, they worked out a daily and weekly schedule that is serving them all well. Kohm feels good about what her school has accomplished by working together. She notes:

> I'm not less powerful because we used a committee process. The issues of leadership of schools are the same issues that teachers face in the classroom. I try to use the same principles that good teachers use with students—fostering choice, decision making, and independence. When the principal is the one in control, teachers feel the need to conform and please the principal. When teachers participate in decision making, they assume responsibility for the way their school works. Blaming and complaining begin to melt away and wonderful ideas take their place.

Change cannot be successful with a we-they attitude. Strong leadership, one of the aspects of effective schools, has to be a partnership. Sometimes teachers have the authority to make change, but not the power. In a true partnership, the power is shared.

And although change may happen one teacher at a time, a group process and balance of top-down, bottom-up is necessary if change is going to be school- or districtwide. In my district and in other places I've been, teachers have been supported in the change process with the hope that they'd move along when ready. But in some cases, teachers have barely budged. I believe we need to give those teachers a gentle nudge. At some point we need to say—teachers and administrators together—*This is what we expect. This is the direction we're going in*. Otherwise, huge gaps are created, and parents get different philosophies and curriculum from one year to the next. Ultimately, for change to be successful, I believe it must be school- and districtwide. It must also be parent supported. One of the ways for this to happen is through support groups, parent education meetings, common planning times, and mentoring of new and developing teachers.

Another necessary working partnership in the politics of education is the local teachers union and administration. Teachers unions can help or inhibit the change process. Locally and nationally, teachers unions must responsibly use their power to help create the best schools and learning environments for students and teachers. Union issues are complex and varied, and going into them in depth is not a focus of this book. However, since most of us teachers are union members, I do want to point out the need for more active teacher involvement.

While administration and teachers unions need to work collegially in the best interests of educators and students, this doesn't always happen. Many local teachers unions do not promote innovation in "best practice" and teacher decision making. Unions focus their energy on making and protecting the provisions for collective bargaining, especially wage and benefit increases. Fair contracts, teachers' rights, and working conditions are absolutely necessary, and they usually receive the attention they deserve. Teachers need to speak out to be sure issues related to professional development and improving educational practice also become part of the teachers union agenda.

Since the community views the union as representing all teachers and since teachers unions seem to be here to stay, we have an obligation to be involved and knowledgeable. More than that, we must advocate to be sure our teachers unions create a partnership with school principals, other administrators, and the superintendent, not an adversarial relationship. We must problem-solve together in a spirit of trust, not just submit contract grievances. Further, it is incumbent on us as professionals to have a vision of teachers unions that includes a focus on instruction and learning.

The old view of labor and management and preserving the status quo must give way to co-educators dedicated to excellence in education and united in problem solving. Otherwise, the change process and innovative, research-based practice will continue to be thwarted.

Finally, partnerships with parents are an absolute necessity for successful reform efforts. We are naive if we think we can make changes in our teaching without the support of the parents in our community. Parents can be our staunchest allies or our worst enemies. It is up to us to make them part of the curricular and change process. Otherwise, resistance from parents can be serious enough to compromise reform efforts. The stories in Chapter 2 from Alief, Texas; Littleton, Colorado; Fairfax County, Virginia; and California inform our teaching and underscore our need to give clear, jargon-free, uniform messages to our school community.

What We Can Do to Foster Parent Support

The specific examples that follow show what conscientious teachers do as they implement changes in their classrooms. For reform to be successful, we teachers must have the support and trust of our parents and community. We *must* take this action to counteract the media bombardment of what is supposedly going on in our schools. We have no time to lose.

• *Communicate effectively.*
We have not done our homework in keeping our parents and communities informed. Parents, accustomed to weekly spelling tests, phonics drills, and worksheets, do not understand why fewer papers are coming home, why misspellings are permitted at times, and why handwriting is not necessarily being formally taught. Whenever teachers and schools change practices without informing the community of the whys and hows of that change, there is likely to be a backlash. By contrast, when parents are included in the change through parent-teacher meetings, curriculum nights, periodic letters from the teacher and/or students, open classroom doors, and open communication, the problems are minimal. In communities where parents have been involved from the beginning, outside forces have not been able to penetrate.

In addition to the weekly newsletter she writes to parents, first-grade teacher Karen McNally has her students write a weekly letter to parents in which they ask parents a question. Parents write back to their students. (See Figures 4–1, 4–2, and 4–3.)

September 1994

Dear Families,

The purpose of my weekly newsletter is to keep you aware of the many fabulous things going on in our class. Let me begin by saying how privileged I feel to be working with your children. They are all so unique and special. We are all very excited about the many learning experiences ahead of us.

This week we have begun writing workshop and are reading many stories and poems. We have developed our classroom rules and discussed how important cooperation is in our lives. Ask your child to tell you about the story *Swimmy* by Leo Leonni and the bulletin board we created for the hall. In math we have begun working with patterns and made a class graph of our eye colors.

At this time I would also like to explain the format for our "Take Home Journal." Your child has decorated a white folder. The folder will contain my weekly newsletter, a note to you from your child, and an area for you to write back to your child. The purpose of the journal is to keep you informed and give you and your child a chance to share the joy of writing. Your child's writing will not have been edited so please be patient with the invented spellings you see. We will add to the folder each week. It will be sent home every Friday and needs to be returned by Tuesday.

It is my hope that this "Take Home Journal" will not only be a memory book of the happenings in first grade, but will also provide a record of your child's growth as a writer.

Sincerely,

Ms. McNally

Ms. McNally

Figure 4–1 Letter to parents about weekly newsletter

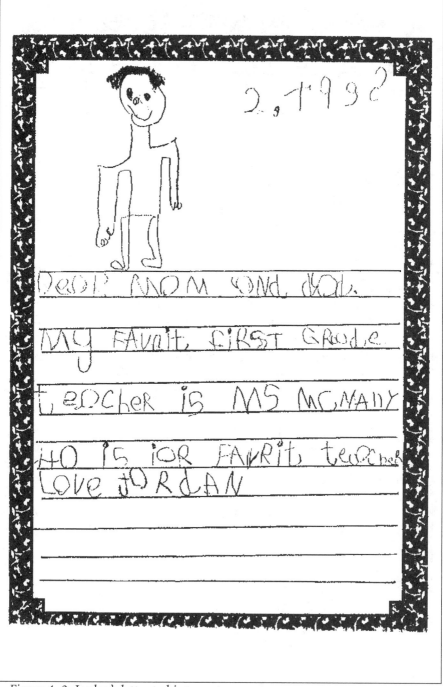

Figure 4–2 Jordan's letter to his parents

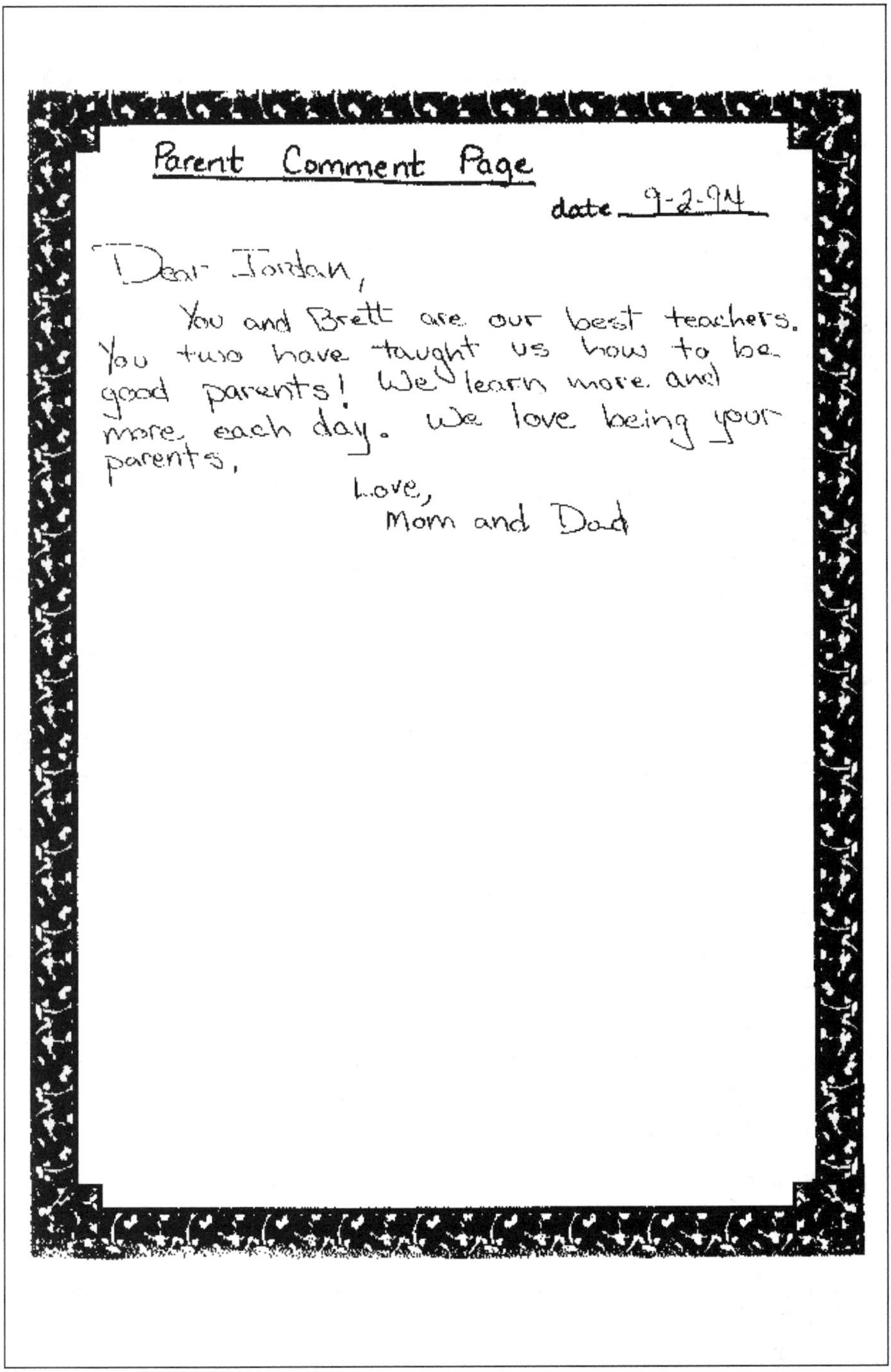

Parent Comment Page

date 9-2-94

Dear Jordan,

You and Brett are our best teachers. You two have taught us how to be good parents! We learn more and more each day. We love being your parents.

Love,
Mom and Dad

Figure 4–3 *Jordan's parents' reply*

Every week, fourth-grade teacher Joan Servis mails parents postcards supplied by our school district that say, "Good Job!" She tells the parents about a positive academic success their child has had in the classroom. Parents respond very positively and are more aware of what is happening in the classroom.

Linda Cooper, who co-teaches an inclusion learning disabilities class, calls all her parents the first week of school to introduce herself and say something positive about each student. Parents are thrilled to get a personal call so early in the year. Trust is established early on. If Linda needs to call at another time about a problem, she finds parents less defensive and more inclined to listen and help. Patsy Bannon, a third-grade teacher, also calls her parents the first week of school and reports something positive about each student.

Holly Burgess is a ninth-grade humanities team teacher (English/social studies/reading) who works a lot with struggling students. Through a newsletter she sends home, she lets parents know what she is teaching and what her expectations are. This past year, she also took the time to call all the parents of her students early in the school year. Knowing that she might need to call some of these parents later with concerns, she made sure her first call was introductory and positive. While Holly did learn about some parents' unavailability, working hours, and custody difficulties, her greatest impression was of the large number of parents who were genuinely surprised and pleased that a high school teacher would call, especially if there wasn't something negative to report.

• *Share current research findings about language learning with parents.*
Let parents know that "the basics" aren't enough.

> Students do less well in programs that focus on discrete units of language taught in a structured, sequenced curriculum with the learner treated as a passive recipient of knowledge; students achieve significantly better in programs that teach language through cognitively complex academic content in math, science, social studies, and literature, taught through problem solving and discovery learning in highly interactive classroom activities.

And we need to underscore that such lofty goals include "the basics," not preclude them as the media would sometimes have parents believe. Being able to share and articulate the research on spelling, grammar, phonics, and other language dilemmas (see Chapters 5, 6, and 7) goes a long way in gaining the support of skeptical parents.

Sixth-grade teacher Sherri Jarvie said that when she shared the NCTE position statement on grammar (see Appendix A) with parents during conferences, parents relaxed about the practice of not teaching grammar in isolation.

• *Speak in jargon-free language; explain terms carefully.*
When talking with colleagues, parents, community members, and the media, we must explain what we do clearly and without jargon. When someone uses a term, we must ask what is meant by the term and not make assumptions. For example, ask a dozen people what they mean by *phonics* or *whole language*, and you'll likely get a dozen different responses. We must be clear when we speak so that our audience understands what we mean.

I don't use the term *direct instruction* any more. I have been using *explicit instruction* ever since I realized some people equate direct instruction to the lecture model, Distar, programmed learning, and/or mastery learning (as described on pages 12–13).

The term *minilesson* has become suspect in some places. Taken literally, some people think we are talking about little lessons with no substance or expectations tied to the lessons. You may want to use *focus lessons* instead as some educators have begun to do. The same is true when we say, *Make a guess*, when we are reading with students and they come to a word they don't know. Some people interpret that to mean, *Take a wild guess*. What we mean is, *With all the information you have, make a smart guess*. But we're misinterpreted. So, it's probably better to say, *Make a prediction* or *What do you think it is?*

Some other loaded terms include *outcome-based education, standards, invented spelling, benchmarks*. When you use these terms, define them so you're not misunderstood. And don't forget to use the *p* words—*phonics, performance-based*, and *portfolios*—judiciously.

• *Schedule a curriculum night for parents early in the school year.*
Each year the elementary-grade teachers and principals in my district move our curriculum open house closer to the beginning of the school year. By having the parent night several weeks after school has begun, questions and possible misconceptions are cleared up before they become problem issues.

• *Let parents know we're teaching the "basics."*
Even when parents are highly supportive of our teaching, they still want to know that the "basics" are being taught. Joan Schaefer is a parent in my school district. Of our whole language program, she says:

> Shaker Heights has a fabulous program. I'm thrilled at how enthusiastic children are about reading and writing. I'm impressed with my children's

ability to interpret literature of various types. I've also seen that in the language arts, teachers who are well-trained in whole language can help all young children shine in heterogeneous groups within the classroom.

However, Joan also values instruction in the "traditional" disciplines. This is the letter she sent to her daughter's teacher at the end of the school year:

> Dear Mr. Young:
>
> I want to tell you once again that Kelly had a super year in your class. I've told Dr. Stokes every year that Kelly works especially well with teachers who are goal oriented and well organized, and also energetic and hands on. You were a good choice for Kelly. She was happy, busy, and challenged, and I'm delighted to know that she's done well.
>
> I'm very happy with the balance you strike between traditional and newer teaching methods. For example, there seemed to be plenty of problem solving in math, but also a real emphasis on learning math facts. I was also pleased to see that you reviewed cursive writing—although "penmanship" may be outdated, my fifth-grade daughter and her classmates have miserable handwriting, to the extent that they routinely combine messy cursive and printing in the same sentence. I was glad you found the time to help the third graders with this (and hope it continues into fourth grade).
>
> Thanks again for a great year. Have a relaxing summer!

Note that half of the letter deals with the importance of handwriting and "skills." The message this parent sends is clear: *Literature and free choice writing are wonderful, but I also want my child to learn to spell and to have good handwriting.*

• *Make instructional programs and teaching practice explicit to parents.*
Parents do not automatically understand "how innovative practices will help students learn 'the basics.'" A report in *Education Week* suggests that parents support innovative practice when they understand how the practice is being implemented. The author notes, "It was clear to me that parents did not understand the process approach to teaching writing." Among other things, she suggests conducting focus groups with parents before making curricular change and making sure students know the what and why of learning.

Susan Mears, a kindergarten teacher (and former first-grade teacher) in my school district, tells the story of being confronted by a parent with a copy of the science curriculum from a nearby private school. The parent was upset with the public school because she believed Susan wasn't teaching science. Because Susan integrated her curriculum throughout the day and didn't talk of separate subjects with her students or parents, the parent erroneously assumed science wasn't being taught. When Susan shared our explicit science curriculum with the parent, she was reassured and satisfied.

• Include parents at the beginning of the change process.
Too often we make changes first and then inform parents. Parents need to be part of the process *before* change is made. If parents do not understand why we seek change, let alone understand the changes, they can oppose them.

In my experience, the most vocal parents are usually pretty successful adults. They are the lucky ones who survived and maybe even flourished under the old paradigm. "It" worked for them, so they see no good reason why "the old way" shouldn't work for their kids.

Affluent parents who have Ivy League aspirations for their children can be the greatest resisters. They support "covering all the topics" and getting the good grades that they had in their own schooling. Educational goals such as application of learning, critical thinking about content, and making connections across the curriculum may not be supported if those goals interfere with the "preparation ethic."

• Open our classrooms and schools to parents.
We teachers are not used to inviting parents into our classrooms, and, at first, it can be scary. Second-grade teacher Loretta Martin says it took years for her to feel comfortable with parents in the classroom. Now she doesn't think about it. She depends on her parents not only to support what she's doing but also as experts and teachers in their own right.

I still remember how hard it was for me to come into the public school when my own children were little. I felt I was imposing myself in a place where I had not been invited. And I was a learning disabilities tutor at the time working in another school in our district!

Open time for parents can be limited. As a second-grade teacher, Jeannine Perry tried a "celebration/sharing hour" one morning a month where parents were welcome to share along with the students. Parents often brought favorite poetry and picture books to read. Some brought the family pet. Because the time was so limited, Jeannine did not feel threatened. She enjoyed the hour as well as the open "drop in" time she extended to parents.

Nell Cangiano, a first-grade teacher, invites parents to half-day visits each month. Classroom demonstrations are drawn from parent concerns and have included spelling, guided reading, and other literacy activities. These classroom visits contribute to the confidence the parents have in this teacher.

First-grade teacher Chris Hayward uses five parent helpers during his weekly journal-writing sessions. Before these parents began to support students with writing, Chris met with them and explained how he uses these writing sessions to evaluate and teach phonics skills. Parents in his room are very clear on how skills teaching occurs.

Third-grade teacher Julie Beers has several parents work both individually and with small groups in her spelling program, which views the teaching of spelling in the context of writing. Some of the activities that parents lend their weekly support to include having students choose misspelled words from their writing, attempt the spellings of those words ("have a go"), and edit their writing.

To orient parents to our classrooms, Holly Burgess suggests preparing a one-page synopsis of our teaching program. As an alternative, students could work collaboratively to write an explanation of classroom activities, procedures, and expectations.

• Start "parents as readers" groups.
Ann Mc Callum reports that Teachers as Readers groups started in Fairfax, Virginia schools. As the Virginia State Reading Association extended the program throughout the state, parents were added to the groups. Fairfax and other districts now have Parents as Readers groups that help parents gain a deeper understanding of the value and importance of book discussions about quality children's literature. Educators interested in starting such Teachers as Readers or Parents as Readers groups can contact the International Reading Association for information.

• Create volunteer activities that matter.
In my school district, the book publishing program, our book fairs, the WEB room (where much of the literature used in our reading program is housed and organized), and the opportunities we offer parents to work—and sometimes teach— in our classrooms and libraries help parents feel like their children's school also belongs to them.

Final Perspectives

Educators, parents, and children need to be knowledgeable and outspoken about the actions that will help children thrive and those that won't, especially in the early years of school. A child's most permanent memory of school often comes from the early grades. We need to be articulate, well informed, and act from a research and experience base. If we are also clear about our goals and purposes—as well as responsive to the parents of the children we serve—most parents are very supportive of our practices and the changes we are attempting.

One parent, when testifying as a parent at a State Board of Education meeting said, "We sent you our children eager to read, write, and learn. All we ask is that you return them in the same condition."

Part II

Back to Basics and Other Teaching Dilemmas

5

Back to Basics

WHAT DOES IT MEAN?

It's impossible to miss the rhetoric. Newspapers, television programs, radio shows, school boards, special-interest groups, and parents are clamoring for "back to basics" more loudly than ever. What that phrase means and how it is interpreted depends on who is using it and for what purposes. As educators we must understand the jargon and the politics because, like it or not, we are all affected by it. By knowing what's going on in the public arena, we are better equipped to deal with our local public and make our teaching purposes clear and understood.

One thing's for sure: whenever test scores are used as the main measure of how our kids are reading and writing, there is a call for "back to basics." As I understand it, that means, *Let's go back to the old days when everything was rosy*. The problem is that in the old days, the literacy rate was not as good as it is today, and lots of kids had trouble learning to read.

Those Were the Good Old Days

I remember the "good old days" well. I was teaching then, using scope-and-sequence charts, phonics drills and worksheets, linguistic readers with contrived stories, red pencils to correct all the worksheets, assigned and copied-from-the-board writing. And lots of kids were failing to learn to read successfully. In the school where I was teaching, almost 50 percent of our students needed extra support in reading by second grade. As a reading specialist, I was told to give the kids "the basics"—sight vocabulary; isolated phonics exercises; "comprehension" exercises that involved identifying the main idea, finding details, and pointing out cause and effect. We didn't use real books or interesting stories then. We used made-for-teaching-reading stories in the vocabulary-controlled, commercial texts. We used "comprehension" workbooks that had myriad multiple-choice questions following the dull stories, and we had a ready supply of red pencils to mark all the errors. We spent far more time on practice exercises than we did on actual reading and writing. So much time, in fact, that our hands were always purple from the number of "dittos" we ran and used. We kept track of all the things our struggling readers couldn't do. And then we gave them more of the same—more "skill, drill, and kill."

We damaged the self-esteem of a lot of kids, especially those who couldn't hear sounds in words or "get" phonics. Lots of those kids were African American; many were from low socioeconomic backgrounds. There was nothing wrong with their ability to learn; the problem was how we were teaching them.

Our kids didn't need more phonics; they were drowning in all the phonics we gave them. They needed a reprieve. They needed to find joy and success in reading to repair their self-esteem from all the bits and pieces and worksheets we loaded on them, literally thousands of them.

Frustrated and bored along with the kids, some of us—in the late seventies and through the eighties—tried to teach reading more authentically, with real books and wonderful stories written and illustrated by children's authors. Spurred on by a belief that kids deserved better and grounded in the knowledge of what made reading pleasurable at home with our own kids, some of us took risks and broke new ground. For me, that's the story I tell in *Transitions*. It's a story of transformation of teachers and kids, of what happens when phonics and "the basics" are put in a literacy context of wonderful books, stories, and poems; when teachers truly believe that all kids can and must learn—and so they do—when they read, read, read, all day long, for the joy of it and to make sense of the world; when kids write every day on topics they're interested in and publish texts that all their friends and family value and can't wait to read; and when the test scores of struggling readers soar—for the first time ever—and lots of people take notice and realize, *We're on to something here*. It's the best school story of all, kids becoming readers and writers for their own purposes—choosing to read and write for pleasure and information in their free time and all the time, in and out of school, because they want to.

Using Real Books
and Paper and Pencil

I was able to make changes in my teaching because I had the support of a large body of research on language learning that came to light in the seventies. Sure, I was having success teaching reading using the best of children's literature and building on kids' strengths. But it was the sharing of that research with our superintendent Mark Freeman and my principal Delores Groves (along with a written proposal and their faith in me) that made it possible to take the risk. What would happen to our struggling readers and all of our other kids if we set aside the commercial basal reading texts and workbooks and used real books and paper and pencil—the most basic teaching materials of all? Fortunately, we found out.

What seemed revolutionary at the time seems like common sense now. Building on a transactional model of how young kids learn to read and write at home in their natural settings before they start school, educators translated that model to the classroom. The details of how that was implemented have become muddied at times (as I discuss in Chapters 2 and 3), but the original intent and research remain as solid as ever.

It's important to look at that research again and think about how to apply it to teaching in our classrooms:

> Certain environmental factors emerged as common to almost all early readers:
>
> • *Reading to children*, often the same book repeatedly. (This is the factor mentioned most often in the research literature.)
>
> • *Seeing a reading model* such as a parent, teacher, or sibling reading.
>
> • *Availability and utilization of a wide variety of reading materials*, especially storybooks.
>
> • *Involvement with writing* such as scribbling, copying, printing, and writing with paper and pencil.
>
> • *Positive, quality interactive responses with the child* in the reading-writing process.

Based on teaching experience and reflection, to those I would now add:

> • *Choice, purpose, and intention* by the learner.
>
> • *Reading and writing as closely related language processes and always as a search for meaning.*

- *Learning as a social, collaborative endeavor that requires feedback and response.*

- *Building on the strengths of the learner with just the right amount of support from an expert* (parent, teacher, student, family member).

- *Sustained time to read and write.*

Reviewing the Language-Learning Research of the Seventies

When I conduct workshops with educators, I am often surprised by how few of us seem to be aware of the research that supports how to teach reading and writing as cognitive social processes. When I ask for a show of hands of how many know Don Holdaway's ground-breaking work on how children's acquisition of oral language can be used as a developmental model for all language learning or Brian Cambourne's conditions of all successful literacy learning, only a small percentage of us seem to know, understand, and apply these principles. We *must* know them, in order to operate our classrooms successfully, to evaluate our teaching, and to continue learning. We must know so that we can be professional, talk intelligently with parents and the community, make rational and wise decisions about our teaching, and do what's right and just for kids.

The best way to understand Holdaway's work is to read or reread his timeless book *The Foundations of Literacy*. Everything you want to know about how to set up the classroom environment, how to teach reading with books, how to incorporate shared reading and writing, how to develop activities to go along with reading and writing, is there, by the educator-researcher who invented, if you will, the "big book." There is even a chapter, "Teaching Basic Strategies," that includes detailed phonics and skills lessons in the literacy context. Primary teacher Peg Rimedio says, "Before I read this book, how children learn to read was a mystery. Then, I suddenly learned how it happens."

To become familiar with Cambourne's conditions—as they have come to be known—and how to apply them to the classroom, read *The Whole Story* and/or his recent article "Toward an Educationally Relevant Theory of Literacy Learning: Twenty Years of Inquiry."

You may also want to read the works of Ken Goodman and Frank Smith, whose brilliant thinking and research have contributed much to our understanding of how children learn and process language. I have written a summary of this research and how I apply beliefs about language learning to the classroom in *Invitations*. You may also want to send for the excellent brochure and position statement, "Elementary School Practices: Current Research on Language Learning," which is also useful to share with other educators, parent groups, and legislators.

Understanding Language Learning by Looking at Ourselves

One of the easiest and most powerful ways to understand and be able to apply the principles of language learning is to look closely at our own learning.

From Andrea Butler, I learned a powerful exercise that I have used in workshops with small groups, in and outside my school district. You can use this activity in your school, in a support group, or with several colleagues to demonstrate that all learning employs similar conditions. Here is a quick, abbreviated version:

1. Think about something important to you, outside of education and teaching, that you wanted or needed to learn. Think through what happened: how you learned it, why you learned it, how you felt while you were learning it, what helped you learn it, and how you felt after you learned it. (Some past examples: riding a bike, learning to drive, making curtains, refinishing woodwork.) Quickly jot down your thoughts. (Allow several minutes.)

2. Share your thoughts with several people around you. Make sure everyone gets a chance to tell his or her story. What do you notice? What qualities do you have in common? Have one person in your group write those qualities down. (Andrea Butler now suggests that the small group of three or four might also represent these common elements in a visual way. Drawing gets us away from a linear concept of learning and toward a more comprehensive one. She notes, "What comes out is a dynamic, interactive, complex level of learning rather than a list.") (Allow up to ten minutes for this, more time if the visual is included.)

3. As a whole group, share these common learning factors. Have the facilitator write down what is said, exactly as it is spoken and in the order given, on a chart or overhead transparency.

4. Note what this all means for the classroom. Discuss the role of an expert, trial and error, time for practice, choice, the need to learn, and much more.

Here is a list of common qualities generated in one workshop in which this exercise was used: pride, trial and error, learn by doing, perseverance, frustration, self-initiated, motivation, need, desire, learn by demonstrating, inspiration, determination, practice, success. Yours will be similar, yet slightly different. No matter how many times I use this activity, the important conditions for all learning, in and out of school, surface every time.

Deborah Meier, winner of a MacArthur award and an exemplary educator, makes the following observation about learning:

> There are, in the end, only two main ways human beings learn—by observing others (directly or vicariously) and by trying things out for themselves. Novices learn from experts and from experience. That's all there is to it. Everything else is in the details.

We must apply what we all do—in the real world whenever we learn anything—to learning in our classrooms, where our business must be to prepare our students to live in the world successfully. You can't get more basic than this.

What We Can Do to Provide Good, Solid Reading Instruction

Drawing on the work of other researchers, Michael Kibby makes two specific recommendations for teaching reading:

1. Literacy instruction at all levels should move beyond teaching students to find main ideas and details in texts to the higher-level skills of applying "logic, inference, and synthesis" to texts.
2. There should be greater use of multiple texts in reading instruction. In particular, the studied texts should be not only narrative, but also expository, such as history, science, math, and so on.

In my own school district, I am part of a committee of teachers, librarians, and administrators working together to do this very thing. Rather than continue to use "core" literature to teach reading as a separate subject in each of the elementary grades, we will be using multiple copies of exceptional fiction and nonfiction trade books—what we are calling "anchor" books—to support the study of authors and illustrators, various genres, and "big ideas." These anchor books will be used with teacher guidance across the curriculum—in reading and writing, but also in social studies, science, and mathematics. Literature will still be used to teach reading. However, that literature—the anchor books—will also be used to support the discussion and analysis of key concepts that connect to district curriculum objectives and children's interests.

Based on my work as a classroom teacher, reading specialist, Reading Recovery teacher, and language arts resource teacher and my experiences as a reader, writer, and thinker, I offer the following broad recommendations for developing solid reading and writing programs that are grounded in how children learn language most easily. These recommendations are not all-inclusive; they are meant as a self-evaluation tool for thinking about our teaching.

• Match children with appropriate books.

In selecting books to use in teaching reading, we need to consider text difficulty and students' interests and experiences. When a child makes many miscues (unexpected responses during oral reading), it usually means that the book or text is too hard and that the child should be given an easier selection. Developing readers make no progress in reading when they are continually given texts that are too difficult. In fact, they may regress. Yet, in many classrooms, children are regularly given books that are too challenging for them.

• No matter what the grade level, read aloud every day.

Introduce children to different genres (types of literature), authors, writing styles. Choose books with wonderful language, vocabulary, stories, and information. Hearing stories and discussing stories promotes reading at every age. There is also much evidence to show that reading aloud positively impacts vocabulary growth and comprehension. If children read a million words a year (which is considered an average amount for middle-class children), they will likely gain the meaning of one thousand new words from context.

Also encourage parents to continue reading aloud. Some of us teachers have discovered that many parents stop reading to their children once their children begin to read.

• Provide sustained time daily for free-choice reading.

From second to fifth grade, time spent reading books is the best predictor of a child's reading achievement. Also, "Children read more when they see other people reading, both at school and at home." Be sure to read for your own purposes at least several times a week. Not only is this a necessary model for students, it's a great way to get professional reading done. In the course of a school year, you could complete several professional books (or many journal articles).

Maintain a well-stocked classroom library. If your classroom library has only a few books, have each student check out several books from the school library and keep them in the classroom library during the time they are checked out. That guarantees seventy-five books or more.

Strongly encourage and expect independent reading at home (see Appendix B). Discourage overuse of television, video, and computer games (see Appendix C).

• *Respect children's rights as readers and allow them the same rights we have.*
"If we want our sons, our daughters, all young people to read, we must grant them the same rights we grant ourselves." Stipulating that only chapter books can be read or that magazines aren't allowed can work against developing a love of reading. Think about incorporating The Reader's Bill of Rights into your classroom: "the right to not read, the right to skip pages, the right to not finish, the right to reread, the right to read anything, the right to escapism, the right to read anywhere, the right to browse, the right to read out loud, the right to not defend your tastes."

Along the same lines, think about the importance of the reading setting. Have a cozy reading corner. Physical comfort, a peaceful room, and an attractive space impact the amount of reading we do.

In terms of encouraging reading and growth in reading, it matters little what students read as long as they read. Although we might be reluctant to condone "light reading," this statement holds true for comic books and teen romances. Light reading, in fact, often leads to more substantial book reading. This is true for adults too. "Romances make up half of all the paperbacks churned out in the United States and bring about $1 billion a year to their publishers."

It is, in fact, the popular series books—which are easy reading for kids—that often cement reading as a lifetime practice. This was certainly true for me. I still remember "sneaking" the reading of comic books as a kid and doing only light reading, including the entire Nancy Drew and Hardy Boys series.

• *Spend most of language arts reading time reading.*
While assigned written responses and activities that draw the child back to the text are familiar activities for working with small reading groups, more reading or rereading (especially for emerging and developing readers) is often the most beneficial means for becoming a better reader. This independent reading can be done individually or with a partner or small group. Struggling readers do well when they support each other through a familiar text.

**• *Give all children an opportunity to discuss excellent literature
in a small group.***
A review of the research validates the benefits of discussing literature.

> Research points to the positive connection between extensive reading and
> improved reading comprehension. Providing opportunities for children to
> discuss what they have read—to become active participants in making
> meaning from written text—has also been proven to help students' reading
> skills to grow. This second approach also has positive effects on the first
> since students who are provided with time and opportunity to share their
> thoughts about reading tend to read more.

Expecting and encouraging students to hear and value others' insight
and understanding often opens up a whole new world in reading. Even struggling readers have good ideas and, with support, can understand and discuss
a book that is above their instructional reading level. Some teachers use
books on tape and partner reading as aids for developing readers.

Small-group discussions are necessary to hear all the students' voices.
Whole-class or large-group discussion does not allow the equal and lively
participation by all students that small-group discussion promotes.

• *Do more guided silent reading.*
"The basis of guided reading is a teacher and a child or a group of children
reading a story together silently, with periodic discussion."

We still do far too much oral reading. Oral reading is great for spot-
checking students' needs and for enjoyment, but most of the reading we do
in real life is silent. Kids need to be taught how to do this. For example, they
need to see us thinking aloud and problem-solving when we come to a word
or paragraph we don't know the meaning of or rereading to make sense.

• *Pull small groups and individuals for explicit instruction.*
Explicit instruction—as long as it arises from ongoing, authentic assessment
(classroom-based data gathering and observation) and evaluation (making
judgments and decisions, and taking action based on the assessment)—is
integral to all good teaching.

Don't be afraid to "ability-group" for short periods of time as needed.
It's our job to teach kids how to effectively orchestrate a whole range of
strategies and problem-solve when they read. You can't teach reading to a
whole class. Working with the whole class is okay occasionally, but you can't
get to know your students as readers and thinkers that way. A "one size fits
all" approach rarely helps students make progress. In most situations, only
some students are "with you" and interested.

• *Ignore most oral reading miscues, especially when they don't interfere with meaning.*
This is difficult for most of us to do but important. Many of us still spend too much time expecting word-perfect reading. A child can read fluently and still not comprehend, what some call "barking at the page." If the student is getting most of the words, reading for meaning (as evidenced by meaningful substitutions. rereading to make sense, fluency), and able to retell the text, we don't need to overfocus on correctness. In fact, small miscues that do not alter the meaning are characteristic of good readers.

This does not mean we don't teach. Of course we do. We notice patterns of miscues in oral reading and use them as teaching points for future—or on-the-spot—instruction. When we see a student repeatedly making the same kinds of miscues, and they are interfering with fluent reading and understanding, we need to stop and teach whatever the student needs.

• *No matter what the grade level, do some shared reading regularly.*
Shared reading is great for building community, supporting struggling readers, and enjoying poems, songs, raps, chants, and stories together. Poetry, especially, lends itself to enjoyable repeated reading, and shared readings of poems can be led by students, even young ones. I define shared reading as any rewarding reading situation in which a learner or group of learners sees the text, observes an expert (usually the teacher) reading it with fluency and expression, and is invited to read along.

What We Can Do to Provide Good, Solid Writing Instruction

First of all, establish a classroom community. Take lots of time with your students to work out the procedures, rules, room arrangement, and expectations. Unless your students care about and respect one another and can manage and control their own behavior most of the time, it will be very difficult to have a "workshop" with some sustained writing time, teacher-student conferences, peer conferences, and self-direction by your students. Without community, the following recommendations cannot be incorporated.

• *Give daily time to writing.*
Don Graves says, "If students are not engaged in writing at least four days out of five, and for a period of thirty-five to forty minutes, beginning in first

grade, they will have little opportunity to learn to think through the medium of writing." Kindergarten teacher Peg Rimedio says, "Start in kindergarten."

Teachers say, *Where will I find this time?* The only way is to integrate the curriculum, to stop the artificial separations between reading and writing and the other subjects. For example, kids can be reading and writing in science or social studies during language arts time. This is what some call the "seamless" curriculum and, of course, this integration requires fewer separate classes and longer uninterrupted blocks of time. In some places, restructuring will be necessary for this to become a possibility.

• *Find out what students "ache with caring" about.*
Allow students to choose their own topics most of the time. (Some of these choices will be within a required curriculum framework—choosing the subject for a mandatory research report, for example.) Help students find books and resources to expand their knowledge. Writing and reading will often overlap.

Find out what students know a lot about, care a lot about, or want to know a lot about. Encourage sticking with the same topic for a while. Mem Fox reminds us, "I have about four ideas a year, and I'm a proficient, professional, published writer, yet we ask children to write story after story."

• *Model yourself as a writer.*
As much as possible, however, do not do "role model" writing for your students; do your real writing of letters, poems, stories, texts for your own life purposes. Students need to see us struggle, think out loud, revise, edit, and write in front of them. Nancie Atwell reminds us, "We only have to write a little bit better than they do for them to take something away from our demonstrations."

• *No matter what the grade level, do some shared writing regularly.*
Use shared writing—the teacher and student compose collaboratively but the teacher scribes—for newsletters to parents, class rules, expectations for editing, retellings of shared experiences (field trips, special visitors), thank-you letters from the class, science observations, and much more.

• *Encourage students to write in many genres.*
We have become overfocused on journal writing, especially with primary-grade students. Teach students—even kindergarten students—to write poetry, notes, messages, letters, greeting cards, lists, book reviews, stories, memoirs, interviews, "how to" books, more.

Use excellent literature (fiction and nonfiction, including pieces written by your students) to notice what authors do: leads, voice, style, interesting vocabulary, format, endings, sentence constructions, powerful adjectives and verbs.

Having students keep track of what they have written helps them become more independent about setting goals for themselves to write in many genres for many purposes. Figure 5–1 (p. 89) is one third grader's record of the writing she's done.

• *Teach more conventions.*
Don Graves suggests, "Far more conventions need to be taught than they have been. Lucy's [Calkins] approach with minilessons has been a great service to the country in that it really focuses on conventions. I like to use the word *conventions*. As Frank Smith says, 'Everything you do in writing is a convention.' Conventions exist to allow for good, crisp thought. If they are missing, then the thinking can be sloppy. The writer needs them just as much as the reader."

• *Be realistic about revision.*
There's no incentive for a student to revise unless the writing is for a purpose the student chooses and/or values. Remember, too, that much of the writing we as adults do never gets revised. Don't expect kindergarten and first-grade children to do much revision. The act of writing and transcription is challenge enough.

• *Model sharing and response.*
Kids cannot conference effectively with each other until we show them how to do it. Use sharing time, at the end of writing time, to model genuine and helpful responses to the content of students' writing.

Reenvisioning "Back to Basics"

If we look at the NAEP test scores for reading (and math) over the last two decades, the overall scores show very little change. And recent NAEP data (for 1992 and 1994) on how students read reveals that most of them can decode the words; the problem lies in understanding and critical thinking.

We need to reenvision and relook at what we define as basic. All of us teachers will continue to have students who have difficulty learning to read and write, regardless of the method we use. Those kids won't just need phonics to become proficient readers, writers, and thinkers. In order for reading and writing to make sense to their lives and enrich their lives, they will need a whole lot more than "basic skills."

Rexford Brown reminds us that we need to be looking for a higher literacy:

Kelly's Writing Journal #1

Date	Genre	Title
9-7-94	Poem	Seasons
9-7-94	Poem	The World
9-12-94	non-fiction	The Phantom Of The Opera
9-12-94	non-fiction	Colorado
9-14-94	report	Colorado
9-21-94	fiction	The Underground Room
10-28-94	Songs	The Song Book
11-2-94	fiction	Teacher Don't Come From Outer-Space

Writing Journal #2

11-9-94	fiction	Teachers Don't Come From Outer-Space
11-21-94	poem	Thanksgiving Day
12-14-94	fiction	Mary Brown: Wanted Dead Or Alive
1-10-95	song	Martin Luther King
1-11-95	field trip summary	What Would you do on the Moon?
1-20-95	non-fiction	What's Happening?
1-24-95	song	Report Cards
1-25-95	core-book writing	Swan Steals Trumpet From Music Store
2-8-95	non-fiction	The Ice Show
2-9-95	biography	George Washington Carver
2-10-95	poem	The World
2-10-95	poem	Africa, England and Spain
2-10-95	poem	Shoes

Figure 5–1 Writing record of a third grader

that goes beyond basic skills and includes enhanced abilities to think critically and creatively; to reason carefully; to inquire systematically into any important matter; to analyze, synthesize, and evaluate information and arguments; and to communicate effectively to a variety of audiences in a variety of forms.

Without such a "literacy of thoughtfulness," basic skills have no meaning. Unless our students can read and write for their own purposes—to make sense of their world, to understand and critique the media and all they read, to create beauty—we will have what many have asked for: a "basics" society, dull and unimaginative. That's not good enough for any of us.

6

Phonics Phobia

It would be irresponsible and inexcusable not to teach phonics. Yet the media are having a field day getting the word out that many of us ignore phonics in the teaching of reading. It just isn't so. Some of us may not be doing as good a job as we need to be doing, but I don't know a knowledgeable teacher who doesn't teach phonics.

Some years ago during a conference talk I said, "Phonics is a lot like sex. Everyone is doing it behind closed doors but no one is talking about it." Not true anymore. Phonics has come out of the closet and into the living room. Everyone is talking about it. In fact we're talking too much about it.

The question is not, nor has it ever been, *Should we teach phonics?* It is common sense and common knowledge that successful readers must have sound-letter knowledge in order to read. The question is, *How should we teach phonics and how much phonics teaching is necessary?* How phonics knowledge is acquired and taught is a debate that has gone on for much of this century and shows no signs of ending. Discussions around phonics tend to become emotional and highly charged. Even among people I respect, there are differences of opinion.

Don Graves notes, "The phonics debate gets polarized, and you're forced to defend things that you don't even believe in, like the notion that kids don't need to know relationships between sounds and symbols. We attack rote phonics, and then all phonics is seen as suspect."

Beyond "Sounding It Out"

Go into almost any classroom and ask kids what they do when they come to a word they don't know, and they will say without hesitation, *Sound it out.* If you push them for another strategy, they will likely say, *Ask the teacher.* After that, they are fresh out of responses. And we're not just talking about the struggling readers. These one-dimensional responses are surprisingly typical even in classrooms where teachers are emphasizing meaning and structure cues along with phonics. So how is this possible, and more important, what can we do about it?

Parents, accustomed to their own reading history of "sounding it out" fall back on this familiar strategy when working with their children. It's how many of us were taught. To ensure that parents are supporting the teaching we are doing in school, it is our job to give them information about the reading process—including the whats, whys, and hows.

Parents are usually supportive when you explain that decoding skills are a natural part of the reading process; it's just how you approach teaching reading that is a little different from what they did in school. We need to explain to parents that phonics is not a method of teaching reading but rather one means of decoding words. Parents also need to know that phonics is but one of several strategies that readers use to make sense of text, and that phonics is most effective when it works hand in hand with meaning and structure.

What Does the Research Say About Phonics?

Intensive, early phonics instruction does produce students with superior word-identification skills but it does not necessarily improve their comprehension:

> Data on the long-term effects of phonics instruction are scanty. In one of the few longitudinal studies, children who had received intensive phonics instruction in kindergarten or first grade performed better in the third grade than a comparison group of children on both a word-identification test and a comprehension test. By the sixth grade, the group that years earlier had received intensive phonics instruction still did better than the comparison group on a word-identification test, but the advantage in comprehension had vanished. The fact that an early phonics emphasis had less influence on comprehension as the years passed is probably attributable to the increasing importance of knowledge of the topic, vocabulary, and reasoning ability on advanced comprehension tests.

So while children who are taught lots of phonics may have an early advantage *as measured by standardized tests*, that advantage disappears by sixth grade when we look at comprehension. If we define reading as getting meaning from print and not just reading the words, overemphasis on phonics is not necessary, and it is inordinately time-consuming. Something else in the curriculum will have to go. What often gets left out are authentic language activities, such as reading for pleasure (independent reading) and discussing literature. Teachers can't do it all. If you spend twenty to forty minutes a day on intensive phonics instruction, there will be little time to actually read books.

The aforementioned research results might have something to do with a shift of teaching emphasis. In the early grades, lots of kids still get the message that it's important to get every word right. Then, in the later grades, we sometimes have to unteach "word reading." The students who struggle the hardest seem to have the most trouble moving from *I've got to get each word right* to focusing on *What meaning am I getting out of this text?*

One of the more recent research findings deals with *onsets* and *rimes* and comes from the work of linguists. Onsets and rimes are easier for beginning readers than vowel sounds in isolation. The patterns remain stable and similar words are easily made for reading and writing. The onset is the part of the syllable that comes before the vowel and is usually a consonant or consonant blend. The rime is the rest of the unit. For example, in the word *bright*, *br* is the onset and *ight* is the rime. Nearly five hundred common words can be derived from only thirty-seven rimes. It is much easier for children to detect and apply familiar letter/spelling patterns than it is to state and apply rules.

Commonsense Views About Phonics

• **Phonics is a tool in the reading process and not an end in itself.**
Phonics instruction must always be used to help students make sense of what they read and not as an end in itself. There is no reason to be able to decode words if you are not reading meaningful, connected text. Decoding words and "sounding out" are not reading. Reading is a meaning-construction process that requires connected, relevant text.

• **Phonics knowledge is necessary to be a competent reader and writer/speller.**
There is no question that kids need to know sound-symbol relationships. To become successful readers and writers, all children need what is called *phonemic awareness*, the ability to hear and differentiate between different words,

sounds, and syllables in speech. What *is* debatable is how phonics knowledge is acquired and how it should be taught. Some of the best ways to develop children's phonemic awareness are through repeatedly singing, saying, and hearing traditional nursery rhymes, simple poems, and songs, as well as through word play. Using invented spelling in daily writing also helps develop phonemic awareness and sound-letter knowledge.

Many students seem able to garner phonics knowledge independently and effortlessly, especially if they have had rich, early language and literacy experiences. Other children seem to benefit from and need some explicit instruction somewhere along the way. These students don't, however, need to be drilled on individual sounds for long periods of time. Explicit teaching is relevant when it is based on students' needs and occurs in the context of writing, or reading literature—not as isolated exercises. Two examples of explicit teaching follow.

Let's say I am working with a small group of beginning readers and I notice they are having difficulty with the high-frequency word/pattern *all* in the book we are reading. After the reading and before the next day's reading we will do some specific word work—writing *all* on individual slate boards, manipulating magnetic letters, creating and writing other words that have the *all* rime (*ball, call, mall*), making a chart and having kids add to it, posting *all* on the classroom word wall, and expecting kids to spell it correctly in their writing.

Or again, second graders in Loretta Martin's class were reading a book about Martin Luther King in a small guided-reading group. Some children were getting stuck reading words with *ch* in them. Loretta supported the children's reading so as not to stop the meaningful flow, but afterward she took time to explicitly teach them the *ch* digraph. She guided the children to notice, talk about, and write down the *ch* words in the text they had just read (see Figure 6–1).

Indirect and direct teaching of phonics, pointing out features of text and discussing words and patterns, occurs all day long though shared reading and writing, through daily free-choice writing, through word play, and as part of other language activities. There are times, however, when the only way to figure out a word is through phonics. When I made that statement to a reading specialist, she hugged me and said, "Thank you for saying that. I've felt so guilty whenever I teach phonics."

• *It is easier to decode a word that you have heard before and know the meaning of.*
In fact, it's impossible to get meaning from a word that you've never seen or heard before just by decoding it. Students need a working listening-speaking vocabulary for decoding/phonics to make sense.

• Phonics can be taught and reinforced during shared reading and shared writing.

I use shared reading—where I read poems, rhymes, stories, raps, songs, and chants and the students follow along and join in—to teach phonics. After we have enjoyed the text several times, I may pull out features of text I want to highlight. I also use shared writing—where I scribe as the students and I orally compose messages, rules, letters, retellings of events and stories—to assess what students know and to teach what they need.

• Phonics can be assessed and taught during writing time.

Daily journal writing, free-choice writing, or assigned writing is a perfect time to note what the child is doing and to talk about it one-to-one. Children's ability to associate spellings with sounds tells us much about their developing literacy skills. Indeed, children's acquisition of spelling skills is closely allied with their growing word-recognition abilities. Here is where children's invented spellings tell us much about their phonics knowledge.

• Most of the time set aside for reading in school should be spent reading meaningful texts.

Children do not become readers through practice exercises and skill sheets.

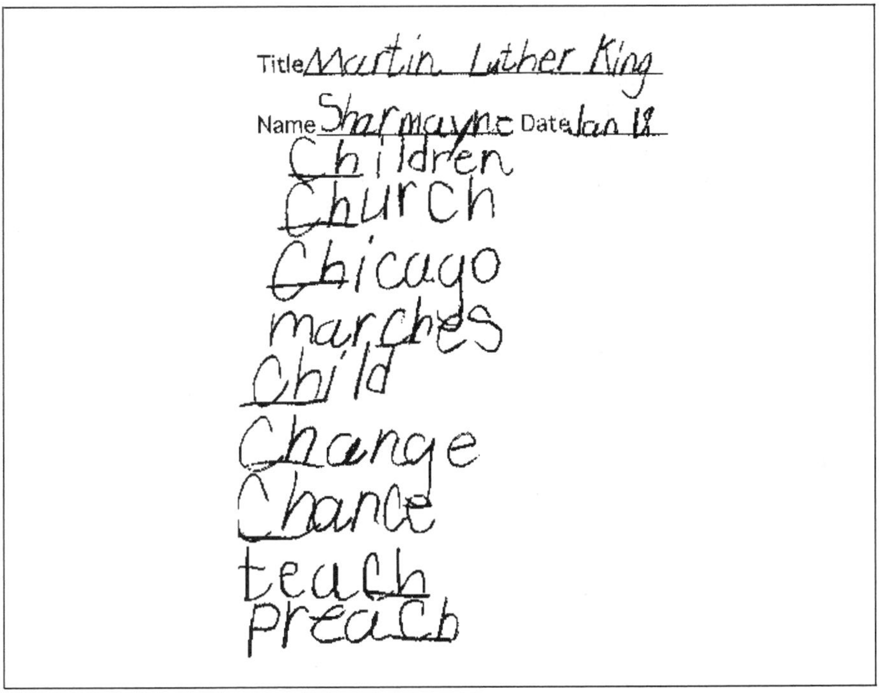
Title Martin Luther King
Name Sharmayne Date Jan 18
Children
Church
Chicago
marches
Child
Change
Chance
teach
preach

Figure 6–1 Explicit phonics teaching in the context of reading meaningful text

With guidance and teaching and time to read and enjoy predictable books, they learn to read by reading. Time spent on phonics should be brief in relation to time spent reading.

The Push for Intensive Systematic Phonics: Why and How?

The Ohio legislature (like the legislatures in North Carolina, New York, Pennsylvania, California, Wisconsin, and other states) has pushed hard to mandate a course in systematic intensive phonics as a requirement for teaching certification in undergraduate education. (It is ironic that in Ohio and many of those other states a course in children's literature is only optional.) Apparently, this push for required phonics courses for teachers is not limited to the United States. The controversy also rages in pockets of British Columbia and New Zealand.

There is no question that this widespread phenomenon is a move to control how we teach. In no other profession would such a mandate be given credence. Imagine states making such dictates to doctors or lawyers! Such a mandate also invades the already crammed curriculum at the university level.

Fortunately, in response to a possible mandate for intensive systematic phonics, some local and state reading councils have begun to pass resolutions that counteract the mandate and put common sense back into teaching. For example, in my state, Ohio, the importance of phonics in teaching children to read is acknowledged along with the belief that teachers as professional educators should select teaching strategies that best meet the needs of their students.

I am in total agreement with the notion that phonics instruction needs to be part of teacher education. However, I do not believe a separate course is necessary or warranted. A separate course sends the message that phonics is the most important strategy in learning to read. A separate course separates phonics from reading as an integrated meaning-making process. Phonics needs to be taught as one of the cueing systems, along with the meaning and structure of language, in an authentic literacy context.

A Workshop in Intensive Systematic Phonics

I attended a local workshop, sponsored by the Ohio Department of Education, on intensive systematic phonics. I went as a curious observer because I believed it was important to know what was being prescribed to teachers. The presenter was polished and knowledgeable, using such popular phrases as "in context" and "children's literature" while recommending sequential lessons in isolation and never mentioning a children's book. Her talk was peppered with references to "research" but the specifics of that research were never stated. (Research was included with our handouts, and I read that research later.) We were told over and over that as teachers we haven't been taught phonics at the university level. However, in my training as a reading specialist twenty years ago, phonics was the only strategy I was taught.

I was very upset when I left the workshop. I was disturbed by the overemphasis on phonics, the highly prescriptive nature of the phonics recommended, and the effect the workshop would likely have on the children the participants teach. Even though I was on overload at work and had no extra time, I felt—as a responsible educator—I had to voice my concerns. Because this workshop was sponsored by the Ohio Department of Education, I wrote a long letter to our superintendent of schools at the Ohio Department of Education with copies to about twenty people, including the presenter and all members of the Ohio Board of Education. I tried to be constructive in my criticism of the workshop and made some suggestions for future workshops. Excerpts from the letter follow:

> In her opening remarks, the speaker implied that the State Department endorses and recommends "intensive systematic phonics," i.e., the prescribed program she presents, as the best way to teach phonics. According to Susan Gardner, reading consultant for the Ohio Department of Education, the State Department endorses and recommends several strategies for teaching phonics and does not state that "intensive systematic phonics" is the best way. While I believe phonics knowledge is absolutely necessary to the reading-writing process, there are many ways for young children to acquire that knowledge. Since the speaker seems to speak for the Ohio Department of Education on how phonics should be taught and since educators take information from the Ohio Department of Education very seriously, it is important that the speaker's message is clear, balanced, and developmentally appropriate.

> I spoke at length with the speaker after the workshop and made the following suggestions to her for future phonics workshops:

> • *Balance the perspectives on the research articles that are shared.*

> For example, the research articles shared are slanted to phonics in isolation and against meaning-based approaches. Using an article that questions the effectiveness of Reading Recovery as the only article about Reading Recovery is very biased.

• *Delete inflammatory and opinionated language in the handouts.*

Address only the teaching of phonics, and do not pit whole language against other teaching approaches by writing about "the controversy." For example, printed statements such as, "Whole language students often develop a false confidence that can interfere with their attention to skills instruction" and ". . .the whole language philosophy implies that effective readers use context first and phonics last (Pryor, *Ohio Reading Teacher*, Fall, 1990)" do not belong in a workshop devoted to teaching phonics.

• *Connect the reading process to the teaching/learning of phonics.*

Using the "intensive phonics system" presented, all first graders are to spend about twenty-five minutes with daily phonics (whether they are ready for it or not). This period of exposure is to be followed by related spelling and dictation—essentially, more phonics. Unless children and teachers understand phonics as a necessary cueing system to be integrated in the process of real reading, phonics knowledge is meaningless. The presenter repeatedly stated, "This is phonics; this is not reading." In the course of a five-hour workshop, there was only one brief reference to a children's book. It appears that first-grade children are to spend more time learning phonics than they are reading books and hearing the language of stories.

• *Connect the writing process to the teaching/learning of phonics.*

Recognize that assessing and analyzing children's daily writing is one of the best ways to teach phonics. On the handout that states, ". . . phonics skills are best assessed in the reading process. . ." add "writing" to the statement.

• *Be open to children's different learning styles.*

In answer to a participant's question, "What about the student who comes to school already reading?" the response was the student "learned to read because of an excellent visual memory." While this is undoubtedly true, the presenter refused to acknowledge that this same student has also internalized many of the rules of phonics and has much phonics knowledge. This is just one example of the varied needs that students have when learning to read. Teachers must constantly make instructional decisions based on the individual learning styles of their students.

I request that the Ohio State Board of Education take a close look at the information and the "handouts" educators receive in the workshop to be sure the information is accurate and gives a balanced perspective on the teaching of phonics.

Thank you for your attention. I look forward to hearing from you.

Sincerely,
Regie Routman

I received one response, from the state superintendent. It was a politically correct, skillfully worded letter that basically took no stand for or against the workshop nor acknowledged that any changes would be made with regard to future workshops. Still, I was glad I had made the effort to write the letter. I can hope that at least it generated some conversations and new thought. Even more than that, perhaps future presentations offered more balanced perspectives, even if I never heard about them.

A Few Disabled Readers Benefit from Intensive Systematic Phonics

Several years ago, I worked with a second grader (I'll call him Michael) who was having a terrible time learning to read. He was smart, had a great attitude, comprehended everything, but he couldn't make any sense of the written code. Even though he was being taught lots of meaning-based strategies along with phonics—in the literature context—he could not make any sense of the written text unless he had heard it over and over again. In the small group I met with daily in his second-grade classroom, he was struggling mightily with reading and spelling, and most of his writing was illegible. His parents were justifiably very concerned. They felt we in the public school weren't doing enough for their child.

Michael's parents had him privately tested by a reading clinic, and he was officially declared reading disabled and dyslexic. The reading diagnostician at the clinic recommended a private school for severely disabled readers where he would receive intensive systematic phonics. She also recommended to our administrator and director of elementary education that our school system needed to create a special class for kids like Michael, that she was seeing too many kids who couldn't read (her implication was clear; it was because of whole language.)

The interesting thing was that Michael was the most severely disabled reader I had ever worked with in twenty years. In the eight or so years since we'd been teaching reading with literature and teaching most strategies (phonics being one of them) in the context of the reading, we'd had very few kids who hadn't learned to read successfully. But, and this is a big but, the reading diagnostician saw *only* kids like Michael, from our district and from surrounding districts. I believe that because she saw a disproportionate number of readers with very severe problems, she generalized about the need for intensive systematic phonics for many students and sent a message to our administrators that was misleading and damaging.

I've been teaching reading too long to deny that kids like Michael exist. But I believe we are talking about a very small percentage of kids, the truly learning-disabled kids, about 5 percent. The rest, a whopping 95 percent, do just fine with good, solid reading instruction as described on pages 82–86. As a former learning disabilities teacher and as a reading specialist, I've worked with those few kids who needed the intensive systematic phonics, and we have an obligation to give them what they need. These are the few who have a terrible time with reading until they "break the code." These are the kids who also need lots of rhyming games, multisensory experiences, mnemonic devices, and other "gimmicks" to help them read.

Barbara Speer, an outstanding teacher of children with learning disabilities in my district's elementary grades, agrees. Although Barbara had been working with students on a pull-out basis for almost twenty years and was used to it, she now works mostly in the classroom, and this has changed her perspective. (All the second graders in our school that have been identified as learning disabled are assigned to the same second-grade inclusion classroom, where Barbara co-teaches with Linda Cooper.) She comments,

> Your 5 percent estimate is probably right—maybe it's slightly higher. I also agree with your observation about the reading diagnostician's perspective being skewed, as was mine, from only working with that 5 to 7 percent of the kids. After this year's experience of seeing how very well—in fact, sensational—the other 93 to 95 percent of all second graders read, we're obviously doing something right. Out of the twenty-two second graders in our class, sixteen are good to excellent readers. Of the six who are not, five have been identified as learning disabled.

What We Can Do to Keep Phonics in Perspective

• **Become knowledgeable. Articulate clearly that we do teach phonics.**
Talk about how and why. Educate yourself about the role of phonics in the reading process. Send for the issue of NCTE's *School Talk* entitled "Phonics Fuss: Facts, Fiction, Phonemes, and Fun." Share the publication with your colleagues and use its resource bibliography to extend your own knowledge of teaching phonics. (You do need to know how to teach phonics, but you don't need a special course!) Many primary-grade teachers have found Don Holdaway's "A Simplified Progression of Word Recognition Skills" very useful for knowing what and when to teach.

Discuss your beliefs and the strategies you use at curriculum evenings, open houses, conferences. Be sure your administrator knows how you include phonics as part of your teaching of reading and spelling/writing.

Include talk of phonics and skills in your newsletters to parents. Appendix E is a second grader's weekly review (Appendix D is a blank version of the form, which you can photocopy). Note that teacher Loretta Martin has been smart and political by including skills and phonics in the "I've worked on these skills—" section. Parents readily see that phonics is being taught. In the student sample in Appendix E, "r-controlled vowels" are listed. Loretta taught these when she observed that about 85 percent of her students were confusing the spelling of "r-controlled" vowels as they were working on independent reading and writing projects about the solar system. They were having difficulty with words like *solar, orbit, Saturn, Mars,* and *Uranus.* The students and teacher jointly made wall charts of words that highlighted "r-controlled" vowels.

• *Share research, fact sheets, and information about phonics with parents, administrators, other educators, and community members.*
Read, discuss, copy, and distribute "Facts: On the Teaching of Phonics" (see Appendix F). When parents ask about "Hooked on Phonics" and other questionable commercial programs, send for and distribute the IRA position paper "Guidelines for the Evaluation of Commercial Reading Programs" and the IRA resolution "'Buyer Be Wary' Cautions International Reading Association." Also, contact the International Reading Association for a set of criteria both teachers and parents can use for judging and evaluating phonics kits before purchasing them. Share alternative reading strategies to "sound it out" with parents. See Appendix G for "Reading Strategies for Unknown Words."

• *Help parents see the big picture of reading.*
Let parents know that actually reading books contributes more to reading achievement—comprehension, vocabulary, and speed—than any other factor. Some of my district's kindergarten and primary-grade teachers route the video *Parents, Kids and Books* to parents and ask for their feedback. After viewing it almost all parents comment that they have newly realized or had confirmed the importance of discussing stories and responding naturally to questions as they read with their children. This helps put phonics in perspective by focusing primarily on the joy of reading and listening to their children's questions and responses about the story.

• *Post phonics charts visibly in the classroom.*
As you do lessons—in the context of spelling, writing, and reading for real purposes—have the students hypothesize rules and make charts with you of patterns that are *worth learning.* I am not talking about the old scope-and-

sequence charts made by a commercial publisher. I am talking about charts used across the curriculum that are newly constructed each year, based on that year's students and their needs and inquiries.

• *Spend most of reading time reading.*

While phonics and spelling activities and games can help students develop phonics knowledge, caution must be taken to spend most of language arts time reading and writing authentic texts. Developing readers need to be able to automatically read and write simple, easy words—those high-frequency words that successful readers recognize immediately and correctly when reading and writing. One of the most expedient ways to promote this fluency is through reading lots of easy and familiar books—individually or with a partner—in which these words occur repeatedly. Years ago, I did an analysis of the words in a popular, predictable text for developing readers and found that almost 40 percent of these words, which we used to call "basic sight words," were included, many of them over and over again.

• *Tape-record reading conferences with children.*

A successful strategy I used when I was working daily in second-grade class-rooms with small groups of struggling readers was to tape-record each child's oral reading several times a year. While the taping was done for evaluation purposes so the child, the family, and I could note progress and needs, an unexpected side effect were the comments from parents. In the course of tap-ing the child reading orally, my voice was also present offering support and suggestions to the child. I might say, *What else could you try?* or *Say the begin-ning sound of that word, then skip it, read on, and come back to it. Now try it again.* Or, when the child was able to work out some difficult part, *Tell me what you did. What worked for you?* Many parents told me that my comments served as models for them. For the first time, they understood they could offer help beyond phonics and "sounding it out."

• *Invite parents in.*

Another strategy that worked well for me was to invite parents into the read-ing group. I told parents the time we met and gave them an open invitation to come in and join the reading group with their child so they could see the kind of teaching going on and ways to support their child at home. I asked them to call me a day ahead to let me know they would be coming. Since the invitation was not for a specific day, parents were usually able to arrange to come in on a day off. Then they saw exactly what strategies, language, and supports I was using to help children become independent readers and left feeling more confident to try multiple strategies at home.

• *Share informal, direct assessments as alternatives to standardized testing.*
Children who are developing readers and who are learning to use a range of strategies to make sense of text may do poorly on "word study skills" in isolation. Some parents, teachers, and administrators panic when that happens. To assure a balanced, accurate picture of the child's reading, I take a running record and a retelling of a child's oral reading of a familiar book and an unfamiliar book and share those results with the student and parents as well.

• *Lobby state departments of education against required courses in intensive systematic phonics.*
We teachers typically do not lobby about important educational issues, and we need to. Lawyers and doctors look after their special interests. So do social workers and human services personnel. We have power only if we use it.

• *Make our voices heard to change teacher education in phonics.*
In my role as a language arts resource teacher, I work with all new teachers in our K–4 classrooms. Many of those coming out of our universities say that they have the big picture, that they know about literature and response, but they don't have a clue about how to actually teach reading—the phonics, the strategies, the cueing systems. Several of them have told me that phonics was barely mentioned in their courses. See pages 130, 133–35 for more on phonics in teacher education.

Final Perspectives

Anne P. Sweet, director of learning and instruction in the office of educational research and improvement for the U.S. Department of Education, puts the continuing controversy over phonics in perspective.

> Although learning phonics is essential, research has shown that it is not sufficient. Effective teachers ensure that phonics teaching is done in conjunction with connected, informative, engaging text. Embedding phonics teaching within whole language instruction is a sound, balanced, commonsense approach to literacy learning.
>
> Getting past the emotion attached to this polarizing debate is requisite to making strides in our children's literacy learning. We know that students need to do a lot of reading and writing, study letters and words, and be exposed to whole selections of literature that confirm what they know about how language works. We know that able teachers carefully orchestrate multiple activities that require students to engage in listening,

speaking, reading, and writing in order to meet content goals, skill goals, and literacy goals all at the same time. Let's band together and support good teachers who practice sound pedagogy, while educating a new crop of professionals to do likewise.

The phonics debate is likely to continue into the next century. We need to add our rational voices to the conversation and help the public understand the place of phonics in the reading process.

7

Spelling, Grammar, Handwriting, and Other "Questionable" Practices

I do teach skills. I think correct spelling is important. I believe children need to be able to understand and use correct grammar. I think handwriting matters. Parents, administrators, students, colleagues, and the public need to know we still value these important "basics." However, I do not teach these skills through meaningless practice exercises, separated from actual reading and writing. I teach these skills using language in authentic literacy and literature contexts.

Teaching the Skills

When I teach skills, I am not talking about the "skills based" teaching that focuses on isolated, simplistic, and decontextualized bits of information. I am talking about all the conventions of written and spoken language—spelling, handwriting, punctuation, structure, grammar, and more—that enable students to communicate more effectively in their lives. In the global sense, Frank Smith says our repertoire of skills allows us to interact with the world, comprehend it, and change it. "Skills, in other words, are the way we get things done."

"Teaching skills in context" has become a popular phrase. But what does it mean? Some teachers have misinterpreted "teaching skills in context" to mean that, instead of using language textbook exercises, you create your own skills activities. For example, in teaching a skill such as quotation marks, some teachers will create sentences without quotation marks and ask students to add the marks. This is still an inauthentic activity that is a waste of students' time. To teach the same skill in an authentic context, the teacher might make an overhead of a student's writing done for a real purpose and audience (with the student's permission) and talk through with the class and demonstrate where, why, and how to use quotation marks. (See Appendix H, "Facts: On Teaching Skills in Context," for a summary of research and practice. Share these facts with educators, parents, administrators, boards of education, and policy makers.)

Skills are "best taught through meaningful communication, best learned in meaningful contexts. . . . Yes, if minority people are to effect the change which will allow them to truly progress we must insist on 'skills' within the context of critical and creative thinking." So writes Lisa Delpit, an African American educational scholar and writer, who speaks passionately about the need to teach skills in order to give all students equal access to "the culture of power." She defines skills as "useful and usable knowledge which contributes to a student's ability to communicate effectively in standard, generally acceptable literary forms." While Delpit's positions are often criticized by language purists, I find many of her arguments persuasive: "Writing process advocates often give the impression that they view the direct teaching of skills to be restrictive to the writing process. . . . Black teachers, on the other hand, see the teaching of skills to be essential to their students' survival." She cautions us that "those who are most skillful at educating black and poor children do not allow themselves to be placed in 'skills' or 'process' boxes. They understand the need for both approaches." Fluency and free writing are not sufficient. Like it or not, we are judged by how we look, act, and speak. If our writing and speaking patterns are careless and sloppy and are furthermore incorrect grammatically and full of misspellings, the public will likely assess us as inept and barely literate.

We must also be careful that we do not judge students' literacy solely on their school performance. For low-performing students, the school setting (being placed in a low track, for example) may foster presenting themselves as less skillful than they actually are. For example, outside school, the language skills of a student may be quite different from—and more proficient than—those they demonstrate in the classroom. Holly Burgess, a high school English teacher, learned the importance of valuing oral language skills in a broad context. She tells the story of receiving a phone call from one of her seniors who was confused about the due date for an assignment. She says,

> I knew immediately who was on the other end of the phone, but I was surprised at how *clearly* he spoke. In the classroom, he mumbles any response, and, when reading aloud, he seems to think speed is of the essence. I realized that I had judged his spoken English only on my classroom interaction with him, never having had a phone conversation with him.

We Need to Do More Teaching

I get paid to teach. Yes, I also facilitate, coach, guide, lead from behind, suggest, mediate, support, intervene, and scaffold. But mostly, I teach. And I don't apologize for it. In some circles, teaching has become a dirty word. It shouldn't be. It's what we do and who we are. I once heard Frank Smith say, "Either you say to the child, *Great job* or *Let me show you how to do this.*"

By teaching, I do not mean standing up in front of the room and lecturing, conducting a monologue while students are silent, soliciting "right" answers, and calling on students only when they raise their hands. By teaching, I do mean constantly instructing, assessing, evaluating, and goal-setting based on the needs and interests of students. I do mean demonstrating for the whole class, small groups, and individuals. I do mean setting up a community of learners who (with modeling and encouraging) learn how to collaborate and value and respect each other. So how do I teach? Mostly through demonstrating over and over again in authentic literacy contexts. Judith Newman says it best for me: "Teaching involves intentionally helping to extend another's knowledge or skill."

Sometimes, It's Okay to Tell Them

And I don't always wait for students to exhibit a need. As a knowledgeable practitioner, I know students will require certain skills and strategies in order to use language successfully. I teach these skills and strategies to make the learning path easier to navigate.

I don't want to discover everything. I don't have the time, the patience, or the inclination. Sometimes, I just want an expert to show me how. Let me give you an example.

A while back, I needed to purchase a new printer for my computer. (My computer, which I use for all my writing, is a small portable called a Powerbook. In my desire not to have my "space" dominated by technological hardware, I prefer small machines.) Given my lack of confidence about all things mechanical, I was feeling pretty good about the initiative I had taken to read about portable printers, check prices, and make an intelligent decision about which model would best serve my needs. I was proud of myself for calling ahead and getting the computer store manager to agree to align my purchase with a demonstration of exactly how to set up and operate the printer. I entered the computer store with my anxiety in check.

The manager kept his promise, but it was a Saturday, and the store was packed with browsers and shoppers full of questions. The manager would no sooner show me a procedure than we would be interrupted. Given the demands on his time and my insecurity, I was embarrassed to ask him to show me a step again. I left the store thinking that with a little luck, I could probably get the printer working.

That Saturday evening, with the manual by my side, I began the assembly/connection. It was a disaster. When I tried to activate the printer, my computer froze; then, no matter what I did, I couldn't turn off the computer. Straight to the manual. To my dismay, I found I couldn't understand or follow it. These writers must be engineers, I thought. It was like reading a foreign language. I tried to restrain my growing panic and called the Macintosh hotline, only to be greeted by the recorded message that the hotline was open Monday through Friday. My last resort was either my computer-savvy neighbor or my computer-expert son Peter. Both were enjoying a Saturday evening out, I realized with a touch of envy. Desperate to get the computer turned off, because I was afraid it would be damaged, I forced myself to painstakingly read the manual and guess at the difficult vocabulary. Three hours later, my anxiety out of control, I was finally able to turn the computer off.

That evening taught me a valuable lesson. First, I don't have to discover everything or be competent at everything. I don't even want to. And second, while some anxiety is okay, or even beneficial for learning, too much anxiety shuts down the learning process. If I had it to do again, I would have hired (or tried to bribe) someone from the computer store to come to my home and set up the printer and show me exactly how to operate it. It was not a good use of my time to spend an entire evening on a project I was not interested in (even though I needed the knowledge or someone else's knowledge). And my overwrought anxiety was unnecessary and harmful to my health.

What does this mean for the classroom? We constantly need to assess what is achievable. I was out of my league trying to assemble the printer because I had no understandable context, no support, and no other strategies to try other than to consult the manual. Kids (and adults) shut down when the task feels overwhelming. Good teachers know how to provide a combination of just enough challenge and support to keep students engaged and willing to problem-solve.

With this in mind, I sometimes think we overdo it when we tell the child, *Do the best you can. Figure it out yourself. Don't worry about it.* Sometimes it may be easier and less anxiety provoking to just tell him. For example: suppose your students are writing and you are walking about the room, conferring briefly with this one and that. If someone needs the spelling of a word he will be using repeatedly in his writing, it's okay just to give it to him. Or, if you are reading with a small group of children and a child comes across a word you would not expect her to be able to figure out, it's appropriate to supply the word. Or, if a child seems particularly anxious about not being able to figure something out on his own, give him a gift; just tell him.

What's Happened
to the Teaching of Spelling?

If there is anything that will sink the whole language movement and fuel the "back to basics" trumpeters, it is spelling. Too many times we have said, *Spelling doesn't matter*. Parents interpret this as, *We're not teaching spelling*. We need to get smart, and we need to get political about spelling.

In many cases, what happened was that we went to extremes not to intervene with kids' spelling. Even when we knew kids should be spelling better, we worried about interfering with their fluency and shaky confidence. Some of us even got the message that we weren't allowed to intervene, that it would interfere with students' creativity.

We've also lumped all of our students' different vocabularies together—reading, speaking, spelling, and listening—expecting kids to spell words beyond their developmental level. While it's appropriate to help kids develop a spelling sense for all these vocabularies so they can use resources effectively to find them, the words are not all appropriate as spelling words to be mastered.

Putting Invented Spelling in Perspective

Many parents fear that their kids will never learn to spell correctly and that they will keep their "bad habits." Unless we inform parents of the developmental nature of learning to spell—along with the strategies and activities we are employing to teach spelling—parents are unsupportive of what they view as a nontraditional, questionable practice.

Reports by the media and professional writers support their worst fears. In *Dumbing Down Our Kids: Why America's Children Feel Good About Themselves but Can't Read, Write, or Add*, Charles J. Sykes, a journalist who writes about educational issues, says we are turning out spellers who are "seldom competent" and that "many educationists in charge of teaching reading and writing no longer believe that it is necessary to teach or to correct spelling." While we read this and cry nonsense, worried parents become alarmist.

And teachers who find older children in their classes who are still misspelling basic words also think we are not teaching spelling. In some cases, of course, they are correct. In other cases, however, I believe that kids are writing more, taking more risks with vocabulary and forms, and writing more interesting pieces. But if a teacher values correct spelling and conventions before content and quality, the writing will look worse to that teacher. Then, too, one of the problems has been that teachers at different grade levels and schools within the same district don't talk much to each other. Primary teachers may not realize all that upper-grade teachers are dealing with, and vice versa.

There's no doubt that students are doing more writing today. Unfortunately, there are still too many classrooms where much of the writing is illegible, sloppy, and filled with misspellings of basic words. I welcome and accept that learning to spell is developmental and that learners develop spelling competency gradually and need lots of time and encouragement to practice and take risks through daily reading and writing experiences. However, I do not accept misspellings that occur because of carelessness, lack of teaching, or low expectations. When we teachers do not continually model reading and writing processes, provide lots of opportunities for guided practice, help kids discover and notice features of words, have high expectations, and hold kids accountable for what they do know, some students will continue to have trouble with spelling and reading despite our use of "writing process" and real literature.

As I see it, invented spelling was never meant to be "anything goes." Its purpose was to free kids to write. In a class of twenty-five to thirty students, children who depend on the teacher's help to spell every word correctly are unable to express themselves freely. Invented spelling (and with it, the teacher saying, *Do the best you can. That's fine for now. Spell it like it sounds*) allows kids to concentrate on their messages without overconcern for correctness. That has allowed even kindergarten children to see themselves as writers early in the school year—and that's been a wonderful thing.

However, I also believe children should only be inventing those words we would not expect them to be able to spell, based on where they are in their literacy development. That means sometimes we have to nudge and expect basic words to be spelled correctly. For example, while it is unrealistic to expect a first grader to spell all words correctly, it is realistic to expect *some* words to be spelled correctly all the time. Older children should be inventing only new vocabulary words, uncommon words, and words we wouldn't expect them to be able to spell correctly for their age or grade level.

We need to continue to celebrate children's invented spellings while keeping our expectations for students reasonable and high. We also need to communicate clearly with parents, by sharing the research on invented spelling—sometimes called developmental spelling—and by explaining the what, why, and how of our spelling programs.

So, How Should I Teach Spelling?

This is a question that everyone is asking. Used to relying on scripted spelling programs and weekly tests, most of us lack the knowledge to teach spelling "on our own." Even as we move toward more holistic teaching, giving up the spelling basal seems to be the last thing that most of us do as we endeavor to make spelling part of writing.

This is understandable. When we use a published spelling series, we get used to the easy management of built-in "skills," to all students studying the same list of words at the same time. Not only is tailoring spelling instruction to meet individual student's writing needs challenging and time-consuming, but successful practice depends on extensive teacher knowledge. The notion of attending to students' instructional levels in spelling (like we do in reading) has all but been ignored in practice, despite the fact that "focused, small-group work on word patterns will enhance not only spelling but also reading development."

When we teachers do give up the published spelling series, a first step has often been taking words from the literature just as some of the literature-based published reading programs do. This is contrived, time-consuming, and doesn't work—as we soon find out. Some teachers I know tried this approach after their principal declared that spelling workbooks would no longer be allowed. Expected to plan their own spelling programs without being trained in how to do so, most teachers floundered and did the best they could. Several teachers I know tried to create their own spelling programs one year but went back to the spelling basal the next because they realized they didn't know enough to do an adequate job. They felt they weren't teaching rules and patterns and didn't know how to teach them.

While explicit teaching of spelling is necessary, we need to remember that spelling ability, like all language functions, develops gradually, and that most of the words children eventually learn to spell come incidentally through wide reading.

> Just as we learn how words are pronounced by hearing them spoken in meaningful ways by people around us, so we learn spellings by encountering them in meaningful contexts when we read. (I must be very clear

here—I am not saying that reading guarantees spelling ability, but that spelling ability depends on reading.)

Building on the positive impact of reading on spelling development, Sandra Wilde suggests first attending to the general literacy development of a struggling speller rather than focusing on a particular spelling program.

• Set up classroom environments that encourage children to become good spellers.

A classroom environment that encourages children to become good spellers provides:

Lots of opportunities to read and write and talk about words.

Lots of playing around with language and pointing out special features of words (noticing and commenting on surprising letters found in a word, for example).

Time each day in which students mostly choose their own topics and write with clear purpose and for an intended audience.

Lots of lessons to explore and teach word patterns, hypothesize and develop rules, notice unusual features of words, and (for older students) work with meanings of Latin and Greek roots and suffixes. (These lessons arise both from what the teacher notices the children need and from what the teacher knows they will need in future reading and writing.)

Lots of spelling references for children (wall charts, personal dictionaries, other children, classroom dictionaries, print around the classroom, word walls).

An expectation that some common words will be spelled correctly.

Focus lessons and high expectations for proofreading written work—noticing and correcting misspelled words by using a variety of strategies.

Opportunities to share and publish writing for a purpose. (For example, for the past two years, fourth-grade students of Joan Servis have interviewed and written about new staff members, and these interviews are published in the school newspaper.)

• Become more knowledgeable about the teaching of spelling.

Thirty first- through sixth-grade teachers in our school district recently participated in two half-day workshops where we focused on the principles of learning to spell and the developmental nature of spelling, how to look for key indicators in children's writing in order to place students on a spelling continuum, and multiple strategies and activities for teaching and developing effective spellers.

After participating in this *First Steps* workshop and using the accompanying resource books, many of us who attended felt more confident either to create an independent spelling program or to combine what we learned with what we were already doing (which in some cases is using a published series). However we do it, we must take professional responsibility for educating ourselves to become more effective spelling teachers.

• *Become writing models for our students.*

When I write in front of a group of students on the overhead projector or chart paper, I think out loud, vocalize slowly as I am writing, and constantly reread. In my rereading—first of several lines, then of the first paragraph, and then, again, of most of a page—students witness the ongoing revising and proofreading I do every time I write. It's not just the content and vocabulary or order that I change. It's also the spelling. It's much easier for me to fix up simple spelling errors on the spot for words I already know or almost know than to save all the editing for the end. Done naturally, in the process of writing, writers come to develop a spelling consciousness as they compose.

• *Raise our expectations.*

I believe that we must hold kids highly accountable so they can take pride in their work. Even in daily writing, we should have appropriate and reasonable expectations such as legible handwriting, skipping every other line (at least for primary-grade children), spelling frequently used words correctly, and rereading to check for meaning, spelling, and punctuation. For editing, setting up expectations through class-composed shared writing works well (see Figure 7–1). Students need to know the teacher will not be a final editor until the student has self-edited.

When I am in a classroom in which writing looks a mess and the teacher accepts all invented spellings (even basic words), the students usually do not take writing seriously. If, too, the students are writing only for the teacher and do not see a purpose for the writing, they have little incentive to do their best, and that includes spelling. Further, if students know their teacher will fix up their errors, they have little incentive to do their own proofreading.

• *Don't accept sloppy drafts.*

I place the same expectations on children as writers that I place on myself as a writer. While I may read aloud a messy draft to a colleague to get feedback

EDITING

Capitalization
at the beginning of sentences
people's names
important places (for example, cities)
titles (of books, movies, TV shows)
days of the week, months
I

Punctuation
periods, question marks, or explanation marks at the
     end of each sentence
apostrophes in contractions (such as, don't, can't)

Spelling
Reread and look for misspellings.
Circle *all* misspelled words.
Correct *all* the ones you can.
     Use the dictionary.
     Sound it out.
     Ask a friend.
*Try writing it another way.

Neatness
Handwriting should be clear.
Corrections should be clear.

Read your paper over again!

Make sure your writing is just the way you want it.

Figure 7–1 Editing expectations by a fourth-grade class at the beginning of the school year

on content, when I want someone to respond to my written draft, I first make sure that draft is legible—and that includes standard spelling of frequently used words. Out of respect for the reader, who I want to focus on the content of the piece, I make sure the draft is easily readable. We should expect no less from our students.

That's one reason why I no longer use the term *sloppy copy* to refer to a draft. Some students have taken the term too literally and use *sloppy copy* as an invitation to turn in messy work with numerous misspellings.

• *Develop core lists of words.*
Teachers in several of our K–4 buildings worked together to develop core lists of spelling words because we became concerned about children's continual misspellings of common words. I think we also got tired of hearing about the students we were sending on who couldn't spell. We wanted it known that we expected students to be able to spell a core group of frequently used words by the time they leave each grade. These lists include words from our students' daily writing in addition to days of the week, months, the name of our school and city, and other common words (*because, enough, through, two, too, to*). We make these lists available to students, parents, and teachers in other grades. These core lists are accompanied by philosophical statements:

> Children will not become proficient spellers unless they are reading and writing daily in meaningful contexts.
>
> Explicit instruction—minilessons, demonstrations—is necessary and is expected (for example, *ed* endings and other suffixes).
>
> It is expected that previous grade-level lists are to be revisited.
>
> Teachers will also expect certain content-area words to be mastered.
>
> It is expected that word families—onsets and rimes—will be taught. For example, along with *right* on the grade 2 list is the expectation that other *ight* words will also be taught.
>
> Just because a word is not on a core list does not mean it should not be taught.
>
> Frequently used words from others lists or experiences should be included.
>
> Contractions are included because they are used so often.

Politically, these lists have been very useful. They have helped show upper-grade teachers, parents, and administrators that we have expectations for correct spelling. Also, because we worked and talked across grade levels over a period of weeks, we came to see what writing and spelling looked like at other grade levels. We were able to stop some of the typical blaming done by the next grade's teacher. We came to realize that while we might teach *to*, *two*, and *too* or *their*, *there*, and *they're* in second grade, it needed to be retaught in third, fourth, and fifth grade—and perhaps, for some, even in middle school and high school—in order for students to own the spellings of certain "tricky" words.

• *Help students produce final copies with correct spelling.*
While we teachers value the process as well as the product in writing, we live in a society that judges on the basis of the final product. Recently, I walked into the room of a third-grade teacher who does an outstanding job teaching writing, and teaching spelling as part of writing. I was very impressed with the high quality of published projects in the reading corner, books in all different formats that reflected the students' inquiries, research, and interests. I was, however, surprised to find many misspellings in these final products. I gently asked the teacher about the misspellings; she said she had final-edited the drafts after the students had edited them but that the students had miscopied some words in preparing the final versions. I mentioned that my editor fixes up my misspellings after I have done my best work and suggested she might want to fix up the misspellings or help the students do so. First, it is distracting to read an otherwise well constructed piece when misspellings are present. Second, it sends the message to parents—and other audiences— that spelling isn't important. Third, to an audience who doesn't understand developmental spelling, it looks as though we're not teaching.

I had a similar experience with an upper-elementary-grade teacher I was working with who was new to our district. She proudly directed me to the published pieces posted in the room. They were so full of misspellings and misplaced conventions that I was astounded. When I asked her about the errors, she replied that the students had done the best they could. I could sense her becoming defensive when, uncharacteristically blunt, I said, "No they haven't. That's not good enough." I was concerned that her principal and parents would think she wasn't teaching writing. I took the opportunity to demonstrate that these students were showing exactly what needed to be taught, and it was our job to teach it.

I offered to work with one of the students, a struggling writer. Darlene sat down next to me, and we worked through her piece together. With nudging and encouragement, she was able to fix up most of her errors. Some techniques I used included:

• Having only the student hold the pencil.

- Telling the student I knew she could do more and that I expected it.
- Reading aloud the first few sentences without taking a breath and then asking, Is this where the first period should go? Is this right?
- Dropping my voice and pausing naturally at the end of the first sentence and asking, What needs to go here?
- Putting a dot or check in the margin for each misspelled word and then expecting her to find them, circle them, and fix up as many as she was able to through "having a go" (trying to write the word other ways), asking peers, using spelling resources.
- Expecting a peer to edit the draft before I looked at it again and having the peer sign his name on the bottom of the paper.

The following week, the teacher told me that kids were taking more responsibility for correcting spellings and conventions. She said she had tried putting a dot in the margin next to those lines where students needed to self-edit, and that in most cases students could do more than she had previously thought. She was also expecting the peer who edited a student's piece to come to the final editing conference. She noted that because peer editors were also being held responsible, they were taking their jobs more seriously.

What We Can Do to Communicate How We Teach Spelling

• *Be sure something goes home in final copy on a regular basis.*
Beyond first grade, my recommendation is that a letter or other short piece of writing go home once or twice a month.

• *When a piece of writing goes public, be sure it's correct.*
This is a social obligation and responsibility. (I would make an exception for kindergarten and first grade here. However, when their student writing is posted in the hall, include an explanation about invented spelling so the public understands we are doing our job.)

• *Stamp or label writing that has not been teacher-edited as "unedited" or "student edited."*
This lets parents and administrators know that we have looked at the piece of writing even though we haven't corrected it. We may be focusing on the content at this stage or be working with young writers who cannot produce a totally correct paper without teacher intervention.

• *Include the what and how of your spelling program in parent newsletters.*
Let parents know your expectations are high and that standard spelling is important. Place spelling in the context of authentic writing. (See Appendix I for one teacher's letter.)

• *Share the research on how children learn to spell.*
Let parents know that there is a twenty-five-year-old research base that reflects the complex, organized way children learn to spell—including the use of invented spellings, which are rule governed.

• *Share the developmental stages of spelling that all children go through.*
Let parents know where their children are on the developmental spelling continuum and what the specific teaching goals are.

• *Have expectations for editing and spelling visible and accessible in the classroom.*
Use word walls, a big book of spells, lists of content-area words, and charts of hypotheses and rules that you and the students are generating based on students' needs as well as the curriculum.

• *Have students document their individualized spelling work.*
Keep spelling folders, have-a-go sheets (where, with guidance, children thoughtfully try to write misspelled words another way), lists of words being studied and mastered, personal dictionaries, personal word walls of frequently used words expected to be spelled correctly. Have students save all drafts so parents see the process from draft to final copy.

• *Have students save examples of editing work.*
Share these with parents so they see that misspelled words have been circled and corrected.

• *Keep track of the spelling lessons you teach.*
Have this list or record available to share with your principal and parents. Or have it on a chart to remind students that you have worked on, for example, *ed* endings.

• *Speak openly and knowledgeably about the importance of being a competent speller.*
Use all opportunities—curriculum night, open house, conferences, newsletters, and informal conversations with parents and administrators.

• Help students develop spelling strategies, "spelling sense," and spelling resources.
Demonstrate various strategies good spellers use, such as trying to write a misspelled word another way (to see if it looks right), asking a friend, finding another word with the same root, using other resources, looking a word up in the dictionary (this usually requires knowing the first three letters).

• Do not give up the spelling workbook until you have the knowledge, resources, and support to teach without it.

Where Does Grammar Fit In?

Teachers and parents are right to be concerned when they see student writing that has run-on sentences, poor spelling, and no punctuation. The solution, however, is not isolated drill and practice exercises. Although research has been around for a long time that shows the formal teaching of grammar has a negligible or even harmful effect on improving students' writing, most of us have either ignored the research or been unaware of it.

Furthermore, there is no hard data supporting the belief that students' grammar in written language is poor and getting worse. In fact, the data show virtually no change between 1984 and 1992. According to *The NAEP 1992 National Writing Trend Assessment for Grades 4, 8, and 11*, errors in word choice and capitalization were rare even in "good" and "poor" papers. "The results by percentile reveal that three-quarters of the papers at grades 4, 8, and 11 contained virtually no fragment errors and three-quarters of the 8th- and 11th-grade papers contained virtually no run-on sentences."

Still, it's difficult to convince someone who believes in the formal teaching of grammar that it's a waste of time. Marcia Bliss is an experienced, conscientious fifth-grade teacher in my school district. She freely admits that she got out the workbooks with the grammar drills "just so I felt better and could say I was teaching grammar." Only after seeing for herself that sentence drills did not work in improving students' writing—and being able to acknowledge what she saw—did she begin to feel comfortable with teaching grammar in the context of writing. Marcia acknowledges that this was not an easy transition. She says, "Now that I had this new awareness, I had to think a lot about how I could teach grammar differently." Without the knowledge of current research, we tend to fall back on the familiar, on the way we ourselves were taught.

My teaching experience tells me that students first need to get a sense of and a feel for how language works and sounds through extensive reading and writing before the study of grammar makes sense. Most of us seem to manage to learn how to speak and write grammatically without being able to state the rules. What seems to help students most is teaching and discussing word usage and sentence construction in the context of writing with intention for a specific audience. This means, for example, that we don't take our red pen and put in the commas for a high school student but, rather, that we demonstrate how commas are used and then support the student as he applies these principles in his own writing.

That does not mean that we don't talk about parts of speech like nouns and verbs, make lists of powerful verbs, or point out how authors use specific conventions in the process of reading and writing. Of course we need to do that. Some of us have been reluctant to talk about parts of speech, fearing we were being inauthentic. Nonsense. We just need to keep in mind that "noun-verb agreement, for example, is a convention of English that is learned in the process of tidying up language already produced; the rule makes no sense unless you are already producing nouns and verbs."

What We Can Do About Grammar

• Share the research on grammar with parents and administrators.
Copy and distribute the position statement on grammar exercises and drill from the National Council of Teachers of English (see Appendix A). Share the NAEP results. Get a copy of "Synthesis of Research on Teaching Writing," by G. Hillocks, Jr. In highlighting a review of twenty years of research, among other things, Hillocks found that

> the study of traditional school grammar (i.e., the definition of parts of speech, the parsing of sentences, etc.) has no effect on raising the quality of student writing. . . . Moreover, a heavy emphasis on mechanics and usage (e.g., marking every error) results in significant losses in overall quality. . . .
> The practice of building complex sentences from simpler ones has been shown to be effective in a large number of experimental studies.

This sentence-combining activity is apparently the only isolated grammar exercise that positively impacts the quality of student writing. A group of fifth- and sixth-grade teachers told me that parents felt much more relaxed about the teaching of grammar after they were given copies of the research during a parent-teacher conference.

• *Use the language of grammar. Call nouns and verbs by their names.*
While memorizing definitions of terms in isolation is not useful, students do need to know how to write with more powerful nouns and verbs. Call nouns and verbs by their names when talking about them in writing and reading in the elementary grades. A student can't write a more exciting verb if he can't identify the verb he wrote. Encourage students to keep a notebook where they list powerful verbs, adjectives, and other words and phrases they like the sound of and may want to use in future writing.

• *Teach students how to proofread effectively.*
With students' permission, make overhead transparencies of drafts and demonstrate how to punctuate, fix up spelling, and use conventions correctly.

We Still Need to Teach and Value Handwriting

Handwriting can be an emotionally charged issue. In the language arts support group in one of my district's elementary buildings, we spent several weeks talking about expectations for handwriting. Lots of issues surfaced. Should we teach lowercase letters in kindergarten? Are we asking children to write too much too soon? Is legibility enough? How much time should we spend teaching stroke formation? When should we begin teaching cursive? How much practice and repetition is necessary? Because the research on teaching handwriting is scarce and conflicting, we had difficulty resolving these issues. Nonetheless, most of us were able to agree that handwriting is important to us and to many of our students' parents and that legibility is the desired goal.

When we teach and value handwriting, we are sending a message to students and parents that we value legibility, attention to detail, neatness, correctness, and excellence. To write beautifully by hand takes time, practice, and pride. It is literally a dying art. I welcome a handwritten letter. It seems to be more personal and to have more voice than a word-processed one. I love to get "h-mail—handwritten and heartwritten." I save all personal, handwritten letters and cards in a special file for future reference and rereading. (By contrast, I am much less likely to save a letter received through e-mail.)

When I want to send a personal message, I always handwrite it on special paper or beautiful blank cards.

Yes, we can print out computer-generated, spell-checked material, and this is great much of the time. Indeed, for some students, word-processing has freed up the process of writing, and that has been terrific. We need to remember, though, that just because a finished piece looks professional doesn't mean that it's better written or even well written. For me, these printed pieces can lack the voice and personal style that comes through in a handwritten piece.

Let me give you an example. At the end of the school year, fourth-grade teacher Joan Servis and I worked with her students to write final-evaluation narratives. These "report cards," written by the students, were not supplementary to the teacher's report; they were the official reports (see Chapter 9). The students went through drafts and revisions and took the project very seriously. Almost all final reports were word-processed so they would look professional. They were so well crafted, complete, and official-looking that it "looked" as if the students couldn't possibly have done them. In retrospect, Joan and I noticed that the narratives of the few late finishers, who handwrote their final reports, stood out for their uniqueness. The individual handwriting styles made those narratives look child-centered and personal. This year we are going to have all students handwrite their final narratives.

Or again, third-grade teacher Danny Young—who does a marvelous job with writing workshop—found out that his kids couldn't handwrite very well when they needed to. While his students were publishing pieces of excellent quality, everything that went to final copy was word-processed on the computer. When Danny and I, working together, taught the students how to write book reviews, we found out that their handwriting was sorely lacking. Because the book reviews of their favorite books were going to be displayed at the local book store, the handwriting had to be polished and legible. Therefore, Danny took the time—in a meaningful context and for a mutually valued purpose (not as a copying exercise)—to teach handwriting and to revalue it.

What We Can Do About Handwriting

• *Educate parents about the importance of early play in the home.*
While the research on handwriting is conflicting, one thing is certain. We are seeing more kids who have difficulty with handwriting because they haven't had enough motor experience with their hands. Instead of manipulating and playing with blocks, they have been sedentary—spending excessive time in front of the television.

• *Make sure parents know we teach handwriting.*
Parents, used to the importance of handwriting from their own schooling, expect handwriting to be taught. Use journals or daily writing to diagnose and observe penmanship. Formally teach stroke formation in the lower grades, and give time for practice. Make the goal legibility.

• *Make sure parents know we value handwriting.*
Do mention handwriting in newsletters; post handwritten work; expect students to handwrite some final copies—personal letters, for example. Let parents know we value and expect legibility and quality penmanship.

8

Other Dilemmas

Teaching is full of dilemmas. How we deal with them says a lot about us as educators. We can ignore dilemmas or only deal with them when it becomes necessary, or we can become proactive and attempt to change problematic situations. I like the following definition because it implies taking an active rather than a passive stance: "In its primary sense *dilemma* denotes a situation in which a choice must be made between alternative courses of action or argument."

Becoming politically savvy and asking questions engenders more questions and often poses new dilemmas. However, the word *dilemma* implies a person actively seeking answers and resolution to conflict, a desirable goal for all thinking people. As such, I view *dilemma* as a positive, forward-moving word and situation.

Using a Published Series: Pros and Cons

Most teachers and school districts still use a published series, often referred to as a basal, to teach reading. My best guess, from talking to teachers and publishers around the country, is that an overwhelming majority—75 percent of us, or more—use a basal at least part of the time for reading/language arts instruction. Today, while many teachers are supplementing the basal reading programs with trade books, in many schools teachers still do not have a choice about whether or not to use a basal.

The Good News

The newer basals have done what many dedicated teachers don't have the time or the resources to do. In an anthology, the publisher efficiently organizes thematic collections of mostly unabridged literature by recognized children's authors. The publishers' programs also provide a language arts framework across the grade levels for teachers and districts that are not ready or eager to create their own literature programs. Using a basal also ensures having texts at every grade level that students can read, alleviating the sometimes difficult task of teachers' having to select texts for students that they can actually read. In addition, programs provide guidance for ongoing observation and a variety of assessment options.

The basals also include useful information about authors and often list many quality trade books to go along with a "theme." These literature collections include not only fiction but nonfiction, poetry, and other genres. This variety is important because teachers organizing their own literature programs tend to overemphasize fiction. According to a recent NAEP report, "nearly two-thirds of fourth graders did not report reading information books at school."

While in the past many districts purchased an entire published series that included consumable worksheets, today districts take advantage of the greater flexibility and choice. Many teachers are buying fewer consumables and reproducibles and more paperback books. Often, these trade books, which supplement the published series, can be purchased individually by titles or in sets. Some publishers also offer paperbacks to go along with a basal theme. These paperbacks include the original literature and may also include information about the author and illustrator. One publisher also includes information that relates to and extends the topic of the paperback. This is a bonus, because most teachers do not have the time or knowledge to seek out all the relevant quality literature they may need for integrated teaching.

The Not-So-Good News

An anthology is not the same as a trade book. It doesn't look like or feel like the kind of book we find in our home or library. Even when an excerpt from a published anthology is unabridged, there is no guarantee that the reader will ever see the entire book and the context of the excerpt. Reading a book for pleasure alone is not emphasized.

A myriad of activities and questions overfocusing on "skills" are still included with many published programs, and worksheets and workbooks are often widely used. Indeed, "much of students' reading time in reading class is directed toward activities that are predominantly skills-oriented and do not integrate reading and writing."

Although teachers are expected to pick and choose from all the resources offered—based on their and the children's needs—it is inordinately time-consuming to read the teacher's guide. It took me an hour just to read through the notes and suggestions related to a single literature selection in a new teacher's edition of a popular basal series. This is not a good use of a teacher's time. I was also bothered by the fact that the pages of notes to the teacher were longer, by far, than the actual story. In fairness to the basal publishers, much of what is included is based on market surveys and teachers' articulated requests. Typically, thousands of teachers from around the country participate in developing these series.

Another objection concerns spelling. While spelling was said to be "integrated" into the program, spelling words came out of the literature, creating a contrived program. The words were not related to words in children's daily writing or children's actual needs.

Also, while changes in language and content in the newer basals are now very minimal, changes in illustrations and format are common. Changing, relocating, or omitting original illustrations shortchanges the reader and may possibly interfere with skillful reading in those instances where picture cues are critical for supporting the text.

What We Can Do About Basals

At the very least, we teachers can be sure that we have classroom libraries with a wide variety of books for children to read. We can make sure that most of reading time is spent reading, discussing, and enjoying real books and not in "doing" reading activities. Even when a basal series is mandated, we can be selective about what parts of the published series we use. We can skip the worksheets and meaningless activities and involve students in authentic responses to literature, including literature discussion groups and author study in connection with basal selections and/or supplemental trade books.

Furthermore, we can learn more about teaching reading. Programs don't teach; teachers do, but we have to be knowledgeable. The reason published series are so popular is not just that they're convenient or cost-effective. They attempt to do what too many of us don't know how to do —teach children to read and appreciate literature. That's too important a task to leave strictly to others.

We Must Preserve Our Libraries

I can't imagine not being able to go to libraries. Libraries are part of the fabric of my literary life. Libraries remain one of the few public services available to everyone. Indeed, libraries are a cornerstone of our democracy.

Furthermore, libraries are not a frill; they are a necessity. A substantial body of research tells us that accessibility to and use of school library media centers staffed by professionals have a direct correlation with reading achievement and positive attitudes toward reading. Specifically, students' academic achievement is higher in both poor and affluent communities when library media centers are better funded and when library media specialists are part of the instructional process. In addition, access to public libraries substantially impacts the amount of reading students do.

Yet, across the nation, libraries are struggling to survive as cuts in spending are the trend. According to the U.S. Department of Educational Statistics, as of 1994 less than half of all public school libraries were staffed by a professional librarian or media specialist. "To merely keep their jobs this year, school librarians across the country fought bare-fisted to convince administrators that what they do is crucial to effective learning." Unfortunately, some politicians and administrators believe that public libraries are sufficient and that school libraries are a "noninstructional" option. In California, many of the school libraries that are still in existence are run by technicians who do not have the appropriate theoretical background or the necessary library training. In several cities in other states, where there are no aides to keep the libraries running, the libraries are simply locked. In some places, libraries remain open but are not staffed.

"Teachers are relying more heavily on public libraries in California," agrees John Philbrook, librarian and multicultural literature specialist at the San Francisco Public Library. In other states, this is also true. With funding cuts becoming common, public libraries are being used more than ever to supply books and materials—from preschool through high school. One consequence of dwindling school libraries is that many of us teachers wind up spending lots of our own money so that we can have classroom collections and books to teach with.

Public libraries feel the demise of school libraries dearly. Set up to serve preschoolers through the aged, public libraries face a dilemma when we expect them to provide services that schools have previously assumed. Barbara Jeffus, school library consultant in the California Department of Education, says, "When we cut school libraries, public libraries bleed."

The fact that young people are using our public libraries in large numbers tells us what the tests don't measure and what the media don't report. For 1993, the first year basic statistics on library circulation were collected, 29 percent of total circulation in public libraries in the United States involved children's materials. Specifically, almost 463 million pieces of children's material were checked out of public libraries, most of them books. Additionally, attendance at library children's programs numbered about 35 million.

It is clear that children and adults are reading more books than ever, for pleasure and information. U.S. Commerce Department figures show retail sales for bookstores continuing to increase each year. Purchases in 1993 increased 10 percent from 1992, which were an increase of 6 percent from 1991. Book sales are up in school markets too. In 1994, educational book clubs and book fairs were the fastest-growing segments of print materials sold from kindergarten through high school. So growing numbers of books are coming into schools and homes, and schools are using more trade books. And book buying is not dominated by households in the top income bracket. In 1994, the majority of books purchased were by households with an annual income of less than fifty thousand dollars.

When books are readily available, children read more. We need to protect and expand our library services as part of our heritage and our future. We need to make sure that large numbers of books are in school and classroom libraries.

What We Can Do
to Promote Quality Libraries

• Know what a dynamic school library is.
Many people still see a library only as a room with books. The broader picture of library media centers is one staffed by knowledgeable library media specialists who plan and teach collaboratively with other teachers. This broader vision is necessary to support increasingly integrated curriculums in today's classrooms. Having a knowledgeable library media specialist makes our work easier. Teachers who plan to integrate science, social studies, etc., across the curriculum should be able to rely on knowledgeable librarians to co-plan units, select nonfiction and fiction books, co-teach, and even co-evaluate student work.

• Locate the terrific library media programs in your area in which the media specialist is integral to the teaching and learning process.
Fill a car with teaching colleagues and your principal and go on a field trip. Consider taking a parent and/or board member along, too. Seeing is believing.

• *Send a faculty representative to your state school library association's conference.*
Have the representative share what was seen and learned that might benefit the students at your school if you had such a library program.

• *If you are a library media specialist, take more responsibility for learning and applying current language arts research and practice.*
Become as knowledgeable as possible. The broader vision of a library media center isn't possible without a highly skilled and knowledgeable librarian. Attend educational conferences; read professionally; observe classroom teachers teaching reading and writing; become part of the larger educational community.

• *Reenvision the librarian as a teacher-librarian.*
Librarians must be viewed as coteachers of the language arts across the curriculum; this is a necessary partnership. Librarians need to move beyond the traditional role of story readers and managers of materials into true partnerships in planning and teaching across the curriculum.

• *If you are working successfully and collaboratively with a library media specialist, share that collaboration so others may model it.*
Brag about your program! Share the units you have planned together—your goals, teaching plans, and assessment strategies.

• *Involve parents in your library program.*
Recruit parent volunteers. Parents can serve as good public relations people and catalysts for improving libraries.

• *Promote book clubs and book fairs as one way to get books into schools and homes.*
Book clubs and book fairs are important for they provide easy and affordable access to a wide range of books. In my district's schools, a substantial share of the profits from in-school book fairs—which are organized by parent volunteers—are used to choose books for classroom libraries and schools.

• *Speak out for libraries.*
Let your community know that libraries and library services are indispensable. With a move toward integrated teaching and the use of more nonfiction books in the classroom, a well-stocked, carefully selected school library and a knowledgeable librarian are a necessity.

As Barbara Jeffus, a school library consultant, reminds us,

A "good" school library is a cost-effective investment. There should be books enough to allow rotating, custom-selected classroom collections and still maintain plenty of copies in the library for circulation. If there is duplication of titles this way, it is intentional. It keeps the classroom collections from becoming invisible as happens when the same books have been there all year. It helps avoid artificial grade-leveling of titles. And it means the classroom teacher doesn't have to spend a small fortune on books for his or her room. It also encourages sharing since the collection belongs to everyone.

Teacher Education:
Not Just the Job of the University

I have heard leaders in our field state that a knowledgeable teacher can do a better job teaching than a published textbook series. It sounds great, and it's probably true. The difficulty is that many of us are not knowledgeable enough about the theory, research, and practice of language learning. How to apply that knowledge to orchestrate the many elements that create the successful classroom eludes many teachers. This seems especially true for recent graduates from our education programs.

Betty J. Bush, who coordinates elementary education at Northwest Missouri State, a small regional university with undergraduate and graduate programs, says teacher education has moved too quickly to embrace whole language exclusively. Some of the schools in which the graduates of these programs will teach still maintain the basal approach to reading and are not ready to make the philosophical shift to whole language. Bush stresses the need for a middle ground at universities, an eclectic approach, because students have to be prepared to deal with a variety of approaches when they get into schools. She also notes that "in methods classes, we barely talk about how to implement phonics instruction into whole language or literature-based programs."

That statement is supported by a survey conducted by Louisa Cook Moats. She found that "teachers who are literate and experienced generally have an insufficient grasp of spoken and written language structure and would be unable to teach it explicitly to either beginning readers or those with reading/spelling disabilities."

Ann Mc Callum, who often recruits teachers for Fairfax County, Virginia, has a different view. She believes that most university programs continue to teach a traditional program and that this results in a mismatch when teachers are hired by surrounding districts that support a holistic approach. She says,

> I worry about a middle ground. Let's teach the best of what the research says, and tell teachers that they may need to adapt or adjust based on community expectations. Let's teach teachers to teach reading so they—not the basal published series—are the decision makers. It's easier to learn to use a basal than to learn to work without one.

Betty J. Bush believes many colleges have given teachers the message: *Make your own changes. Do your own thing with portfolios or literature. Don't worry about what approach others in your school are using.* She notes that teachers have not been made aware of the importance of cross-grade collaboration to ensure students' developmental progress.

Jerry Treadway, long-time professor of education at San Diego State University, puts teacher education in perspective when he says, "Every time we don't like the result of a program, we go to teacher training. But the second point is that if the program we're espousing can only be successful with the highest level of teacher expertise, then we've developed a formula for failure."

Of course, we still need to do a better job in teacher education, including providing more time for students as interns. However, that's not enough. Being a successful teacher involves many complex factors. We need to give teachers lots of ongoing support once they become part of a school district. Furthermore, we need to raise the level of our profession by attracting and recruiting more of the brightest students.

We Need to Encourage
Smart Students to Become Teachers

At the wedding of a friend's son, Barbara Berlin—one of the bridesmaids—sought me out to talk about her excitement at becoming a teacher. Now enrolled in a graduate program and reading my book *Invitations: Changing as Teachers and Learners K–12*, she spoke passionately about wanting to work with young children. At Harvard University, where she had been an undergraduate, she had been discouraged from thinking about becoming an elementary teacher. "No one I came into contact with at Harvard was going into elementary teaching, and I knew of no courses that were offered." The not-so-subtle message she received was, *Teaching is not an option for bright women.*

That attitude mirrors society's thinking. Barbara says that when people hear of her intentions, they typically say, *You went to Harvard and you want to be a teacher? Why?* We have given the message that anybody can teach and that if you're a really smart student, you should pick another profession. Only those of us who do teach—and our families and close friends—know how demanding and satisfying teaching can be both intellectually and emotionally.

Now, several years after graduation and jobs in other fields, Barbara is following her heart and her instincts. When she told her mother (who had taught for thirty years) about her decision to teach, her mom said, "I never thought you should be anything but a teacher."

Then, too, we've all heard the story of legions of students going into teaching because they weren't smart enough to "make it" in other professions. Unfortunately, there's probably some truth to this.

Gloria Ladson-Billings tells the story of serving on university interview panels for education candidates. When candidates were asked, *Why do you want to be a teacher?* most responded, *I just love kids.*

> Most of the candidates were at a loss when asked to explain further why they wanted to teach. . . . I cannot recall a single one who talked about loving intellectual activity or who spoke of knowledge as empowering.

I feel sad when I read that statement. One of the things I love about teaching is that it is so intellectually demanding. It's a profession that demands our constant questioning of our practice through professional reading, collegial interaction, attendance at professional meetings, self-reflection, and self-evaluation. What it takes to be a responsive teacher is not about following a manual, as some outsiders would have us believe. Teaching is as challenging and rewarding a profession as any I can think of. We need to let our best and our brightest students know that. I went into teaching because my parents thought it was a "good profession for a woman." I have stayed in teaching because I love the intellectual challenge—with the kids, with other teachers, and for myself.

New Teachers Need Lots of Support

In my district, part of my job is to work with all new teachers in grades K–4. That means that based on their expressed needs, I do lots of demonstration teaching in their classrooms, coach them in their own teaching, plan with them, and talk with them about their goals and concerns. All our new teachers also have mentor teachers. Yet, what I hear over and over again from new teachers—not just in my district but around the country—is how poorly prepared they feel to teach.

Some have been given the message that they can do "their thing" in the classroom. Others freely admit that phonics has not been a part of their education and they don't have a clue how to teach reading. Many say they're well versed in children's literature, but they don't know what to do with it.

Hallie Butze is a bright, energetic first-grade teacher in our district and a brand-new teacher. A recent graduate of a small university with an "excellent education program," she says that her methods courses in reading gave her a strong background in children's multicultural literature. But how to teach reading remained an enigma. Hallie says,

> We never talked about how we would actually teach reading using a book with a group of children and what we would do with emerging readers. I had no idea what the teaching of reading looked like K–6. Fortunately, I had a whole year here as an aide in a grade-1 class so I learned how to teach reading. Without that, I wouldn't have had a clue.

Hallie also credits doing lots of professional reading and observing other teachers as helpful and necessary. In her student-teaching experience, she found the teaching of reading boring, with everyone on the same page at the same time. Remembering how learning to read had been boring for her in first grade, she knew she wanted her students involved and excited.

Robyn Feinstein is a hard-working, smart, caring teacher who spent her first two years teaching in kindergarten. A recent graduate of a well-known college, she felt unprepared to teach reading when she moved this school year to teaching second grade. She describes her university courses as focused on activities to go along with and extend literature—vocabulary, responses, story grammar, and "cutesy" exercises. She learned a lot about how to get kids excited about literature but nothing about how to teach kids strategies so they could actually read the books. She says,

> Discussions about literature were separate from the teaching of reading. Reading for meaning as being primary was not mentioned. We had a phonics workbook to teach us the rules so if phonics came up we knew where to look in the workbook to teach the rule. But I never knew what it meant to "teach skills in context." As students, we got the idea that you couldn't do explicit instruction one-on-one or in a small group but that you read whole class and somehow, the kids would learn to read. The university may not have intended the message to be "no instruction" but that was the message we got.

Robyn had always done lots of professional reading, but she needed to "see" what the teaching of reading looked like. Things started to click for her when she observed me and other colleagues, talked with other teachers, and saw what worked. She came to recognize some key elements of successful practice as being:

- The need for skills teaching has to come from the kids (not, *Today I think I'll teach the long e sound*).
- Kids need to have a variety of strategies and we need to model these in use.
- Partner reading and reading with other peers is powerful.
- Often, the best response to reading is more reading.

How One School District Supported a New Teacher

When you walk into Chris Hayward's first-grade classroom, you see a group of children who love and respect their teacher. You see a room where everyone is engaged and enthusiastic, where kids know exactly what is expected of them, where every corner bursts with literacy. There is an attractively organized reading area with lots of great books and a place for gathering, a writing area with children-authored books on a shelf, a word wall displaying frequently used words, kids working together at tables of four or five at different reading-writing projects. His principal, Rosemary Weltman, says, "One senses that students are all engaging in dynamic and purposeful learning, enjoying one another under the orderly, peaceful routines that Chris has established."

But Chris's classroom did not start out that way. Last year, his first year of teaching, turned out to be unexpectedly difficult and stressful for him. Chris graduated with honors from the college of education of a state university where he had received the Most Outstanding Senior award, an award given to only one student in the graduating class. Chris viewed his undergraduate program as "strong." As part of a small, handpicked group, he had spent his entire junior year in an elementary school where professors taught the two required reading-writing methods courses on site. While he had worked all year with mentor teachers in different grade levels, Chris had spent most of his time in grades 3 and 4. He felt comfortable with the school's eclectic reading program; it was closely aligned with what he was learning in his courses.

Hired after a series of interviews with administrators in our school district, Chris came to his new teaching job feeling well prepared and "very self-assured." Although the kids loved him from the start, "things came crashing down" early in the school year. It started around the time of open house, which serves as our annual curriculum night for parents. In addition to talking about the curriculum, all teachers are expected to give parents a "curriculum packet" to let parents know district and teacher goals and objectives in all subject areas. Rosemary Weltman questioned some of what he was communicating to parents. She then began to look more closely at his reading instruction program. Says Chris, "She found out I was struggling to teach reading using the district's methods."

In retrospect, Chris acknowledges that while he learned some questioning and assessment strategies in his undergraduate courses, he never got the specifics of teaching reading. He didn't know the questioning-teaching strategies to help kids become independent readers, and he didn't have any idea how to teach beginning reading. In November, after his principal observed him teach a small reading group and gave him a poor evaluation, he was crushed. He says,

> I felt very low, like a failure. I had come in at the top. I had worked hard to get a job in Shaker. I came in thrilled and eager to work. I put in long hours, staying till 10 P.M. each night and eating my dinner at school. Then I worked at home until 12:00 or 1:00 A.M. Rosemary was concerned about the amount of time I spent at school. She was telling me to leave earlier and have some fun. But I felt caught. I wanted to keep my job. I was struggling to understand what was expected of me. On top of that, I felt bad that the kids had me instead of one of the other three first-grade teachers. I felt bad for the parents that they had a first-year teacher in an instrumental year. I was very nervous. I knew what I didn't know. I worried the parents would sense this.

Chris had not been without support. Like all new teachers in our district, he had a mentor teacher. His mentor, Laurie Spohn, was an experienced, tenured teacher who was very supportive. She kept in close daily contact with Chris. The two of them talked at least an hour a day, in school and on the phone. As the language arts resource teacher, I worked weekly with Chris in his classroom, mostly demonstrating reading and writing strategies. Additionally, Sherri Grossman, the Reading Recovery teacher, modeled many reading strategy lessons in small reading groups. And, our district math coach, Judy Wells, did demonstration math lessons regularly in his classroom.

Most important, Chris had Rosemary Weltman, a principal with high expectations, rigorous standards, and an excellent, specific plan for improvement. Rosemary Weltman made sure that all the human and material resources our district could provide were available to Chris to help him grow professionally, and she coordinated the effort. Rosemary met with Chris twice a day, on average, talking with him and challenging his thinking in an effort to understand where he was and to support him. She expected him to reflect carefully on everything he did, planned, and read professionally, and she wrote him a lot of positive notes as well.

By February—about midyear—Chris started feeling like things were coming together for him, but he still worried about being rehired (partly because a district levy failed to pass, triggering professional cutbacks). In March, Rosemary Weltman wrote him a glowing evaluation. At the end of the school year, parents of two different students wrote complimentary letters to our superintendent of schools. Chris's students were reading and writing beautifully, and they were excited about learning.

Chris continued to grow professionally during his second year. In December 1995, in the summary portion of his narrative evaluation, Rosemary Weltman wrote,

> Chris is a wonderful first-grade teacher. He is dedicated to meeting the individual needs of his students and nurtures their well-being. He goes well beyond his responsibilities within the classroom, participating in all aspects of professional growth and development. He is thoughtful and reflective about all of the areas of his involvement, and possesses sound judgment. Chris's students are the lucky beneficiaries of his superb, individualized instruction and his genuine care and concern for their total welfare. . . .

So what turned things around for Chris in the teaching of reading and writing after such a rocky beginning?

• Having a knowledgeable and caring principal who supported and monitored his professional development.
Where his teacher education had fallen short, Rosemary Weltman made sure that she and other educators in our district provided the resources and demonstrated the strategies he needed every day.

• Seeing excellent examples of teaching behavior.
Chris found the "endless" modeling of the teaching of reading, mostly through small-group guided reading, invaluable:

> Once I saw the modeling working for me and how much I depended on it, modeling for my students became relevant to my teaching. Before that, I was just telling them what to do without giving them any clear expectations of what I wanted. Now I model everything and set high expectations through the modeling.

• *Doing professional reading and reflecting on it.*
At his principal's request, Chris read *Invitations* and reflected on his reading. He found the professional reading very important:

> When I started to read, I felt I had no time to read anything that wasn't specifically pertinent to what I was doing in my classroom that day. The reading put a lot of extra pressure on me. But in the long run it paid off.

• *Observing in a master teacher's classroom.*
In late winter, Chris spent a day observing expert first-grade teacher Jim Henry:

> It was my first experience seeing a teacher using the methods our district was prescribing and that I was reading about. When I saw Jim, I understood what he was doing because I had just read about it. What I saw made sense, so I could apply it.

• *Receiving guided feedback.*
Chris received important daily feedback from Rosemary Weltman, his mentor, and other support teachers. He received weekly feedback from me. After I had repeatedly demonstrated small-group guided reading, I then cotaught the group with Chris and coached him. Later, we would talk and reflect.

> Having you coach me, watch me, and critique me was a big help. I learned how to word questions to the students, and I learned what I still needed to do.

• *Having many supportive teachers on staff.*
In addition to his mentor, other teachers—at his grade level and across grade levels, both in his home school and at other schools—shared materials and strategies and offered support. Some of this took place during our weekly whole language support group, which Chris attended.

More Help for Novice Teachers: What We Can Do

While Chris Hayward feels his undergraduate education was solid, he acknowledges that an undergraduate program can't possibly teach all the specifics needed for particular school districts. He was more fortunate than most first-year teachers because he had tremendous daily support from many educators in our school district.

Based on his experiences and others like them, I make the following recommendations for supporting new teachers:

• *Where mentor teachers are available, free them up for modeling and meeting new teachers' needs.*
Mentor teachers need to be given time to repeatedly model teaching and management behaviors in the new teacher's classroom as well as to provide curricular specifics to meet new teachers' needs.

• *Create opportunities for collaborative planning.*
Learning how to plan for integrating the language arts across the curriculum is difficult for novices. Viewing an experienced teacher's plans and curriculum maps serves as a model and supports new teachers who do not yet have a developed curriculum framework. Better yet is working side by side with an expert teacher and thinking aloud and talking through the planning process together. As an example of meeting teacher needs, Chris found the curriculum mapping (planning) he did at the end of his first year with his mentor Laurie Spohn invaluable, especially for his second year of teaching. The curriculum mapping and thinking with an experienced teacher helped him understand the what, why, and how of teaching.

• *Provide release time to observe quality teachers.*
Encourage sustained observation and dialogue with experienced, excellent teachers.

• *Provide professional reading relevant to the district's curriculum.*
Required professional reading (if possible, over the summer), followed by study groups and guided discussion, allows new teachers, in a relaxed way, to investigate and reflect on teaching strategies and beliefs the district values.

• *Role-play curriculum nights and parent conferences.*
A practice session with another teacher or a video of a past occasion is excellent preparation.

• *When possible, apprentice new teachers before they begin teaching.*
From district to district, and even building to building, there are vast differences in teaching styles, philosophies, and expectations. When possible, provide opportunities for new teachers to "shadow" experienced ones for extended periods of time, as Hallie Butze was able to do as an aide.

Changing Demographics

I am still haunted by a statement Don Holdaway, the well-known New Zealand educator and researcher, made to me some years back when he was doing some work in our school district. He told me, "In the history of the world, there has rarely been a successful big-city urban school system." A profound statement and a challenge we must meet.

Our country has never been more diverse, and our diversity continues to grow. The last decade brought more changes in our population, by far, than any other decade. Asian-born Americans outnumber European-born, and U.S. residents born in Latin America outnumber both. One out of four Americans says they have African, Asian, Hispanic, or American Indian ancestry. Showing a 38 percent increase over 1980, one out of eight Americans speaks a foreign language at home; in response, the 1990 census created a new category—linguistic isolation. While this category applies to one in twenty-five children nationally, in California one in every seven children speaks a language other than English at home.

Most of America's poor live in major cities, in poor neighborhoods, with blacks and Hispanics disproportionately represented. Nationally, children under age eighteen account for 40 percent of our poor. And as our poorest Americans, many of these children are low performing, or what many call "at risk." By the year 2015, 50 percent of our students are predicted to be "at risk" due to population growth and immigration. "At-risk" students are "those students who are unlikely to succeed in schools as schools are currently constituted because they bring a different set of skills, resources, and experiences than those on which school is traditionally based." Knowing that these students eventually enter the workplace means we must educate all of them, to the best of our abilities.

More than one in ten students from families with an annual income greater than forty thousand dollars attend private school, creating "an emerging two-tiered school system divided even more by class than by race or ethnicity." I'm not sure that as a country we firmly believe that all students should be educated. Rather than work for the good of all children, some of us seem to have only our own self-interest at heart. Yet we must put that self-interest to work. Unless we educate all of our nation's children, we are all in trouble. "By the middle of the next century, no ethnic or racial group will constitute a majority. The number of Hispanic people will surpass the number of Blacks within two decades. Whites will become a minority again around the middle of the twenty-first century."

What Do Changing Demographics Mean for Us as Teachers?

Historically, minority and disadvantaged groups have received a skills-based education that does not focus on critical thinking or on a curriculum of "big ideas." We can't let this happen again because we know it doesn't work. We must keep abreast of the latest research on educating bilingual students and poor and disadvantaged students. We need to make our needs known for these children and speak out for what we know about teaching and learning.

We are teaching in more challenging times. Nationally, since 1970, there has been an increase in the poverty rates for children. Almost 30 percent more children live in households with only one adult.

The good news is that we can educate, and even accelerate, the learning of very poor children, but we need to know what strategies and programs are most effective. Not only classroom teachers need to be knowledgeable; support teachers and those who furnish supplemental instruction must also be aware of the latest research and know how to apply the most effective teaching strategies.

In the first large-scale study of students in "high poverty" classrooms, students who received academically challenging instruction—aimed at high-level understanding—made impressive gains. What is significant is that the students who did best were in meaning-oriented classrooms as opposed to skills-oriented classrooms. This was true not only for reading and writing, but also for mathematics. Mechanics and basic skills were taught in both types of classrooms. However, in the meaning-oriented classrooms, mechanics and skills were linked to the actual reading and writing of text or conceptual understanding of topics, as opposed to being taught in isolation.

> We found clear evidence that students exposed to instruction emphasizing meaning are likely to demonstrate a greater grasp of advanced skills at the end of the school year.

Another significant finding is that "teaching for meaning" produced more understanding and use of advanced skills for all students, both low and high achievers. This is research we need to talk about—with parents, policy makers, and all educators who work in increasingly diverse settings.

Standardized Testing and How to Deal with It

Standardized testing is not going to go away. It is part of the fabric of our schools and our society. It is big business for publishers, and results are still used to sort, select, and place students in—and remove them from—various special programs. Still, we teachers can influence how these tests are given and used.

In the school district where I teach, pressure from first- and second-grade teachers, and thoughtful response from knowledgeable administrators, helped do away with standardized tests in those two grades. First-grade teachers were vocal in conveying what they wanted to the superintendent, director of elementary education, and board of education. These teachers were tired of crying kids, wasted time, and an agenda that did not serve students first.

Now, even when standardized tests are required, we treat them as a separate form of reading that I now call *reading-test reading*. Because our students are unfamiliar with the format, we teach it to them through demonstrations and practice tests. Sure, it's a waste of time that could be better used in other ways, but the reality is students will have to take tests throughout their school careers, and they need to learn how to do so successfully. To ignore this reality is to put them at a disadvantage.

One of my big objections to standardized testing is the emphasis on the "deficit model." Results are used to point up what the child can't do. Rather than build on the child's strengths, standardized tests reinforce weaknesses. Added to that is the well-documented fact that standardized tests are culturally biased toward white middle-class experiences.

If standardized tests are used in perspective, only as a set of numbers from one given day that has little relation to what we are teaching in school, I can live with them. Or when standardized tests are given not to judge students but as a sampling in certain grades, to determine if programs are working, I can live with that, too. It is when scores are used to label and classify that the tests are dangerous.

Judy Wallis, a language arts coordinator in Houston, notes, "In all cases, tests are designed to rank. It seems we measure, rank, and then use what we've done, and the purpose for having done it, as the support for attack. Norm-referenced tests always find one-half above average and one-half below average—no other way!"

Unfortunately, an emphasis on tests continues to drive instruction. As a society, we always want to know how many failed; we rarely emphasize the number that passed. Pressure for higher test scores continues to be fueled by media ranking schools and publishing scores. Some schools spend way too much time teaching for the test. Benefits are only temporary, at best. In Ohio, which has required proficiency tests at various grade levels beginning with fourth grade, some teachers tell me they literally stop meaningful teaching those several weeks or months before the test so that their students will do well. Of course, this translates to less time on authentic enterprises.

On the national scene, lots of people talk about SAT scores and other standardized test scores dropping and point out that college-bound seniors' scores were higher several decades ago. What they fail to mention is that the pool of test takers has changed. Scores were higher because fewer students took the test. Today, we have the multicultural masses taking the test. Saying that scores have dropped is only a small part of the picture.

> In summary, the much-publicized decline in SAT scores might be the result of dramatic changes in the types of students taking the examination, indicating that American education is getting better at inspiring both more students and students with more varied backgrounds to seek advanced degrees.

Putting Standardized Testing in Perspective for Parents

Parents in my school district used to come to fall parent-teacher conferences expecting to spend most of the twenty minutes poring over the numbers and results. No more. We no longer give the message—by the amount of time we spend talking about them—that these tests carry a lot of weight. Now conferences are spent talking about students, sharing work and accomplishments, setting goals, celebrating learning. Very often students are an integral part of these conferences. Parents are handed test results as they leave and asked to contact the principal or teacher if they have questions. Because parents have seen ongoing work—through what has been sent home and possibly a portfolio—they come to see the standardized test for what it is, one isolated indicator on a given day that provides little information for improving instruction and learning.

Another important point to keep in mind about test scores today is that we've raised the standards for what it means to be literate.

> We can estimate that around 85 percent of today's public school students score higher on standardized tests of achievement than their average parent did. But the high-jump bar keeps getting higher and it takes a higher jump today than it did around 1965 to hit the fiftieth percentile.

My own observations tell me that elementary students who have learned to read with predictable literature and problem-solving strategies (including phonics) are doing better than ever. Rebecca Kimberly, a principal in our school district, confirms this:

> I've seen a big change in how students approach reading since I came here eight years ago. Now, I see even kindergarten youngsters are reading for meaning. They self-correct, they understand, they use the context. That's a

result of teachers understanding that reading is reading for meaning, not just decoding. Every year I see an increase in students and teachers understanding that reading is about getting meaning.

Still More Dilemmas

Of course, there are many other important dilemmas we teachers are faced with and for which we need support. According to Public Agenda's surveys, "Americans from all walks of life, in every demographic group and in every part of the country, endorse the very same list of priorities—safety, order, and the basics."

Specifically, lack of discipline continues to be the biggest problem faced by local public schools, as perceived by the public. However, it's interesting to observe that the more meaningful and relevant the curriculum, the less likely discipline will be a problem. If we go back to boring teaching approaches, we'll have bored kids and greater discipline problems.

Nationally and locally, we educators must speak out, write, and lobby for the changes and support we need. Otherwise, we cannot hope to deal effectively with the many complex issues we face—increasing class size, more violence, greater information "to cover," increasing numbers of LEP (limited English proficient) students, more diversity, deteriorating facilities, hard-to-reach parents. And then, too, there are the growing demands to reshape our schools through voucher programs, charter schools, standards, certification programs, and more.

Yet, despite all the complexities, disappointments, and perceived failings of our public schools, most of us—educators, parents, politicians, community members—want the public schools to work, and a large number are willing to support new approaches.

Public schools remain our best hope for the future of all our children. While we can't do the job well without a lot of support, we can become politically proactive about the changes we seek and the support we need. Maybe then we can transform our schools into democratic communities of intellectual excellence.

Part III

Empowerment for Life

9

What Happens When We Empower Students and Teachers

I believe the ultimate in education is reached when learners—both students and teachers at all levels—take charge of their own learning and use their education to lead rich and satisfying lives. That is, as learners, they are able to inquire independently about everything that interests them, choose to read and write for their own purposes, find and use resources to seek the knowledge and information they desire, write to learn, reflect, think, modify their thinking, and take new action. Further, they constantly set goals for themselves, self-evaluate, seek feedback, and go on learning. Even very young children can do this—and they do, when teachers and other experts (such as parents and fellow students) serve as models and mentors.

What has been most transforming about the whole language movement is this empowerment for self-directed, life-long reflection, learning, and action—not just for students but for teachers too. Some people say "whole language" is what they have always been doing, and now they have a name for it. I disagree. I don't know anyone who connected evaluation and teaching in such a way that students and teachers continually self-evaluated their work and set new goals with formulated plans of actions to achieve those goals, all in the course of meaningful-to-their-lives daily instruction. We, as teachers, never went that far because most of us were still trying to control the entire learning process. Also, we didn't have models for ourselves yet—other professionals and resources that redefined teaching and learning from the transmission to the transaction model.

So how did some of us get to the point where students are truly initiating, monitoring, and evaluating their real-world learning; where teachers are experts, mentors, lifelong learners and models; where parents are valued participants in their children's learning? How did we nurture and guide young students, even those in kindergarten, to take charge of their learning and rejoice in their accomplishments? It's what you see in a true whole language classroom, where the term *whole language* is not used loosely or flippantly as a label with no meaning but rather embodies the best of what democracy, freedom, and education need to be about.

Several specific enterprises can serve to illustrate this new empowerment for students as well as show them taking responsibility for their own learning. I will discuss two here. The first one is an example of persuasive letter writing to a newspaper editor. The second involves two evaluation practices: student-led conferencing and students writing their final report cards, narratives on themselves as learners.

Choice with Intention

Last school year, I spent some time working with fourth-grade students in Harryette Eaton's classroom, modeling and coaching student-led literature conversation groups in which the students learned to facilitate and self-evaluate their own "book groups."

One early February morning, before we began our discussion groups, I asked the students to give me their opinions of the book *Smoky Night,* written by Eve Bunting and illustrated by David Diaz. The book had just won the 1995 Caldecott award, a prestigious honor. I loved the gorgeously illustrated book, a personal story set during the Los Angeles riots, and I had brought it to school to share with teachers in our weekly language arts support group. In our meeting, the librarian questioned the book's appropriateness for elementary students, as had a book review in *USA Today.* That made me wonder what these students—used to speaking their minds—would think.

I gathered the class together in the reading area. I told them ahead of time that the librarian wasn't sure *Smoky Night* was appropriate to read to young children, and that some other adults felt the same way. I told them I wanted and needed their opinions. I read the book straight through, twice. The students were riveted by the bold, brilliantly illustrated scenes and the sensitively told story of Daniel and his mother amid the looting and fire setting that took place during the L.A. riots. They loved the book, and it showed. Their rapt faces and minds were engaged in a story they could relate to. Violence and danger are part of children's worlds today—if not in their lives, than through the inescapable power of television. The students declared the book suitable for children. After a lengthy and heated discussion, they decided that some of them would write a letter to the librarian, giving their opinions and suggesting she might want to read the book to students above first grade.

I then read them the book review from *USA Today*. It began, "Should an award-winning child's book require a warning label alerting parents and teachers that the contents within may be deeply disturbing to young children? Well, I'd slap one on the 1995 Caldecott winner, *Smoky Night*. . . ." More lively and opinionated discussion ensued. "How could she say that?" they wanted to know. It was obvious they didn't agree with her.

I asked them, "Do you know what people in a democracy do when they want to express their opinions about something they feel strongly about? One thing they can do is write a letter, a persuasive letter telling what they think and why, and maybe even offering suggestions."

Their response was immediate. "We could do that. Who would we write to?" And so it happened that most of these students *chose* to write to the editor of *USA Today*. They had a real and important reason to learn how to write a persuasive, business letter. They took the task very seriously and wanted the letters to be their best efforts. The powerful voices of these thinking students came through in their letters. See Figure 9–1 for an example.

David Mazzarella was duly impressed, as is evident in his thoughtful response to them (see Figure 9–2). I was particularly struck by the fact that he took the time to recognize and comment on the higher literacy and thoughtfulness of these students, which is, after all, what our schools need to be about.

Seeing Evaluation Through a New Lens

If the goal of assessment and evaluation is to improve teaching and learning, and I believe it is, then ongoing evaluation, classroom-based, must drive instruction and learning.

Several years ago, after I had conducted a workshop on evaluation, a teacher asked, "So are you going to write a book about evaluation?" At the time, I thought I might. I had not yet realized evaluation is not a separate piece or an end in itself. I now know it is part of reading and writing and everything we do in our classrooms and beyond; it is ongoing, on-the-spot, integral to our instructional effectiveness every day. We are constantly evaluating and re-evaluating what we do, where we and our students are in our learning processes, and continually setting and resetting goals.

The difficulty we have now is that many of us have changed—or are in the process of changing—our teaching but we are still mired in the old ways

David
3-16-95

Dear Mr. Mazzarella,

I am writing in response to the book review on Smoky Night dated February 7, 1995.

I think kids should have a choice about what books they read without someone censoring their choice. This book is about the past, so kids wouldn't have to worry about it. If this book needs a warning label, then why don't they put a warning label on history books for older grades? Those books are about the past too. These books could be inappropriate and violent. They shouldn't put a warning label on Smoky Night because they didn't put a warning label on any of the scary stories I've ever seen. So why should Smoky Night have a warning label when it's not half as bad as scary stories?

On T.V. they don't have any warnings. On T.V. they are talking about taking over the world and killing people. In this book they are only talking about people smashing things.

Why should you deprive a child to miss this wonderful book, that has riveting, bold, and elaborating illustrations and collages.

This book is good because it has a moral to the story. The moral is don't judge somebody by their religion, or their color of their skin. Anybody can be friends just like like Daniel's mom and Ms. Kim even though they are different cultures.

Figure 9–1 Letter to the editor of USA Today

David Mazzarella

Editor, USA TODAY
President, Gannett International

GANNETT

USA TODAY

April 10, 1995

Ms. Regie Routman
Language Arts Resource Teacher
Shaker Heights City School District
14900 Drexmore Road
Shaker Heights, Ohio 44120

Dear Ms. Routman:

Thank you for sending all those letters from your fourth grade class regarding
our review of the book Smoky Night.

I do think they were very thoughtful, and of course they exhibit a good deal of
independent thinking and maturity. I can appreciate that the students wish to make
up their own minds on a piece of literary work. This is, after all, what our
educational system is supposed to produce.

The reviewer has an opinion as well. Her intention was to advise parents
that the book could contain some unpleasantness. Your students evidently
feel they are astute enough not to be unsettled by it. They are to be commended
for exercising their right of free speech in stating their opinions, which I will
share with our staff.

Thanks again for making their views known to us.

Sincerely,

David Mazzarella
Editor
USA TODAY

Figure 9–2 Letter from the editor of USA Today

of assessing. While many of us are attempting alternative, authentic assessments that develop out of what we do daily in our classrooms, we are at the same time administering state-required and district-required standardized proficiency tests. While we are trying our hand at self-evaluation and descriptive narratives, we are also having to use district-approved report cards with seemingly endless categories to check off. This is frustrating and inordinately time-consuming.

Nonetheless, we must continue to make these efforts to connect evaluation and instruction because we are professionally obligated to do what's best and just for kids and their families. Our commitment drives us to continue to examine, refine, explain, and change our beliefs and practices.

In recognition of our pedagogical shift and our move toward sharing authority, many of us moved our desks out of the classroom altogether (or shared it with students as a work place), exchanged students' desks for tables where students could work together, gave over the bulletin boards to the students, shared the curriculum agenda through "negotiation," made our classrooms look more like comfortable, homey living spaces and less like institutions. We added rugs, rocking chairs, lamps, and even flowers. We added hundreds of wonderful books—fiction and nonfiction—and attractive shelves and units to hold them. We made students' writing central to everything we did and displayed that writing proudly. We welcomed parents as partners into our classrooms. We began sharing what we were doing with our colleagues.

As our daily practices changed and evolved, we took a hard look at assessment and evaluation and realized the old reporting system didn't fit or work. We started by "fooling around" with portfolios. For years, we have read about portfolios, talked about them endlessly, tried compiling our own, experimented with them in our classrooms, and experienced frustration as well as exhilaration in attempting to get the portfolio process to work for us.

With our guidance, kids began talking about their work in a way that showed more depth and insight. Rather than just saying work was "good" or "excellent," they learned how to apply descriptive criteria to writing, problem solving, and projects in all curriculum areas—criteria that had been jointly written by students and teacher. With practice, they internalized the criteria and genuinely improved their work. They began to understand for themselves, for example, that quality writing had to include voice, a strong lead, interesting words, and details, among other factors. It was no longer, *The teacher says I have to . . .* but *I see I need to work on . . . .* Control of learning was shifting. Students were becoming independent thinkers. They were learning how to ask their own questions and to back up their opinions with research and data. This process of change was—and is—slow and painful for us, requiring years of thoughtful inquiry, risk taking, discussion, and rethinking.

Moving to Student-Led Conferences

Through portfolios (ongoing, reflective selections of in-process and final work samples, projects, and records), genuinely owned by the students to improve their teaching and learning, parents and families finally became part of the process, not just as token team members who listened politely, but as talking, contributing, valued participants. Some of us tried our hand at three-way conferencing, or what we often call *triangular conferencing*. Parents and students were included, but the teacher still was there to lead the conference.

Triangular conferences, which served to celebrate students' accomplishments (largely through sharing and talking about the portfolio) and set reachable and manageable goals with a plan of action, were a breakthrough for some of us in changing forever the traditional teacher-parent conference. Teachers were exhausted after these conferences; they took up to an hour each and required long and intense preparation. But we couldn't go back. Attendance was almost always 100 percent. When parents know a celebration—not a devaluation—of their child is going on, they come, all of them. One teacher noted that for the first time in eight years, "Every parent came at the assigned time." Some kindergarten kids asked if they could "do it again." Some students came dressed up in their best clothes because "my mom and dad get dressed up when they go to an important meeting." Letters and comments from parents and kids touched our hearts, minds, and souls. (Figure 9–3 shows a parent's response after her first triangular conference.) Second graders wrote letters (see Figure 9–4 for one example) urging the next year's crop of parents to keep their children present for the entire conference—that year there had been a private teacher-parent chat after the triangular conference in recognition that parents still wanted some access to teachers alone. (See Figures 9–5 and 9–6 for comments from a second grader and his mother.)

The move to student-led conferences followed naturally. Here kids are truly in charge as they need to be, for only they can make changes in their learning, just as we're the only ones who can change our own practices. Now it seems absolutely ludicrous to me ever to have an assessment conference to which the child is not invited. It is akin to our principal having a conference about us with a central office administrator and then telling us about it later.

March 1993

Dear Mrs. Cooper,

As I went to bed and thought over yesterday's events, I realized what a wonderful gift you had presented to me in the form of our three-way conference.

I had been a bit distressed at the prospect of not having the conference time "all for myself," as I usually have, and thereby not having the opportunity to discuss matters which I really didn't intend for Philip to hear.

What I couldn't anticipate was the pleasure I would derive from this opportunity to observe aspects of my son's personality which I do not have a chance to see at home. It was uplifting to be introduced to the warm relationship that he has established with you. This bond of camaraderie mixed with respect is to be attributed completely to his own efforts, with no involvement from us, his parents. Since this kind of relationship is probably what I would most wish for him in life, it was gratifying to know that it can be within his grasp.

I carried away a message that was wordlessly communicated through your interactions: "This kid is O.K. Go ahead and feel comfortable about your confidence in him."

Chances are, we would have talked ABOUT Philip at great length and in considerable depth at a two-way conference, and yet my maternal concerns would have prevented me from being reassured in the way that I was when we all met together. . . .

Would I have felt the same way if I had had three-way conferences in earlier years? I don't know.

Do I believe that every teacher could promote an experience as successful as the one you provided? Of course not! You're special!

Sincerely,

Harriet K Wallach

Figure 9–3 Parent response after first triangular conference

March 17th

Dear Parents,

We feel very stongly
about parent techer time,
We feel that we shold be
abel to be in the room
at parint techer time,
Becasre we want to know
what you are talking about
at that time. Because We
will know what to do
better,

From,

Ben Z.

Figure 9–4 A student's unedited response to leaving his triangular conference

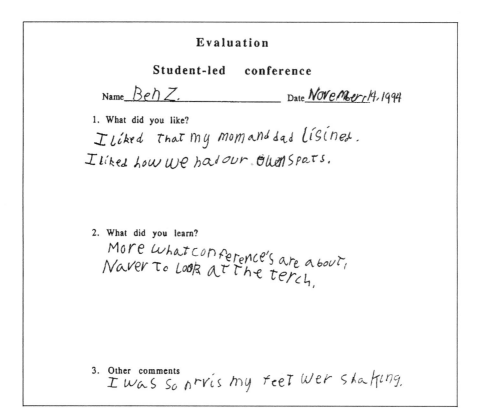

Figure 9–5 Student response to student-led conference

That's exactly what we've done to kids by excluding them from the process. Student-led conferences have the potential for tremendous student empowerment. Parents see that readily, as the following story confirms.

Along with several hundred parents, teachers, administrators, and school board members, I recently attended an evening community meeting in our school district devoted to looking at student achievement. In groups of about thirty, we brainstormed ways to improve student achievement—a big issue in our schools. One of the ways suggested was to relook at assessment, using student-led conferencing as a model for change.

As I was leaving the meeting, I got to talking with a parent whose second grader and fourth grader had just gone through student-led conferencing for the first time during our traditional fall conferences. This mother was effusive in her praise of what these conferences had done for her children. She described her second grader, who had struggled with reading in first grade and lacked confidence, as doing magnificently in talking about his work and accomplishments. What impressed me was knowing that both of

Evaluation

Triangular Conference

Name: Susie Z.   Date: 3/9/95

1. What did you like?

I like the fact that Ben is so comfortable with his progress and his ability to work the problems out so easily, this program keeps his confidence level up so therefor he is positive about his work.

2. What did you learn?

I learned that this way of learning should be taught throughout Bens Elementary Education He is so comfortable. (Please mrs Martin move to 3rd grade next year!) Triangular Conferences show so much more than listening to the teacher. You can really see and understand the whole process

3. Other comments

I am extremely pleased! Thankyou

Figure 9–6 Parent response to triangular conference

her children's teachers had been trying this kind of conferencing for the first time. Both were highly successful. Both teachers had worked closely with colleagues who had worked through the rough spots with them.

Student-led conferences scare some of us. We have to be totally professional, organized, articulate, and clear in our beliefs and practices to carry them off successfully. Initially, they are more work, as is all significant change in teaching practice. These conferences require clear and excellent communication with parents to apprise them of the rationale, goals, and procedures and get them to buy in. Some administrators worry that their weakest teachers will be "exposed." Parents finally know what we're really teaching because what we do and believe is so visible.

If you want to make "back to basics" a nonissue with parents, move to more meaningful assessment practices. When parents "see" what students are learning, producing, thinking, and evaluating—as well as what the expectations are—in spelling, math, phonics, science, all areas, they stop asking for "the basics" because they know firsthand it underpins all that is happening in the teaching-learning process.

At the same time, when we change our "hard copy," as some of our teachers piloting alternative assessment have done, parents need to understand the changes we are making right from the beginning. Otherwise, they can become confused, as did one parent of a first grader, who scheduled a meeting with the principal after she had read the educational narrative report (a departure from the usual checklist) written by the child's first-grade teacher. The language was so similar to the kindergarten report that the parent believed her child had made no progress. Although the kindergarten and first-grade teachers had been conscientious and descriptive in their narratives, they had used terms such as *experimental phase of writing* and *early reading phase* without attaching book titles, sample pages of text, and writing pieces to illustrate what those phases meant. It was clear to the teachers but not to the parents. Further conversation revealed that the parent did not understand why we were changing the reporting system. While we thought communication from the schools had been sufficient, we learned we needed to do a better job in parent education.

Student-led conferences have caused us to reexamine our traditional use of time. We've all known that the use of time and space is out-of-date in most schools. But we haven't pushed hard enough to change the old order. Or we haven't known who, when, and how to push and take action. To make more time for meaningful conferences, the school calendar must be adjusted and revisioned. Teachers cannot add more time after and before school to their already overflowing days.

Some possibilities could include conference evenings for working parents (with compensatory time for teachers) and conference days viewed as instruction days. The procedures for how some of us are beginning to conduct student-led conferences—with students showing what they know through reading aloud or reading silently and retelling what they read, problem solving in math, writing a letter of thanks to their families for coming—could easily be viewed part of our instructional program. As teachers and parents observe the students in performance-based actions, teaching and goal-setting with an action plan follow.

Administrators in my school district have been very supportive of elementary teachers who are willing to participate in triangular or student-led conferences. At the present time those teachers who choose to can take two additional conference days (by hiring substitutes) and can also report by trimester instead of quarterly. Principals have also provided in-school release time (again, by hiring substitutes) for teachers at a grade level to plan together—to develop letters to parents, conference procedures, and "hard copy" forms and to work through the "nuts and bolts" with colleagues.

Moving to successful student-led conferencing requires us to be professional in the highest sense—smart, articulate, and well versed in educational theory and practice. It requires us to focus on students' strengths and use respectful language in their presence. It requires us to know our students very well. It also requires us to assume the role of mentor and collaborator with colleagues who need to be invited to join us. With student and parent permission, some of our experienced teachers have videotaped a few of their conferences and shared them with interested teachers. Others have invited teachers trying the process for the first time to sit in and observe a student-led conference. In a few of our K–4 buildings, we used our language arts support group time to read and discuss a very useful book, *Student-Led Conferences.*

One teacher was so successful with student-led conferences that several of her parents insisted that next year's teacher implement it, causing a teacher to try—and buy into—a practice she wouldn't otherwise have considered. That's one way grass-roots movements begin.

Students Writing Their Own Narrative Report Cards

While a growing group of teachers in our school district have been moving toward more authentic assessment practices—including student-led conferencing—teachers have always controlled the final assessment piece, the report card. Believing that students—who were used to self-evaluating their daily work and setting goals for themselves—could evaluate themselves for a semester as well, I suggested to several teachers that we try to have them do just that.

First, we had students examine a number of written narratives reports to get them familiar with this type of writing. Fourth-grade teacher Joan Servis and I shared copies of narratives written by teachers in our district as well as some narratives we found in professional books on evaluation. I also shared a written self-evaluation of myself as a reader (see Figure 9–7). We brainstormed what their narratives might be called, how they could be organized, what they needed to contain. We talked about audience, purpose, and voice. The students worked diligently for weeks, drafting and revising, rewriting and editing, and staying highly engrossed in a project that they took seriously. We were elated at the professional and complete job almost all the students did.

We learned that parents can have difficulty fully appreciating and understanding student-written narratives unless they have the total context

Informal Self-Evaluation in Reading
by Regie Routman, May 1995

Strengths
read *New York Times* daily for at least 30 minutes
    (read most of national news and editorial page)
read professional journals each month
read every day for at least one hour
read nonfiction and fiction, adult and children's
skim read when I need to
read very fast with good understanding
reread when necessary
read book reviews
keep a monthly reading log
take recommendations of what to read
read mostly "just right" books and an occasional challenging
    book
talk about books and articles with friends
read many books by an author I admire
am presently reading *Pigs in Heaven* by Barbara Kingsolver
recent favorite book, *The Shipping News* by E. Annie Proulx
favorite author, Jane Smiley

Weaknesses
don't read international news carefully
read mostly professional books and journals about teaching
some days I watch TV when I could read
need to read more children's books and Y. A. fiction

Goals
*read more fiction, especially notable fiction
set aside time each evening for quiet reading
read newspaper more carefully, especially international
    issues

Figure 9–7 Self-evaluation as a reader

of what the expected learning goals and outcomes are. A student's saying he is making "wonderful progress" is not enough. Parents want and need to know the grade-level curriculum expectations. One parent found the narratives "very valuable" but still wanted the teacher's evaluation to be sure she had the complete context of her daughter's progress.

Most of the final narratives were so professional that it was sometimes hard to tell that they were written by students. Several parents in Julie Beers's third-grade class commented to their child's next teacher that they read through the entire narrative before realizing their child had written it. (Figures 9–8 and 9–9 are the language arts sections of student-written final narrative evaluations written by a third grader and a fourth grader.)

Educational Report

Student Cassie H. Grade 4
Teacher Mrs Servis School Onaway
Date 6\15\95 Assigned to Grade 5

Absent 0 Tardy 0

Final Report

Language Arts

Reading

In reading She is a developed reader. She is currently Reading "Bridge To Terabitha" by Katherine Paterson. She reads a wide variety of books and She enjoys reading. She reads almost every night for 40 minutes. She is making Progress and Improving.

She does'nt Participate that much in Reading disscussion Group but, enjoy's listening to other's Ideas.

Writing

She enjoys writing. She Piggyback's off author's Ideas. She also likes listening to other students Ideas and Stories and She gladly takes suggestions in Peer confrencing. She also writes every night and writes a variety of different Stories. She also wrote poems.

Figure 9–8 Student-written narrative as the final report card

She is currently writing a story from a dogs point of view and a book of short stories. Her handwriting has improved greatly throughout the year.

Spelling, Speaking, Listening

In Spelling she sounds out unknown words and breaks words up. She is a good speller and she has improved in spelling and can spell longer words. In Speaking she does'nt speak in front of the class that much, and she needs to work on projecting her voice. She listens to others ideas and listens to the teacher.

Figure 9–8, continued

Educational Report

Student Timothy K.   Grade 3
Teacher MS. Beers   School Oraway
Date June 1995   Assigned to Grade 4

LANGUAGE ARTS

Reading

At the beginning of the year Tim hated reading. Sometimes he would not read at night when there was no WEB checker. Now Tim loves reading. When he's in a good part of a book, he usually has to be told again and again to put his book away. Tim reads books at his level and often times he'll get to a word he does not know. First he will sound out the syllables. If that does not work he'll skip the word and read on. If the sentence still does not make sense he will ask a teacher or peer. At the beginning of the year Tim was not reading books at his level. He was reading books like *Max Malone* or *The Littles*. Now Tim is reading books like *Number the Stars* and *James and the Giant Peach*. Tim is now

Figure 9–9 Student-written narrative as the final report card

reading his own series, *The Chronicles of Narnia* by C. S. Lewis. Tim has confirmed that they are his favorite books. Tim is always prepared for WEB interview and is ready for discussion groups. Tim has read 36 books. Tim always has his assignments done on time. He likes fiction books the most. He also reads a little bit of science fiction. Tim needs to read more nonfiction books over the summer. Tim now reads 40 minutes a night. Tim is very proud of his accomplishments in reading. He wants to read the rest of the *NIMH* books.

Writing

Tim's writing is wonderful. At the beginning of the year when it was writing time he would moan and groan. Now Tim says, "Woo Hoo" and at the end he always asks, "Can we have more writing time, please?" Tim now writes fiction things based on nonfiction. Tim is now writing about his trip to Holiday Valley and he said over the summer he will try to finish his story. Tim uses very interesting vocabulary such as "Everybody then said 'good bye, we're going to miss you' in a sarcastic way." Tim has very good detailed writing such as "The clock ticked on and on." Tim uses dialogue at least 5 times on a page of writing. Tim is very conscientious in writing. He always tries his best no matter what.

Figure 9–9, continued

What Makes a Good Teacher?

Effective teachers come in all shapes and sizes. Although I embrace whole language principles and strive to apply them to my teaching, I am well aware that there is no one best, ideal way of teaching. That when you get right down to it, it's not the method or philosophy that's most important, it's the teacher, her knowledge, her relationship with the students, that's always been primary. Without that mutual respect and trust and camaraderie, you can't teach much.

I'd like to quote here from several terrific books by wise thinkers and educators because I believe we can use their observations and thinking to empower and inspire our own teaching practices. We can learn much—if we are open to it—from the wisdom of others. We can come to know in new ways and strengthen and revitalize our teaching.

Talking about successful teachers—one who could be labeled "whole language" and one who could be labeled "basal text"—Gloria Ladson-Billings notes,

Beneath the surface, at the personal ideological level, the differences between these instructional strategies lose meaning. Both teachers want their students to become literate. Both believe that their students are capable of high levels of literacy.

Mike Rose, in his eloquent book *Possible Lives*, critically examines intellectually rich classroom communities in our public schools and makes it clear that it's the teacher, the teacher's knowledge and the quality of life in the classroom, that gets results. He talks about the kinds of knowledge effective teachers are able to apply to their teaching, in spite of the constraints of everyday practice:

> They had determined ways of organizing their classrooms that enabled them to honor their beliefs about teaching and learning. We saw a good deal of variation here; there is no one best way: lecture-discussion, Socratic dialogue, laboratory demonstration, learning centers, small-group collaborative learning, a kind of artisans' workshop where students pursue independent projects. Not infrequently, these approaches existed in combination in the same classroom. In a number of cases, the current organization evolved. Teachers experimented with ways to create a common space where meaningful work could be done. This quality of reflective experimentation, of trying new things, of tinkering and adjusting, sometimes with uneven results, sometimes failing, was part of the history of many of the classrooms in *Possible Lives*.

I love the way Deborah Meier (former principal of Central Park East in East Harlem and a consultant with Ted Sizer in the Essential Schools Coalition) uses kindergarten as a metaphor for how our schools could be. She says:

> Kindergarten is the one place—maybe the last place—where teachers are expected to know children well, even if they don't hand in their homework, finish their Friday test, or pay attention. Kindergarten teachers know children by listening and looking. They know that learning must be personalized. . . . Kindergarten teachers know that helping children learn to become more self-reliant is part of their task. . . . The older they get the less we take into account the importance of children's own interests, and the less we cherish their capacity for engaging in imaginative play. . . . In kindergarten we design our rooms for real work, not just passive listening. We put things in the room that will appeal to children, grab their interests, and engage their minds and hearts. Teachers in kindergarten are editors, critics, cheerleaders, and caretakers, not just lecturers or deliverers of instruction. What

Ted Sizer calls "coaching" is second nature in the kindergarten classroom.

A good school for anyone is a little like kindergarten and a little like a good post-graduate program—the two ends of the educational spectrum, at which we understand that we cannot treat any two human beings identically, but must take into account their special interests and styles even as we hold all to high and rigorous standards.

Finally, we teachers know more than we think we know. It's just that our knowing cannot be measured and quantified, and we feel uncomfortable speaking out without hard data. Because we don't value our experiences and intuition enough, the public doesn't value it. We need to rethink what and how we know and revalue it. I think Lorri Neilsen says it best:

> What I now know about teaching reading and writing, I know not only in my mind, but in my bones. This knowing transcends words on the page and goes deep into that twilight zone that makes all researchers wary: personal knowledge. Because this wisdom of practice is difficult to see, label, measure, count, or stamp, we call it intuition, sixth sense. It is the essence of good teaching, the root source of improvisation, and traditionally the most undervalued knowledge in the educational enterprise.
>
> The wisdom of practice goes beneath, beyond, or through language, and it is profound. This knowing is messy, seldom predictable or generalizable, rarely precise, and known and learned as much through our eyes, ears, hands, heart, and soul as it is through our minds. . . . Teachers, like fish in water, are saturated with this knowing. . . . It is these forms of knowing—the artistic, the intuitive, the social, the nonpropositional—that are vastly undervalued by our profession and the public.

We can and must do even more than reflect on the wisdom of teaching. We can rethink and reenvision our classroom practices and traditional school structures in a new way so that all students can attain intellectual competence and self-respect. That means our classrooms and schools need to be restructured so that we can get to know our students, teach the way we believe, and work collegially. The only way these changes will happen is if we work for them—by becoming political: speaking out, knowing the research, writing proposals, experimenting in our own classrooms and schools, and sharing our results with local and national audiences.

10

Leading the Literacy Life We Want Our Students to Lead

Inquiry, collaboration, community, portfolios, negotiation. These are some of our new power words in education. Important words and goals. However, the talk always seems to center on "how to" incorporate these concepts into our classrooms. The crucial talk needs to start with us, not the concepts. Unless we embody the spirit and deed of what we are teaching—as learners ourselves and as models for our students— we won't be making the impact we need to make.

Several years ago, *The Sunday New York Times Magazine* ran a lead story about a college president, Leon Botstein (president of Bard College since 1975), who was both popular and successful, not a common feat. I was struck by the following remarks Botstein made and think they have relevance for us as educators.

> What makes me a good leader . . . is that the students see that I'm something more than the guy who signs the diploma and pushes the paper and makes some kind of speech. That, in fact, *I live the life I'm asking them to live.* They have more to gain from me that I'm willing to go through the terror of getting out on stage and know what it's like than if I don't.

If we want our students to be thinkers, researchers, collaborators, readers, writers, and evaluators, then they need to see us thinking, researching, collaborating, reading, writing, and evaluating. We need, literally, to live the life we're asking them to lead.

Inquiry and Change:
Become a Teacher-Researcher

A few months ago at a conference, I was talking about the need for teachers' voices to be heard and the need for us teachers to speak out more, write for other teachers, and become more articulate about our beliefs and practices.

"How many of you think of yourselves as teacher-researchers?" I asked the audience of about three hundred teachers and administrators. Not one hand went up. Sadly, I think this is a pretty accurate commentary. Most of us are intimidated by the words *teacher-researcher*. I understand that because I used to feel the same way.

Several years ago, as an invited speaker at a state reading conference, I was asked (along with all speakers) to send along three words to describe myself. Those descriptors would be used in the conference bulletin after each speaker's name. I sent "wife, mother, teacher." I can still remember thinking that I wanted to say *teacher-researcher* instead of *teacher*. But I was afraid if I said *teacher-researcher*, teachers wouldn't identify with me. I was also still struggling with not feeling entitled to say the words. *Teacher-researcher*. Wasn't that the domain of the university? Wasn't that for someone who knew how to collect and report on quantitative data? That certainly wasn't me. It's taken a long time to get comfortable with calling myself a teacher-researcher.

We must begin to see ourselves in that role, and we must begin to say the words without stuttering. I love the following definition of research because it makes the notion of research accessible to us.

> Research is a high-hat word that scares a lot of people. It needn't. It's rather simple. Essentially research is nothing but a state of mind . . . a friendly, welcoming attitude toward change . . . going out to look for change instead of waiting for it to come.

Teacher research goes beyond reflecting about our teaching. Teacher research involves wondering, posing questions, problem solving, trying out new procedures, working out our thoughts through writing, and ultimately acting on our new insights by changing our practices. Reflection alone isn't enough. "What separates those teachers who 'look back on the day' from those who are researchers lies in the notion of change. A researcher considers seriously what he might do differently."

Here's an example of what I'm talking about. Some of my recent wondering about the teaching of writing includes:

• How effective are peer conferences for the quality of students' writing?

- Can kids write well if the teacher doesn't write but uses only great literature as models?
- How can we get kids to raise their expectations for the quality of their writing?
- What makes writing powerful?
- How can we help kids write more for real audiences?
- What should the role of publishing be?

After lots of thinking and reflecting and after observing—and working and talking with—students in writing classrooms, I made some changes in my teaching. Some of those changes include better and more frequent modeling of what a good writing conference looks like; not having kids peer conference until it's been modeled and practiced; using sharing time more as I want my work responded to as an author— not a "what I liked" and "what I need to add or change" formula, but natural feedback that includes some positive responses but mostly involves specific suggestions based on my expressed needs and requests.

Another change in practice for fourth-grade teacher Joan Servis and me came about because of our continuing discussion and reflection about students' daily independent reading, which we call WEB (for "wonderfully exciting books"). We expected students to read for at least thirty minutes each evening, and each morning we had them record the page number they were on in the book they were reading.

But that is not what Joan and I do as readers. We each keep a monthly record of the books we've read, and we've been doing it for several years—for ourselves. Our record includes title, author, genre, and an asterisk if the book is outstanding. Recording the genre is important to us because it helps us keep the balance in the types of books we read, a goal for us both. Before I recorded the genre and then looked at the pattern of my reading, I was reading almost all professional books even though I was always saying that I wanted to read more fiction.

I remember exactly how and when my thinking began to change. Because I was trying to model everything I was expecting students to do, I began recording my daily reading in a small WEB log like our students use. I did this faithfully for about two months until it hit me that what I was doing was inauthentic. It served no useful purpose for me; it was, in fact, a waste of time. The number of pages I read each day was not anything I cared to chart. It was "role model" recording rather than "authentic" recording. At this point, I began questioning what we were requiring of students, but I was still at the wondering stage.

We now use the same recording model with our students; they write down the books they have completed, listing the title, author, genre (type of book), and often some type of personal rating system. Sure, we know there will always be a few kids who "cheat" and put down books they didn't read. But we're not willing to penalize the whole class for a few delinquents. We trust the students, and we want them to know it.

What made the change "teacher research" is that the move to "real world" recording of books read happened thoughtfully, after much personal and collegial reflection, ongoing discussion, trial and error, and modification over several years. The change fit with our developing view of literacy—trusting the learner more and making our teaching more authentic. And now, because I have just written about it, I have taken that small piece of teacher research a step further by sharing it with you, my collegial reader.

I have no doubt that when you think about it, you are also a teacher-researcher. You just need to make the mental shift to thinking like one. And then, take another risk. Think about speaking out and writing. We need to have much more writing by teachers for teachers. Vito Perrone, in his eloquent book *A Letter to Teachers*, encourages us to be more assertive:

> Only when teachers themselves assume the dominant position in regard to issues of teaching and learning in their classrooms, and begin to speak more broadly and authoritatively on matters of education, will we see significant improvement.

If we truly want our students to have their own inquiry questions and to read and write about their pondering, musing, and research findings, we need to model by our own example. We must share our teacher-researcher questions—and our curiosities and discoveries about what fascinates us—with them.

Cultivate Your Interests

Near the end of a recent school year, Leslie Bakkila, a teacher new to our school system who I had been working with, told me, "You know, Regie, there was one thing you said to me that helped me more than anything else." As I do with all new teachers, I had spent a lot of time in her room, supporting her in the language arts—demonstrating and coaching, sharing and talking. Expecting her to say something about small-group reading, writing, self-evaluation, or some other literacy activity, I was totally surprised by what came next:

Remember that day we were talking, and I told you that my husband had just called and said he had tickets for the ballet that night. I told my husband I couldn't go because I had papers to grade. And you said, "Leslie, go to the ballet. *Be an interesting person.*" And I went and loved it and told my students about it the next day. That really sunk in. How we have to lead interesting lives ourselves.

It's so easy for us to become consumed by our work. There's never enough time to do it all; there are always more plans to write, more papers to check, more things to do in the classroom so it's organized and comfortable. I am as guilty as the next teacher. I have to make a concerted effort to balance my life. Some weeks and months I do better than others. Much of the time I fail miserably.

What are some things I like to do that (I hope) keep me interesting? Alone or with my husband, family, and friends, I love to cook and create my own recipes, read great fiction, walk, go to bookstores and browse, spend time in coffeehouses, go to the farmer's market, plant and tend flowers, make preserves, write personal letters and poetry, read *The New York Times* every day, go to the theater, travel. I share these experiences with students and teachers.

In my job as coach (officially, language arts resource teacher), I work side by side with teachers and kids, demonstrating, encouraging, collaborating, sharing, and celebrating successes. When I used to go into classrooms for the first time, I would introduce myself as a reading and writing teacher who worked in different classrooms. My introduction was lackluster, impersonal, and boring. Now, whenever I can, I share my portfolio—and myself. My portfolio, which is ever changing, includes personal and academic goals and keepsakes, accomplishments, and work in progress.

Students and teachers alike love to learn about others' lives. Mem Fox says, "If you don't open up and share who you are with your students, they will not learn to trust you as a teacher and as a fellow human being; this will limit their engagement in class."

I take Mem Fox's words to heart. I am convinced that the reason I am able to get students to write with passion—and they do—is because I talk and write about what really matters to me—missing my grandmother, the trauma of moving after eighteen years in our home, my dad's wife dying, sharing a favorite book, having Peter and Claudine (our son and his wife) come home unexpectedly for Thanksgiving, writing this book.

Our students need to know that we have lives outside school and that as literate people, we are curious about lots of things because we're involved in the world. Perhaps, most important, our lives outside the classroom make us better teachers because we are more interesting, vital, and "real" to be with.

Kindergarten teacher Karen Sher concurs:

Without question, my kindergartners are the most attentive, intrigued, and expressive when I share parts of who I am outside of school. I feel that unless children and teachers can share the whole of who we are with each other, the empathy and love integral to optimal learning cannot exist. My class is familiar with my family, my hobbies, books I read, pieces I write, things that are hard for me, things that worry me, and so on.

Take Charge of Your Own Professional Development and Learning

Veteran teacher Joan Servis tells the story of sharing a flyer about an upcoming workshop with a fellow teacher and encouraging the teacher to go. The teacher said she couldn't go because of the district's recent levy failure and follow-up cutbacks. When Joan explained that she was taking the day and paying her own way, the colleague asked, "Why would you want to do that? You're so close to retirement."

Joan replied, "The day I stop growing is the day I should retire."

We cannot wait for someone else to set up professional growth opportunities for us. My district's superintendent of schools, Mark Freeman, says, "Teachers are waiting to be told what to do. If they wait for the stamp of approval from the superintendent, nothing will happen. If it's right for kids, do it. Start at the building level. This is how change works best."

There's no question that teachers see reform as extra work. Some teachers are willing to spend their own time to move ahead. Others are not. To ensure that all teachers continue to move ahead professionally, staff development days must be built into the school calendar. I am not talking about the model of staff development that relies on experts from out of town. I am talking about lots of time for all educators to work, talk, share, and plan collegially, at grade levels and across grade levels—what is more aptly termed professional development. In many places, including my own district, this has been very difficult to accomplish. While change is never easy, being professional demands that we continue to grow and continually reexamine our beliefs and practices.

Except for my Reading Recovery training, I have never taken a special class in language learning, literacy acquisition, or whole language. What I know, I know because I consciously live as a learner-teacher. I read widely—professionally and personally—take time to observe, reflect, and self-evaluate, am part of support groups and discussions with my colleagues, attend professional meetings, try out new ideas.

As a member of the National Council of Teachers of English (NCTE), the International Reading Association (IRA), the Association for Curriculum Development (ASCD), and The Whole Language Umbrella (WLU), I read their professional journals—*Language Arts, Primary Voices,* and *Voices from the Middle* (Urbana, IL: NCTE), *The Reading Teacher* (Newark, DE: IRA), *Educational Leadership* (Alexandria, VA: ASCD), *Talking Points* (North York, Ontario: WLU). I also subscribe to *The New Advocate: For Those Involved with Young People and Their Literature* (Boston: Christopher Gordon), *Teaching PreK–8* (Norwalk, CT: Highlights for Children), and *Book Links: Connecting Books, Libraries, and Classrooms* (Chicago: The American Library Association). Articles from these journals, and others I see occasionally, stretch my thinking and keep me abreast of the latest research and thinking in the language arts and in education.

I also read professional books published by Heinemann (Portsmouth, NH), Stenhouse (York, ME), Christopher Gordon (Norwood, MA), Pembroke (Markham, Ontario), Peguis (Winnipeg, Manitoba), Jossey-Bass (San Francisco), Teachers College Press (New York), Scholastic Professional Books (New York), and The Wright Group (Bothell, WA), and I make sure I receive their latest catalogues.

I do not read every article or every chapter. I don't have time. I pick and choose, skim and scan, underline and take notes, skip lines and pages, reread certain articles, clip and save others, make copies of articles to share and discuss with colleagues, and recommend books to friends. When I really love a book, I rush out and buy it for a colleague or two, and they do the same for me.

Occasionally, when some part of a text really strikes me so that I don't ever want to forget it, or something is so well written I want to be able to find it easily, I will copy those favorite lines into a special notebook that I carry with me. Then I can, and do, go back to it again and again and think about its meaning or savor its beauty. Students know I keep such a notebook, because I share it with them. Some students have been motivated to start their own notebooks where they record favorite words, phrases, sayings, poetry, and memorable passages from literature.

Make Time for Professional and Personal Reading and Reflection

Teachers tell me they can't find the time to read. I say we must. I could not put my trust in a doctor or lawyer who didn't keep up with current research and practices. It should be no different for us as teachers.

I recently had a talk with a superintendent who spoke of talking to a group of middle school teachers and discussing the work of Howard Gardner, Theodore Sizer, Robert Slavin, and other prominent educators. The superintendent noted with dismay that most of the teachers had no idea who he was talking about. A sobering prospect, that we who are to be modeling scholarly behavior and reading are neither scholarly nor readers.

We must make time to read. My favorite quote on that score, one that I do go back to often, comes from a magnificent book, *Better Than Life*, by Daniel Pennac. Here's part of it:

> If you have to ask yourself where you'll find the time, it means the desire isn't there. Because, if you look at it more carefully, no one has the time to read. Children don't, teenagers don't, adults don't. Life is a perpetual plot to keep us from reading. . . .
>
> Time spent reading is always time stolen. Like time spent writing, or loving, for that matter.
>
> Stolen from what?
>
> From life's obligations. . . .
>
> The issue is not whether or not I have the time to read (after all, no one will ever give me that time) but whether I will allow myself the joy of being a reader.

Furthermore, dealing with the politics of education requires us to be as thoughtful, professional, well read, and educated as possible. "Make time to think. . . . Thinking is difficult. It requires concentration and discipline. Give it the time it deserves. Aristotle would approve."

Be More Collegial

Someone once asked me why I come to school each day. I surprised myself by immediately responding, "My colleagues." And then I really thought about it, and my response held true. Sure, I love the kids—being with them and working with them. However, given the prospect of only seeing kids and working alone each day, teaching holds little interest for me. It's the daily interaction—the deliberating, thinking, talking, reflecting, and growing professionally with my colleagues that keeps teaching intellectually exciting and rewarding for me. It's being part of that community of caring and sharing teachers that I relish. Without it, the learning and changing I would be able to do would be very limited indeed.

There's a lot of talk these days about creating "communities of learners" in our classrooms. To make that phrase more than just part of the educational jargon, we need to first become part of an adult community of learners.

We need to begin by being more collegial with each other. We teachers often feel so much stress and isolation from our profession that we must support each other in word and deed in order to continue teaching. In the course of change especially, when we are grappling with our values, attitudes, and beliefs, we need the collegiality and reassurance of caring and supportive teachers and administrators. I have learned that trust develops one person at a time, and it can take years. However, teachers are more likely to take risks when they trust and feel supported by their fellow educators.

Mike Rose, author of *Possible Lives*, admits that it took him a while to appreciate how important teacher support is:

> The ability of many of these teachers to work effectively within their schools and districts was strengthened by the way they pulled others into their professional lives. You won't find this discussed very much in the teacher-education literature, and, I must admit, it was so obvious that it took me a while to appreciate its full significance.

Collegiality says a lot about us and our schools. When collegiality exists in a school, adults

1. talk with one another about practice
2. observe each other engaged in practice
3. work on curriculum together
4. teach each other what they know. . . .

The quality of adult relationships within a school has more to do with the quality and character of the school and with the accomplishments of students than any other factor.

Human kindness goes along with collegiality. How we treat each other says a lot about the culture of our schools. A teacher in Hawaii, who describes herself as the only whole language teacher at her grade level, says nobody mentions whole language in her school, but she feels the backlash. Articles against whole language are anonymously posted over the copy machine. A teacher in Missouri who is just beginning to use portfolios keeps his door closed all day because he doesn't want to deal with derisive comments from fellow teachers who feel threatened by change. How can we expect kids to be kind to each other when we speak against each other in the halls?

I have visited schools across the country. Where kids seem to be thriving in all ways, socially and academically, educators and parents are closely aligned and working and communicating effectively and respectfully. Take a close look at your own classroom and school. When was the last time you observed another teacher teaching? When do you talk with others about your practice? Are you working on curriculum with others, or are you still doing everything yourself? Are parents and other teachers comfortable and welcome in your classroom and school? We need to make in-house videos of ourselves and teachers we admire and share those videos with each other. We need to have joint planning time with grade-level colleagues, even lobby for release time during the school day to collaborate. We need to build professional and respectful communities of adult learners before we can expect to have effective communities of student learners in our classrooms.

Kindergarten teacher Karen Sher says,

> I never miss an opportunity to share my collegial meetings with my students. Its a part of me that I want them to know about—as I always tell my parents at open house. Children don't do as we say; they do as we do. If we want them to value collaboration and cooperation (as well as reading, writing, etcetera), we have to model it.

Share Knowledge and Materials

Many of us teachers like to hold on to what we've created. Rather than freely and generously sharing with our colleagues, we become stingy and territorial. I understand the feeling; years ago, I was like that too. Looking back, I think it was because I wanted recognition and because I thought new, better ideas wouldn't come to me. I've learned that the more I share with others, the more I continue to learn. In the give-and-take of ideas, interesting conversations and adaptations occur. I have also learned the well does not run dry; the ideas keep coming.

It's ironic that we teach our students to share and collaborate, yet don't live that model with our colleagues. We hoard, and we keep silent. When we do share an idea, we become resentful when it is used in the same way we used it. One new teacher angered a veteran teacher by copying his newsletter, almost verbatim. Yet, that is how many of our students learn. When I model a new writing genre—a thank-you letter or a bit of memoir—my students' initial attempts often resemble mine very closely. This imitation of my words or style only lasts a short time, just until students feel comfortable. Eventually, with support and encouragement, their own styles emerge.

We must give the same respect and trust to our colleagues. We must be mentors and share our knowledge even though we are not paid to do so. I believe mentoring and supporting other teachers is a professional responsibility. The only way we continue to grow is to support, teach, and share with each other.

Likewise, we need to be generous with our books. We all know teachers whose cupboards burst with wonderful books and materials, but nobody except that teacher and her students get to use them. I have been in schools where teachers have complained bitterly to me about not having books to teach reading while the teacher down the hall has shelves overflowing. We tell our students to share. Yet, many of us don't practice what we preach. We need to.

Collaborate as Learners: Start a Support Group

Working alone all the time is an awful business. It's lonely and frustrating. It's hard not to share the high and low moments with someone and to have support and recognition. It's difficult to have to create everything yourself. Yet, that's exactly how most of us still work. One of the best things that ever happened to me as a teacher was beginning to work and talk with others regularly. That happened as part of my journey to becoming a whole language teacher.

One way we break the isolation of teaching and continue to grow professionally in my school district is through weekly whole language support groups. Since 1987, in all our K–4 buildings—and now in our 5–6 building—teachers have been meeting voluntarily every week for one half hour before school begins. It has been our best staff development effort because it's ongoing, and because we focus on what we need professionally to keep learning and growing. One year, because of increasing curricular demands, we met every other week. That didn't work. We needed the sustained and frequent conversation and collegial interaction that weekly meetings provided.

We read and discuss current journal articles, share ideas and new books—professional and children's literature—and focus on teaching issues. We listen to each other and support each other. We exchange ideas and concerns. Some recent topics that we have focused on at length include portfolios, student-led conferencing, and spelling.

In several of our buildings, teachers have opted to spend their own money to purchase books to read and discuss over a period of weeks. In an effort to understand and work more effectively with all of our students, this year we read and discussed *The Dreamkeepers: Successful Teachers of African American Children*, by Gloria Ladson-Billings, and *Kwanzaa and Me: A Teacher's Story*, by Vivian Gussin Paley.

One of the benefits of our support groups has been getting to know each other across the grade levels, learning and understanding how and what we are thinking, trying out, and teaching. At one time, I remember thinking that we would run out of topics and concerns. Almost ten years later, that has never happened. As teacher-learners, we always have new questions.

Even if there is only one other teacher you know who is interested, start a support group and invite everyone. Be nonjudgmental, open, and patient. It took one teacher eight years to come to a meeting. Trust builds slowly. Being part of a support group will change your teaching. Lots of educators have told me or written me that being part of a support group transformed their professional lives.

Using Our Literate Selves as Models for Teaching

Although many of us don't believe it, we are our own best experts on how to teach reading and writing in our classrooms. We need only to look to, trust, and think about our own literacy and literacy development.

Looking at Ourselves as Readers to Inform Our Teaching

Even though many teachers now use literature in teaching reading, in many cases the teaching is as it has always been; that is, the materials have changed, but the literal questions, responses, and vocabulary words still persist. By the time the students and teachers are "done" with a book, many of them—and us—dislike it because of "overkill."

We need to look closely at what we ourselves do with a well-loved book to inform our classroom practice. Think about the last time you read a book you loved. Remember how you felt when you finished the book. Imagine how you would have felt if you had then been required to write a book report or a summary that had to include the main idea and supporting details. Or, if at the end of chapters, you'd been required to write answers to questions. For myself, that would have been enough to turn me off to reading the book. And if that practice persisted throughout my school career, it would have taken me a long time to become a reader in the true sense—one who chooses to read for my own purposes. In fact, that is exactly what happened to me and to many of us and what continues to happen to our students. Without time set aside for reading for pleasure, reading can become another dreaded assignment. Figure 10–1 is an essay by a graduating high school senior who loved reading and writing in first grade and who came to hate it as he progressed through school.

Recently, at a workshop for teachers and administrators of all grade levels, I asked the participants to reflect on their most recent favorite book and to jot down how they happened to read it, what they did while they were reading it, and what they did after they finished it. After everyone had talked about his or her responses with a partner, I took down comments from the audience exactly as they gave them to me. Here is what they said:

- ***How did I choose the book?***

  someone recommended it

  favorite author

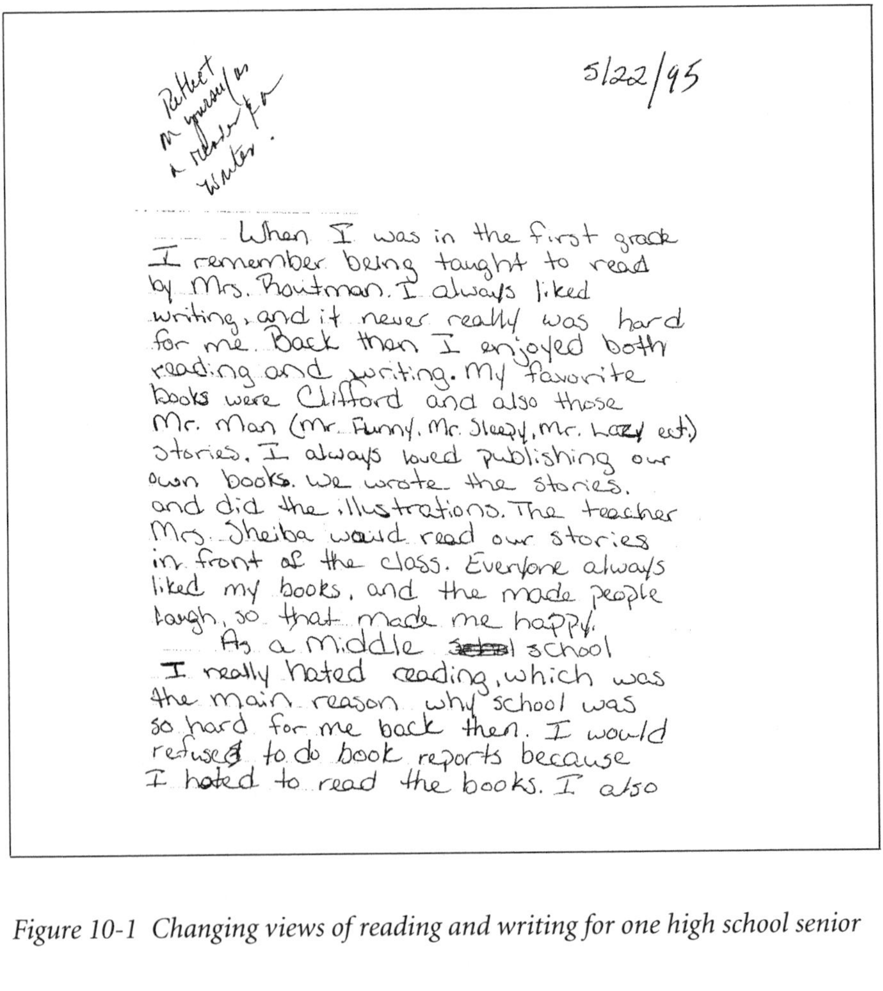
Reflect on yourself as a reader & writer.

5/22/95

When I was in the first grade I remember being taught to read by Mrs. Routman. I always liked writing, and it never really was hard for me. Back than I enjoyed both reading and writing. My favorite books were Clifford and also those Mr. Man (Mr. Funny, Mr. Sleepy, Mr. Lazy ect.) stories. I always loved publishing our own books. We wrote the stories. and did the illustrations. The teacher Mrs. Sheiba would read our stories in front of the class. Everyone always liked my books, and the made people laugh, so that made me happy.

As a middle school I really hated reading, which was the main reason why school was so hard for me back then. I would refused to do book reports because I hated to read the books. I also

Figure 10-1 Changing views of reading and writing for one high school senior

topic I wanted to know more about

found it browsing in the library

somebody put it in my hand

good title and/or cover

good book review

great illustrations

• *What did I do while reading?*

related book to my own life

laughed or cried

took notes so I could remember it

---

did not really care then either. my
interest in writing was the only thing
that made me pass (and also Summer
School). I was always writing. I would
ask my teachers to give me writing
assignments, instead of book reports

If I was not writing for a class,
(which was most of the time) I was
writing raps. I used to be the
best rapper in the middle school.
All through study hall, and most of
my classes that was all I would
do.

Now I am in high school
and everything has changed, except
for one thing. I still hate reading.
In my high school career there
has only been about six or seven
books that really interest me. I
still like writing but the topics are
all stupid to me now. I don't rap
anymore because it became harder than
what it was so instead of me working
to keep it up, I just left it alone.

Figure 10-1, continued

made predictions

shared a special part with someone

tried to get more comfortable

hid so no one could bother me

got lost in the story

ate

changed my practice

fell in love with the characters (or didn't fall in love with the character)

reread parts

• *What did I do afterward?*

shared it

bought it

told others about it

looked for another book by the same author

reread it

looked for a similar story

tried to implement the ideas from it

talked with others about it

asked questions about anything I didn't understand

watched movie or video and compared it with the book

wrote the author

related it to myself

What do these responses about our own literate behavior suggest for the classroom? Above all, there must be time each day—twenty to sixty minutes—when students can read, mostly books of their own choosing. In middle school and high school, it's difficult to take time out of periods that are already too short, but committed teachers manage to create blocks of time, at least on some days, for "choice" reading. Here are some other things that come to mind as important for helping students become readers, that is, students who choose to read critically for pleasure and information. You'll think of others.

• *How do I choose the book?*

• Give students time to talk about books with each other and to hear about favorite books classmates are reading. (One way is through a "Critic's Corner"—see *Invitations*, p. 50.)

- Allow time for browsing. Many of us love to browse in bookstores. Why not encourage browsing of books in the classroom and make time for it, such as an occasional free reading period devoted to browsing? Some teachers promote this by placing boxes or crates of books—grouped by author, topic, genre, or some point of interest—all around the classroom.

- Help students find more books by a favorite author. Literally, put the books in their hands.

- Talk about book reviews—how and why they're written in the world outside school. Give an oral book review to entice students into a book. If you have a school librarian, invite her in to discuss the school's book review process. (Most kids have no idea how books wind up in the library.) Write book reviews for the school library, public library, or local bookstore. Students in some of my school district's second- and third-grade classrooms wrote reviews of favorite books. The students took the project very seriously because it mattered; their book reviews were to be displayed at a local bookstore (and they were).

- *What do I do while reading?*

  - Make sure your room has some comfortable reading areas, perhaps some cushions and cozy corners where readers can curl up with books. How our rooms look tell a lot about how much we value reading.

  - Occasionally, allow time for students to describe or read a memorable section aloud to a friend.

  - Help students notice what authors do, and encourage them to attempt similar goals when they write. Once in a while, ask them to "flag" a paragraph that is especially well written—one that uses exciting language or describes a character or setting in vivid detail, for example. Allow time for sharing these paragraphs with the whole class, a small group, or a partner.

  - Ask students to predict, orally or in writing, what today's reading will be about.

  - By modeling, encourage students to generate their own discussion questions about what they see as important in the text.

  - Show students how we as adults figure out words we don't know. Riveted by a story, most of the time we either ignore the word or figure it out using the surrounding context (as well as our prior knowledge).

- Demonstrate how to take notes for a discussion. For example, in preparing to participate in an adult book group, I mark sections of the book I want to highlight, try to learn more about the author, take notes, think about how the book relates to my life. With demonstrations and practice, many of these literature discussion groups can be successfully student-led. (See Notes, p. 215, for resources.)

- *What do I do afterward?*

  - You don't have to do anything with the book. Sometimes the best response to a wonderful book is quiet contemplation. Savoring and appreciating the book is the best response of all.
  - Encourage reading another book by the same author.
  - Compare the book just read with similar books or other books by the same author. Comparisons can take the form of discussions; Venn diagrams, charts, or other graphic representations; seeing and discussing the movie or video. Keep written responses to a minimum.
  - Discuss students' questions and confusions. Other students can often respond thoughtfully to peers' questions before we say what we think.
  - Have students talk to each other about their books. (See WEB interviews, *Invitations*, pp. 43–50.)
  - Encourage students to write to favorite authors when they have questions.

Seriously consider award-winning author Flannery O'Connor's warning when she found out students were being assigned her work: "If teachers are in the habit of approaching a story as if it were a research problem for which any answer is believable so long as it is not obvious, then I think students will never learn to enjoy fiction."

Envisioning Ourselves as Writers

We as a profession do not see ourselves as writers. For many of us, the lack of writing confidence goes back to our own school experiences where we wrote for the teacher (never ourselves) and judged our competency—or lack thereof—according to teacher comments and red correction marks on our papers. Certainly that was true for me.

Despite the fact that we all write letters, cards, newsletters, lists, notes (and research papers, if we are taking a college course), we rarely share these with our students to show them we are writers. Our lack of writing confidence is so deep that when I ask a teacher to share her writing with her students, she replies, *What writing? I've never written anything.*

Why We Must Write

There are several reasons why we teachers must take the risk and write. First of all, nobody can tell our classroom stories with our voice. No matter how many articles or books have been written about a topic, your story is different and important because only your voice can tell it. I believe we have a responsibility to share our knowledge and talents with others. The exciting things going on in your classroom are too good to stay only within your classroom and school. Teaching is a complicated, lonely business, and our own stories give confidence, insights, practical suggestions, and inspiration to our fellow teachers in a way that nothing else can.

Second, writing makes us better teachers. When our students see how we struggle, organize, think, reread, revise, edit, and get ideas with and through our own writing, they are supported in their writing. When they see our process—because we show it to them, speak it aloud, do it in front of them—we are demonstrating the most powerful of practices while giving them a lifelong gift and tool—using writing to remember, to organize our thinking, to reflect, to communicate effectively, to problem-solve, to understand our world, to inquire and make new meaning.

Third, writing informs our practice and pushes our thinking deeper. I didn't understand Don Murray's words "You write to figure out what you know" until I began writing. Then, I finally understood "writing to learn." Yes, I had ideas in my head, but they only crystallized and began to make sense after I wrote them down, thought about them, shifted them around on the page, read some more, wrote, rewrote. It was through the hard work of writing that I learned what I knew and needed to know. And here's a bonus: writing makes you smarter. Working out and thinking through tough issues stretches your brain cells. Writing also makes you a better listener. Because you're closely observing and noting, you have to listen harder. When you begin to write, you start to live your life differently. You become more observant and reflective. To help me do that, I fill up notebooks. When I am working in a classroom and something happens that I want to remember or think about further, I write it down within a few hours. Otherwise, it's gone. So many new things keep happening that I lose the insight unless I record it promptly.

The fourth and most compelling reason to write is that writing changes the world and makes a difference. Having written, I have been astounded at the power of the written word. People take your ideas seriously when they know you are knowledgeable and truthful. You have taken the time and trouble to say what you think and feel and believe, what you honor and know and cherish, what you have researched and observed, what you question and don't understand, what you have learned in your heart and mind and whole being.

Yes, it takes courage to write, but mostly it takes grit, perseverance, and will. One of the best books to read to get you thinking and writing is *Writing Down the Bones: Freeing the Writer Within*, by Natalie Goldberg. She says,

> Basically, if you want to become a good writer, you need to do three things. Read a lot, listen well and deeply, and write a lot. And don't think too much. Just enter the heat of words and sounds and colored sensations and keep your pen moving across the page.

Enter the Public Debate

Like the students who wrote to the editor of *USA Today* (pp. 148–50) to protest and speak out, we teachers must now do the same. We need to do what we are having our students do—write and speak out for real reasons in order to make a difference. We need lots of us writing in the public arena so that our voices are heard loudly. An occasional letter here and there won't do it.

Right now, the urgent educational climate demands that we become political, that is, that we enter the local and national debate in a clear and reasoned manner, that we share our beliefs and classroom stories publicly. Writing for our own professional community is a start, but it is not enough. The national outcry criticizing, confusing, and misunderstanding current educational practices demands that we become publicly articulate. If we want to influence the course of public education, and we must, then we as educators must clarify issues for a wider public audience—the media, parents, school boards, local and federal government. Democracy gives us the freedom and opportunity to speak out and be heard. We must seize that right. Otherwise, much of what we know and believe about teaching and learning may be lost, simply because we didn't make the effort to raise our voices.

Make Time for Reflection, Writing, and Action

I know what you're thinking. All this reflection, collaboration, reading, writing, and professional development sounds great for others, but you don't have the time or the energy for it. And it's true, teaching demands everything we have. Only our families and friends know how much we care about our kids and colleagues and how exhausted we are most of the time.

I wonder, though. If we were able to lead our lives differently, if we were more professional and articulate, more collegial and reflective, more outspoken and visible, we might at least be heard and respected to the same degree our critics are. Even better, we might be able to influence practice and policy that does not serve the best interests of our students.

As I was finishing the writing of this book, I received a letter from a teacher in Wyoming, who said, "Change is not easy and although I want it, I am held back by the fear of what must be done to achieve it." Yet with courage, this teacher stood up in her school district and proposed a change in the direct reading instruction approach she had been told to use with her low-achieving students. The classes she works with no longer chant sounds and read meaningless passages. They are now involved in meaning-based and holistic reading of real literature because of her strong beliefs and action.

Serving as an advocate for children and a true teacher-researcher, this teacher moved beyond reasoned thought to decisive action. We must all be willing to do the same. Our future depends on it.

Appendices

Appendix A: On Grammar Exercises to Teach
Speaking and Writing 187

Appendix B: Encourage Independent Reading at Home 188

Appendix C: Discourage Heavy Use of Television
and Electronic Media 189

Appendix D: Blank Weekly Review 190

Appendix E: Weekly Review 192

Appendix F: FACTS: On the Teaching of Phonics 194

Appendix G: Reading Strategies for Unknown Words
Beyond "Sound It Out" 198

Appendix H: FACTS: On Teaching Skills in Context 199

Appendix I: Explanation of Spelling Program 203

Appendix A

On Grammar Exercises to Teach Speaking and Writing

Background: This resolution was prompted by the continuing use of repetitive grammar drills and exercises in the teaching of English in many schools. Proposers pointed out that ample evidence from fifty years of research has shown the teaching of grammar in isolation does not lead to improvement in students' speaking and writing, and that in fact, it hinders development of students' oral and written language.

Resolved, that the National Council of Teachers of English affirm the position that the use of isolated grammar and usage exercises not supported by theory and research is a deterrent to the improvement of students' speaking and writing and that, in order to improve both of these, class time at all levels must be devoted to opportunities for meaningful listening, speaking, reading, and writing; and

that NCTE urge the discontinuance of testing practices that encourage the teaching of grammar rather than English language arts instruction.

National Council of Teachers of English. "Resolution on Grammar Exercises to Teach Speaking and Writing." Urbana, IL: National Council of Teachers of English, 1985.

Appendix B

Encourage Independent Reading at Home

Children get Wonderfully Exciting Books (WEB) from home, school, the library, the bookstore, and from friends and relatives to read independently. The main purpose of this nightly reading is to develop the lifetime habit of reading for pleasure and information. Nightly reading also reinforces the reading strategies and habits being developed at school and at home. Students also learn to self-select books that are appropriate to their reading level and interests, take responsibility for reading these books and carrying them between home and school each day, and take proper care of their books.

Students are expected to read each night for about fifteen to thirty minutes, depending on their age level and other commitments. The books students choose to read independently should, for the most part, be books they can read easily, with very little assistance. Occasionally, students may choose to tackle a "hard" book, but this should be the exception. Students develop reading skills, vocabulary, and confidence by reading materials that can be handled easily, or with a little help; difficult material often causes students to feel frustrated. Students are also encouraged to read other materials, such as magazines, newspapers, recipes, directions, instructions.

While the requirement is that students read nightly, teachers and parents must take care to encourage the reading without making it a dreaded assignment. Above all, we want our students to choose to read because they want to, not because someone is mandating it. Let's help students focus on the pleasure that reading can bring.

by Regie Routman

Appendix C

Discourage Heavy Use of Television and Electronic Media

SHAKER HEIGHTS CITY SCHOOL DISTRICT
15600 Parkland Drive
Shaker Heights, Ohio 44120

Dear Families:

As you begin to plan your child's summer schedule, please carefully consider the impact of electronic media. We strongly suggest you limit TV/VCR viewing and video games for the following reasons:

1. Research demonstrates that the highest achieving students in classrooms watch the least amount of television.

2. Over involvement with electronic media encourages passivity and inhibits social and language growth.

3. Without extended quiet time, children lose the ability to imagine and make up stories.

4. Unlike books, which require readers to ponder, imagine, analyze and question, TV programs invite no active response. Additionally, questions and answers are often superficial and require little reflection. A habit of inquiry is fostered when you encourage your child to read nonfiction as well as fiction books.

5. Because the rules of video games are predetermined, they restrict a child's ability to make up their own rules and to develop the important social skills of compromise and negotiation.

Take your child to the public library. Our library summer programs are recognized as some of the finest in the country. Don't forget to take advantage of this wonderful resource. Also, encourage active play outdoors, talk, think, wonder, read and tell stories to each other, and TURN OFF THE TV . . .

Sincerely,

Composed by the language arts support group at Fernway School, Shaker Heights, Ohio

Appendix D

Blank Weekly Review

WEEKLY REVIEW

Name ———————————   Date ———————————

Here are some things I've done this week:

Here are three things I've learned:

1.

2.

3.

I've worked on these skills: ————————————————

————————————————————————————————

————————————————————————————————

I have been reading: ————————————————————

————————————————————————————————

————————————————————————————————

I am most proud of my work on _____

_____

because _____

_____

Next week I plan to work on _____

_____

Student comments:

Teacher comments:

Family comments:

I have read this evaluation with my child and added my comments.
(date) _____

by Loretta Martin

Appendix E

Weekly Review

WEEKLY REVIEW

Name *Clare* Date *april 21/1995*

Here are some things I've done this week:

I made a poster about me.

I did my book review

I meet Floyd Cooper

Here are three things I've learned:

1. *I learned how to write a book review*
2. *I learned about the sun.*
3. *I learned how to do a story map.*

I've worked on these skills: *R controlled vowels*

I have been reading *The Aventures of Spider*

I am most proud of my work on *my book reviews*

because *I used good language*

Next week I plan to work on *my poems*

Teacher comments:

Clare, your book review is
outstanding! I can't wait to
see them displayed at Booksellers.

Family comments:

Clare,
    I always enjoy your poems!
I look forward to seeing or hearing
some soon.
    Book reviewers of the world, look
out! Clare Malone writes a very
good review.
    Keep up all of your great learning,
you are doing a wonderful job in
2nd grade.

I have read this evaluation with my child and added my
comments.
(date)   Mrs. Malone

Appendix F

FACTS
On the Teaching of Phonics

Through critical attention to relevant research and careful observa-
tion of children in the reading-writing process, we teachers can intel-
ligently decide how to teach phonics. . . . I prefer to teach phonics
strategically, in the meaningful context of the predictable stories chil-
dren read and write every day. In the context of written language,
phonics instruction facilitates meaning making and independence.

(Regie Routman, 1991)

Background

Educators generally agree that children learning to read and write English
need to understand that there is a relationship between letter patterns and
sound patterns in English (the alphabetic principle), to internalize major
relationships between letter and sound patterns, and eventually to develop an
awareness of the "separate" sounds in words (phonemic awareness): In other
words, educators agree that emergent readers and writers need to develop a
functional command of what is commonly called *phonics*. However, this does
not necessarily mean that children should be taught phonics intensively and
systematically, through special phonics programs or even through phonics
lessons in basal reading books and workbooks. Indeed, various lines of
research argue for helping children develop phonics knowledge in the context of reading and enjoying literature and in the context of writing, rather
than through skills lessons. Many of these reasons are listed below, followed
by a list of ways that teachers and parents can help children learn phonics
while reading and writing interesting texts.

Comparative and Naturalistic Research

• Despite extravagant claims found in the popular media, research does not
strongly support the teaching of phonics intensively and systematically. At

194

best, systematic phonics (in comparison with traditional basal reader/whole word approaches) may produce better scores on reading comprehension tests, but only through grade 3 (Chall, 1967/1983).

• From 1985 onward, the body of experimental research has typically compared traditional skills instruction with whole language instruction in reading and writing, in primary grade classrooms. Though many of the differences are not large enough to be statistically significant, the children in whole language classrooms scored the same or higher on virtually every measure in every study, including standardized tests and subtests that assess phonics skills (Weaver, 1994b; Tunnell & Jacobs, 1989; present other studies comparing literature-based with skills-based reading instruction).

• Research on how children learn to read and write in the home indicates that children become literate in much the same way as they learn their first oral language, though of course the processes are not exactly the same. Just as we do not teach babies and toddlers the rules for putting words together to make grammatical sentences, so we do not need to teach children phonics rules if we give them plenty of guided opportunities to learn letter/sound patterns (Holdaway, 1979; Cambourne, 1988; Stephens, 1991; Weaver, 1994b). In short, phonics is best learned and used *in the course of learning* to read and write, *not as a prerequisite* (Goodman, 1993).

• Many—indeed, most—young readers are not good at learning analytically, abstractly, or auditorily (e.g., Carbo, 1987). Therefore, for most young children it is harder to learn phonics through part-to-whole teaching (phonics first) than through whole-to-part teaching (reading and writing first, and learning phonics from and along with the words in familiar texts).

Research on the Reading Process and on the Effects of Reading Instruction

• Of course fluent readers can identify many words on sight, yet identifying words by letter/sound patterns alone does not seem to be the way readers process words in the normal reading of texts. Rather, proficient readers use prior knowledge and context along with letter/sound knowledge as they identify words and construct meaning (e.g., Goodman, 1973).

• Many poorer readers are ones for whom phonics was overtaught, with little or no emphasis on trying to make meaning while reading (e.g., Chomsky, 1976; Carbo, 1987; Meek, 1983).

• Too much emphasis on phonics encourages children to use "sound it out" as their first and possibly only independent strategy for dealing with problem words (Applebee, Langer, & Mullis, 1988).

• Programs for teaching phonics often emphasize rules, rather than patterns; teach not only common and consistent relationships but also uncommon relationships between vowel letters and sounds, rather than the more stable patterns in "rimes"; and emphasize the patterns of letter/sound relationships for vowels, although consonants provide much more useful information for identifying words in meaningful contexts. In contrast, effective phonics instruction focuses children's attention on noticing letter/sound patterns in the major components of syllables: that is, on noticing the letter/sound patterns in initial consonants and consonant clusters and in the rime, which consists of the vowel of a syllable plus any following consonants, such as *-ake, -ent, -ing, -ure* (Adams, 1990).

• Without using phonics programs, parents and teachers can do various things to help children gain phonics knowledge in the context of reading and writing. The following are some of these: (1) reread favorite poems, songs, and stories and discuss alliteration and rhyme within them; (2) read alphabet books to and with children, and make alphabet books together; (3) make lists, word banks, or books of such words that share interesting spelling/sound patterns; (4) discuss similar sounds and letter/sound patterns in children's names; (5) emphasize selected letter/sound relationships while printing something children are dictating; (6) help children write the sounds they hear in words, once they have begun to hear some separate sounds; (7) when reading together, help children use prior knowledge and context plus initial consonants to predict what a word will be, then look at the rest of the word to confirm or correct (Mills et al., 1992; Powell & Hornsby, 1993; Freppon & Dahl, 1991; Griffith & Olson, 1992; Weaver, 1994a, 1994b).

References and Resources

Adams, M. J. 1990. *Beginning to Read: Thinking and Learning About Print.* Cambridge, MA: Harvard University Press.

Applebee, A. N., J. A. Langer, & I. V. S. Mullis. 1988. *Learning to Be Literate in America: Reading, Writing and Reasoning. The Nation's Report Card.* Princeton, NJ: National Assessment of Educational Progress, Educational Testing Service.

Cambourne, B. 1988. *The Whole Story: Natural Learning and the Acquisition of Literacy in the Classroom.* New York: Scholastic.

Carbo, M. 1987. "Reading Style Research: 'What Works' Isn't Always Phonics." *Phi Delta Kappan* 68: 431–35.

Chall, J. 1967/1983. *Learning to Read: The Great Debate.* New York: McGraw-Hill.

Chomsky, C. 1976. "After Decoding: What?" *Language Arts* 53: 288–96, 314.

Freppon, P. A., & K. L. Dahl. 1991. "Learning About Phonics in a Whole Language Classroom." *Language Arts* 68(3):190–97.

Goodman, K. S. 1973. *Theoretically Based Studies of Patterns of Miscues in Oral Reading Performance.* Detroit, MI: Wayne State University. ERIC: ED 079 708.

Goodman, K. S. 1993. *Phonics Phacts.* Portsmouth, NH: Heinemann

Griffith, P. L. & M. W. Olson. 1992. "Phonemic Awareness Helps Beginning Readers Break the Code." *The Reading Teacher* 45: 516–25.

Holdaway, D. 1979. *The Foundations of Literacy.* Portsmouth, NH: Heinemann.

Meek, M. 1983. *Achieving Literacy.* London: Routledge & Kegan Paul.

Mills, H., T. O'Keefe, & D. Stephens. 1992. *Looking Closely: Exploring the Role of Phonics in One Whole Language Classroom.* Urbana, IL: National Council of Teachers of English.

Powell, D., & D. Hornsby. 1993. *Learning Phonics and Spelling in a Whole Language Classroom.* New York: Scholastic.

Routman, R. 1991. *Invitations: Changing as Teachers and Learners, K–12.* Portsmouth, NH: Heinemann.

Stephens, D. 1991. *Research on Whole Language: Support for a New Curriculum.* Katonah, NY: Richard C. Owen.

Tunnell, M. O., & J. S. Jacobs. 1989. "Using 'Real' Books: Research Findings on Literature Based Reading Instruction." *The Reading Teacher* 42: 470–77.

Weaver, C. 1994a. "Phonics in Whole Language Classrooms." ERIC Digest: ED 372 375.

———. 1994b. *Reading Process and Practice: From Socio-Psycholinguistics to Whole Language* (2nd ed.). Portsmouth, NH: Heinemann.

Appendix G

Reading Strategies for Unknown Words Beyond "Sound It Out"

- Skip the difficult word.
  Read on to end of sentence or paragraph.
  Go back to the beginning of sentence and try again.

- Read on.
  Reread inserting the beginning sound of the unknown word.

- Substitute a word that makes sense.

- Look for a known chunk or small word.
  Use finger to cover part of word.

- Read the word using only beginning and ending sounds.
  Read the word without the vowels.

- Look at the picture cues.

- Link to prior knowledge.

- Predict and anticipate what could come next.

- Cross check.
  "Does it sound right?"
  "Does it make sense?"
  "Does it look right?"

- Self-correct and self-monitor.

- Write words you can't figure out and need to know on Post-its.

- Read passage several times for fluency and meaning.

Use errors as an opportunity to problem solve.

by Regie Routman

Appendix H

FACTS
On Teaching Skills in Context

Basic skills belong in context.

(Lucy McCormick Calkins, 1980)

Background

Teachers, researchers, parents, and the public agree that children need to develop and use what are sometimes called "basic skills," such as the ability to use phonics knowledge in reading, the ability to spell conventionally, and the ability to use grammatical constructions effectively and according to the norms of the communities with which they want to communicate. What many people do not realize, however, is that the ability to use these skills is best fostered by teaching them in the context of their use. Research demonstrates that skills taught, practiced, and tested in isolation are not used as consistently or effectively as skills taught when children are actually reading and writing.

Phonics

- Recent research demonstrates that in classrooms where phonics is taught in the context of rereading favorite stories, songs, and poems, children develop and use phonics knowledge better than in classrooms where skills are taught in isolation. Similarly, phonics knowledge is developed by encouraging and helping emergent writers to spell by writing appropriate letters for the sounds they hear in words (for a summary, see Weaver, 1994).
- Effective phonics instruction focuses children's attention on noticing the letter/sound patterns in initial consonants and consonant clusters and in rimes (the vowel of a syllable, plus any consonants that might follow, such as -ake, -ent, -ing, -ure). Focusing on rimes rather than on vowels alone is particularly important in helping children learn to decode words (for a summary, see Adams, 1990).

199

• Effective reading instruction helps children learn to use phonics knowledge along with their prior knowledge and context, rather than in isolation. For example, children can be encouraged to predict words by using prior knowledge and context along with initial consonants, then look at the rest of the word to confirm or correct their prediction.

• Both teachers and parents can do various things to help children gain phonics knowledge in the context of reading and writing. For example: (1) reread favorite poems, songs, and stories and discuss alliteration and rhyme within them; (2) read alphabet books to and with children, and make alphabet books together; (3) make lists, word banks, or books of such words that share interesting spelling/sound patterns; (4) discuss similar sounds and letter/sound patterns in children's names; (5) emphasize selected letter/sound relationships while printing something that children are dictating; (6) help children write the sounds they hear in words, once the children have begun to hear some separate sounds; (7) when reading together, help children predict and confirm as explained above (Mills et al., 1992; Powell & Hornsby, 1993; Griffith & Olson, 1992; Weaver, 1994a & 1994b).

Spelling

• Children who are encouraged to spell words as best they can when they write typically score as well or better on standardized tests of spelling by the end of first grade than children allowed to use only correct spellings in first drafts. Meanwhile, the children encouraged to spell by writing the sounds they hear in words seem to develop word recognition and phonics skills sooner (Clarke, 1988).

• Emergent writers benefit from help in writing the sounds they hear in words. Gradually, with extensive writing experience, their early invented spellings will give way to more sophisticated invented spellings and to conventional spellings.

• Extensive exposure to print and reading helps children internalize not only the spellings of particular words, but spelling patterns. Just as children learn the patterns of the spoken language from hearing it, children learn patterns of the written language from reading and rereading favorite texts. Texts with regular patterns like "Nan can fan Dan" are not necessary, however, nor are they even as readable as texts written in natural language patterns.

• In the long run, teaching children strategies for correcting their spelling is far more important than giving them the correct spelling of any particular word. Such strategies include: (1) writing the word two or three different ways and deciding which one "looks right"; (2) locating the spelling in a familiar text or in print displayed in the classroom; (3) asking someone, consulting a dictionary, or using a computer software program or a hand-held electronic speller (Wilde, 1992).

- Discussing spelling patterns and drawing spelling generalizations as a class will also help children develop an ever-growing repertoire of words they can spell correctly in first drafts.

Grammar

- Decades of research demonstrate that teaching grammar as a school subject does not improve most students' writing, nor even the "correctness" of their writing (Hillocks & Smith, 1991). What works better is teaching selected aspects of grammar (including sentence variety and style, punctuation, and usage) in the context of students' writing—that is, when they are revising and editing their writing (Weaver, 1996).
- For improving editing skills, it is most effective and efficient to teach only the grammatical concepts that are critically needed for editing writing, and to teach these concepts and their terms mostly through minilessons and writing conferences, particularly while helping students edit their writing.
- Research shows that systematic practice in combining and expanding sentences may increase students' repertoire of syntactic structure and may also improve the quality of their sentences, when stylistic effects are discussed as well (Hillocks & Smith, 1991; Strong, 1986). Thus sentence-combining and expansion may be taught as a means of improving sentence variety and style. However, isolated activities are not necessarily any more effective than minilessons and writing conferences in which teachers help students rearrange, combine, and expand their sentences for greater effectiveness.

References and Resources

Adams, M. J. 1990. *Beginning to Read: Thinking and Learning About Print.* Cambridge, MA: Harvard University Press.

Calkins, L. M. 1980. "When Children Want to Punctuate: Basic Skills Belong in Context." *Language Arts* 57: 567–73.

Clarke, L. K. 1988. "Invented Versus Traditional Spelling in First Graders' Writings: Effects on Learning to Spell and Read." *Research in the Teaching of English* 22: 281–309.

Freppon, P. A., & K. L. Dahl. 1991. "Learning About Phonics in a Whole Language Classroom." *Language Arts* 68(3):190–97.

Griffith, P. L. & M. W. Olson. 1992. "Phonemic Awareness Helps Beginning Readers Break the Code." *The Reading Teacher* 45: 516–25.

Hillocks, G., Jr., & M. W. Smith. 1991. "Grammar and Usage." In J. Flood, J. M. Jensen, D. Lapp, & J. R. Squire, eds., *Handbook of Research on Teaching the English Language Arts.* New York: Macmillan.

Mills, H., T. O'Keefe, & D. Stephens. 1992. *Looking Closely: Exploring the Role of Phonics in One Whole Language Classroom.* Urbana, IL: National Council of Teachers of English.

Powell, D., & D. Hornsby. 1993. *Learning Phonics and Spelling in a Whole Language Classroom.* New York: Scholastic.

Strong, W. 1986. *Creative Approaches to Sentence Combining.* Urbana, IL: ERIC and the National Council of Teachers of English.

Tunnell, M. O., & J. S. Jacobs. 1989. "Using 'Real' Books: Research Findings on Literature Based Reading Instruction." *The Reading Teacher* 42: 470–77.

Weaver, C. 1994a. *Phonics in Whole Language Classrooms.* ERIC Digest: ED 372 375.

———. 1994b. *Reading Process and Practice: From Socio-Psycholinguistics to Whole Language* (2nd ed.). Portsmouth, NH: Heinemann.

———. 1996. *Teaching Grammar in Context.* Portsmouth, NH: Boynton/Cook.

Wilde, S. 1992. *You Kan Red This! Spelling and Punctuation for Whole Language Classrooms, K–6.* Portsmouth, NH: Heinemann.

Appendix I

Explanation of Spelling Program

Dear Families,

Your child will not be using a spelling book this year, but I will be teaching spelling! My goal is to move your child from invented spelling to conventional spelling through daily reading, writing, and spelling activities using the rules and patterns found in traditional spelling programs.

During daily writing workshop the emphasis will be on content first, with an understanding of the importance of correct work. Many pieces will show evidence of invented spelling and drafts which have not been revised or edited. When students are required to correct and recopy every written paper, they become discouraged and write as few words as possible. However, in our classroom the writing will be balanced. You will see examples of both kinds of writing: drafts and work that has been revised, edited, and corrected.

Each week your child will bring home 5–10 new words that he/she has chosen (sometimes with my help) to learn. The weekly personal list is a combination of words chosen from journal entries, writer's notebook, class focus, themes, interests and *high frequency words* used in reading and writing activities. This week's words were pulled from the first grade core list and science vocabulary. A spelling check will be given each Friday. If the words are not mastered, they will be added to your child's list next week.

Letter writing is one of the choices during writing workshop that is enjoyed by the students, if the audience is real and familiar. To assure responses and interest, please have your child bring in a name and address of a friend or relative that he/she would like to correspond with during the school year. This person will become your child's pen pal.

Sincerely,

Loretta Martin

Loretta Martin

by Loretta Martin

Notes

page

Introduction
xvii "No Frills Drills," *20/20*, aired on October 13, 1995, by the American Broadcasting Corporation.
xvii *Nightline*, ABC News, aired on October 18, 1995, by the American Broadcasting Corporation.

Chapter 1
3 United States Department of Education, National Commission on Excellence in Education, *A Nation at Risk: The Imperative for Educational Reform* (Washington, DC: U.S. Government Printing Office, 1983).
4 "largely true because . . .": David C. Berliner and Bruce J. Biddle, *The Manufactured Crisis: Myths, Fraud, and the Attack on America's Public Schools* (Reading, MA: Addison-Wesley, 1995), p. 144
4 The statement that a majority of parents believe the public schools are doing a good job is supported by Stanley M. Elam and Lowell C. Rose, "The 27th Annual Phi Delta Kappa/Gallup Poll of the Public Attitudes Toward the Public Schools," *Phi Delta Kappan* (September 1995), p. 410.
4 The comments about *The Sandia Report* are based on Berliner and Biddle, p. 26 and pp. 165–67.
4 The comment by Ann Landers is taken from her syndicated column as published in *The Plain Dealer* (Cleveland, Ohio), November 30, 1995.
5 "One thing is sure . . .": Michael W. Kibby, *Student Literacy: Myths and Realities* (Bloomington, IN: Phi Delta Kappa Educational Foundation, 1995), p. 16.

5   The second-out-of-thirty-two statistic comes from W. B. Elley, *How in the World Do Students Read? IEA Study of Reading Literacy* (Hamburg: The International Association for the Evaluation of Educational Achievement, 1992).

5   The data from the three "then and now" studies have been summarized in National Council of Teachers of English and International Reading Association, *Standards for the English Language Arts*, October 20, 1995 Draft (Urbana, IL: National Council of Teachers of English; Newark, DE: International Reading Association).

5   "Thus, evidence suggests . . .": Ibid., p. 7.

5   List beginning "more reading instruction . . .": Kibby, *Student Literacy*, p. 7.

5   The statement that U.S. students do not do well when asked to apply knowledge is supported by Barbara B. Gaddy, T. William Hall, and Robert J. Marzano, *School Wars: Resolving Our Conflicts Over Religion and Values* (San Francisco: Jossey-Bass, 1996).

5   "asking students for simple responses . . .": Kibby, *Student Literacy*, p. 20.

5–6   The statements about the national assessment of reading are based on findings from the 1992 and 1994 (draft) NAEP Reading Reports. States not reporting were Alaska, Oregon, Nevada, South Dakota, Kansas, Oklahoma, Illinois, Ohio, and Vermont. Findings for 1994 were for Grade 4.

6   All the quotations in the paragraph beginning, There are signs . . . , are from Miles Myers, *Changing Our Minds: Negotiating English and Literacy* (Urbana, IL: National Council of Teachers of English, 1996). In order: pp. 144, 145, 159, 120.

7   Sandra Wilde, *You Kan Red This! Spelling and Punctuation for Whole Language Classrooms, K-6* (Portsmouth, NH: Heinemann, 1991).

7   Sandra Wilde's comments were presented in her talk, "Where Are We with Invented Spelling?" at the annual fall meeting of the National Council of Teachers of English, San Diego, California, November 1995.

7   Richard Gentry, *Spel Is a Four-Letter Word* (Portsmouth, NH: Heinemann, 1987).

7   Richard Gentry, *My Kid Can't Spell* (Portsmouth, NH: Heinemann, 1996).

8   "Students in grade 4 . . . ": *1992 Writing Trend Assessment* (Princeton, NJ: Educational Testing Service, July 1994).

8   The statements regarding the Texas spelling series are based on an article in *Texas Education News*, November 25, 1995, p. 1.

9   "Specifically, current research indicates . . .": Barbara B. Gaddy, T. William Hall, and Robert J. Marzano, *School Wars: Resolving Our Conflicts Over Religion and Values* (San Francisco: Jossey-Bass, 1996), summarizing a review of the research on whole language versus skills instruction from *Educational Psychologist* 27(4)(1994), entire issue.

10 The comment about *Sesame Street* is supported by Barbara Fowles Mates and Linda Strommen, "Why Ernie Can't Read: *Sesame Street* and Literacy," *The Reading Teacher* (December 1995/January 1996), pp. 300–306.

10 The Hooked on Phonics sales figures are as stated in *Reading Today* (December 1995/January 1996), p. 26.

10 "is based on the philosophy . . .": Susan Estrich, "A Novel School Plan: Back to Basics," *USA Today*, September 21, 1995.

10 "A major battle brews . . .": Anthony Flint, "It's Phonics vs. Whole Language," *The Boston Globe*, November 7, 1995.

11 "What whole language does . . .": *The Boston Sunday Globe*, October 29, 1995.

11 "Many of the more glossy . . .": Peter Applebome, "Fads at School: Buzzwords for Failure," News of the Week in Review, *The New York Times*, December 17, 1995, p. 3.

11 "More and more schools refuse . . .": *Washington Post*, July 2, 1995.

11 "Unfortunately, many school critics . . .": Gerald W. Bracey, "The Fifth Bracey Report on the Condition of Public Education," *Phi Delta Kappan* (October 1995), p. 151.

11 "What if somebody . . .": Hugh Downs, Introduction to "No Frills Drills," *20/20*, aired on October 13, 1995, by the American Broadcasting Corporation. Transcript # 1541. All other statements quoted from the segment were made by John Stossel, except for the one beginning "No, teachers do what they're told . . . ," which was made by Zig Englemann.

12 The *20/20* viewing audience is the fourth quarter 1995 average, as reported to me by Robert Wohler of ABC's marketing and research department in December 1995.

13 Shelly Lewis and Maeve Kenny made their statements in separate telephone conversations I had with them in December 1995.

Chapter 2

18 The statistic that one out of four Americans is born outside the U.S. is from Sam Roberts, *Who We Are: A Portrait of America Based on the Latest U.S. Census* (NY: Random House, 1993), p. 62.

20 "(1) a strong literature. . .": *Every Child a Reader: The Report of the California Reading Task Force* (Sacramento, CA: California Department of Education, 1995), p. 2.

21 California's books-per-pupil library-hours statistics are as presented in "Collection Data for Elementary Schools," *School Library Media Quarterly* (Fall, 1990), p. 21.

21 The other statistics in this listing come from Roberts, *Who We Are*, pp. 75 and 80; Jeff McQuillan, "Did Whole Language Fail in California?" *Communicate: A*

Newsletter for the California Association of Teachers of English (November 1995); and Dennis R. Parker, "Politics and Pedagogy: The Bookends of California's Literacy Crisis," *Clips: A Journal of the California Literature Project* (November 1995).

22   The statement that reading test scores can be directly correlated to per-pupil spending is based on McQuillan, "Did Whole Language Fail in California?"

22   Even California officials seem to realize . . . : the statement was made in *Education Week,* June 14, 1995.

23   However, a growing body of research favors . . . is supported by David C. Berliner and Bruce J. Biddle, *The Manufactured Crisis: Myths, Fraud, and the Attack on America's Public Schools,* p. 206 (Reading, MA: Addison-Wesley, 1995).

23   "In particular, when the money is used . . .": Gerald Bracey, "Debunking the Myth About Money for Schools," *Educational Leadership,* November 1995, pp. 65–69.

26   "At that time . . ." and the following paragraph: Alan Davis and Catherine Felknor, "The Demise of Performance-Based Graduation in Littleton," *Educational Leadership,* March 1994, pp. 64–65.

26   Most of the material on Littleton High School comes from conversations I had with teacher Sandy Redman and former Superintendent Cile Chavez.

26   However, in the November 1995 school board elections . . .: *Education Week,* November 15, 1995, p.12.

29   Daniel Yankelovich's ideas are taken from his book *Coming to Public Judgment: Making Democracy Work in a Complex World* (Syracuse, NY: Syracuse University Press, 1991).

29   The quotation from *The Popcorn Report* (New York: HarperBusiness, 1991) is from page 27.

30   "Seek first to understand" is one of Stephen R. Covey's *Seven Habits of Highly Effective People* (New York: Simon and Schuster, 1990).

30–31 The material on the Fairfax, Virginia, school district is taken from an interview I had with Ann Mc Callum on December 3, 1995.

Chapter 3

38   "The whole language movement . . .": Marilyn J. Adams and Maggie Bruck, "Resolving the 'Great Debate,'" *American Educator: The Professional Journal of the American Federation of Teachers* (Summer 1995), p.18.

41   One of the best one-stop sources of whole language research is C. Weaver, L. Gillmeister-Krause, and G. Vento-Zogby, *Creating Support for Effective Literacy Education* (Portsmouth, NH: Heinemann, 1996).

41   Yetta Goodman's remarks were made in her closing presentation on the day of whole language held during the annual fall meeting of the National Council of Teachers of English in San Diego, November 1995.

42 Norma Mickelson, an educator in Vancouver, British Columbia, included her definition in a presentation at the annual meeting of the International Reading Association in New Orleans, April 1989.

43 For discussions and suggestions for language arts instructions that support Dorothy Strickland's comments, see D. Strickland, "Educating African American Learners at Risk: Finding a Better Way," *Language Arts* (September 1994), pp. 328–36, and the video *The Reading/Writing Connection, Dawn Harris Martine, 2nd Grade, Mahalia Jackson Elementary, Harlem, NY.* The video is available from the Center for the Study of Reading at the University of Illinois, Urbana-Champaign.

43 Research to support the need to go further than the basics can be found in Rexford Brown, *Schools of Thought: How the Politics of Literacy Shape Thinking in the Classroom* (San Francisco: Jossey-Bass, 1991).

46 The Ralph Peterson statement is on page 2 of his *Life in a Crowded Place: Making a Learning Community* (Portsmouth, NH: Heinemann, 1992). The italics are his.

47 SCANS five competencies are presented in *Learning a Living: A SCANS Report for America 2000* (Washington, DC: U.S. Government Printing Office, 1992).

47 The quotation from *Negotiating the Curriculum*, by Garth Boomer, Nancy Lester, Cynthia Onore, and Jon Cook (London and Bristol, PA: The Falmer Press, 1992), is from page 21.

49 For a discussion and demonstration of skills and strategies teaching, see Chapter 7, "Teaching for Strategies," in my book *Invitations* (Portsmouth, NH: Heinemann, 1991 and 1994), pp. 134–59.

52 For information and data on Reading Recovery, write to The National Diffusion Network for Reading Recovery, The Ohio State University, 200 Ramseyer Hall, 29 West Woodruff Avenue, Columbus, Ohio 43210-1177.

Chapter 4

54 Liz Crider teaches in the Shaker Heights, Ohio, City School District.

55 "The change process in contemporary American schooling . . .": Daniel J. Walsh, "The Defeat of Literacy: Tragedy in Albemarle County," *The New Advocate* 6(4)(1993): 251–63.

56 "Getting Reform Right: What Works and What Doesn't" is by Michael G. Fullan and Matthew B. Miles and was published in *Phi Delta Kappan* (June 1992), pp. 745–48.

68 "Students do less well . . .": Wayne P. Thomas and Virginia P. Collier, "Research Summary of Study in Progress: Results as of September 1995. Language Minority Student Achievement and Program Effectiveness" (Washington, D.C.: National Clearinghouse for Bilingual Education, operated by The George Washington University, December 1995).

70 The *Education Week* article, "Is Innovation Always Good? Parents Have to Be Prepared to Accept the New Ideas," was written by Anne Wescott Dodd and published in the May 3, 1995 issue.

71 The term *preparation ethic* and the ideas expressed in the paragraph in which it is used come from Ronald D. Anderson's "Curriculum Reform: Dilemmas and Promise," *Phi Delta Kappan* (September 1995), p. 35.

Chapter 5

78 Regie Routman, *Transitions: From Literature to Literacy* (Portsmouth, NH: Heinemann, 1988).

79 "Certain environmental factors . . .": *Transitions*, pp. 17–18.

80 Don Holdaway, *The Foundations of Literacy* (New York: Scholastic-TAB, 1979), available through Scholastic or Heinemann.

80 Peg Rimedio is a kindergarten teacher in the Shaker Heights, Ohio, City School District.

80 Brian Cambourne, *The Whole Story: Natural Learning and the Acquisition of Literacy in the Classroom* (Toronto: Ashton Scholastic Ltd., 1988).

80 Brian Cambourne, "Toward an Educationally Relevant Theory of Literacy Learning: Twenty Years of Inquiry," *The Reading Teacher* (November 1995), pp. 182–90.

81 Regie Routman, *Invitations: Changing as Teachers and Learners K–12, Updated, Expanded, and Revised* (Portsmouth, NH: Heinemann, 1994), pp. 8–21.

81 "Elementary School Practices: Current Research on Language Learning" (Urbana, IL: NCTE, 1993). Single copies are available upon request. Bulk rate is $7.00 per 100.

82 "There are, in the end . . .": Deborah Meier, *The Power of Their Ideas: Lessons for America from a Small School in Harlem* (Boston: Beacon Press, 1995), p. 181.

82 "1. Literacy instruction . . .": Michael Kibby, *Student Literacy: Myths and Realities* (Bloomington, IN: Phi Delta Kappa Educational Foundation, 1995), p.18.

83 For the evidence on how reading aloud impacts vocabulary, see John W.A. Smith and Warwick B. Elley, *Learning to Read in New Zealand* (Katonah, NY: Richard C. Owen, 1995), p. 39.

83 The one million–one thousand statistic is taken from Stephen Krashen's *The Power of Reading: Insights from the Research* (Englewood, CO: Libraries Unlimited, 1993), p. 9.

83 The statement about time spent reading books in second to fifth grade is supported by Richard. C. Anderson, Paul T. Wilson, and Linda G. Fielding's "Growth in Reading and How Children Spend Their Time Outside of School," *Reading Research Quarterly* (Summer 1988), p. 297.

83 "Children read more . . .": Krashen 1993, p. 42.

84   Checking out books from the school library to keep in the classroom library is an idea suggested by Norris Ross, third-grade teacher in Shaker Heights, Ohio.

84   "If we want our sons . . .": Daniel Pennac, *Better Than Life*, translated by David Homel (Toronto: Coach House Press, 1994), p. 171.

84   The complete Reader's Bill of Rights can be found in Pennac 1994, pp. 175–207.

84   The statement that light reading leads to more substantial reading is supported by Krashen 1993, pp. 46–68.

84   "Romances make up half . . .": Walter Goodman, "A Nation of Readers, and That's Not Good," Television Review, *The New York Times*, October 26, 1995, The Living Arts, p. B10.

85   "Research points to . . .": James R. Squire, "Language Arts," in *Handbook on Improving Student Achievement*, edited by Gordon Cawelti (Arlington, VA: Educational Research Service, 1995), p. 71.

85   "The basis of guided reading . . .": For the source of this quotation and the procedures involved, see Smith and Elley 1995, pp. 35–38.

86   "If students are not engaged . . .": Donald Graves, *A Fresh Look at Writing* (Portsmouth, NH: Heinemann, 1994) p. 104.

87   "I have about four ideas . . .": Mem Fox, *Radical Reflections: Passionate Opinions on Teaching, Learning, and Living* (San Diego: Harcourt Brace, 1993), p. 18.

87   "We only have to write . . .": Nancie Atwell, "Taking Off the Top of My Head," presentation at the annual fall meeting of the National Council of Teachers of English, San Diego, November 1995.

88   "Far more conventions . . .": Regie Routman, "Donald Graves: Outstanding Educator in the Language Arts," *Language Arts* (November 1995), p. 523.

88   For the procedures and benefits of shared writing, see *Invitations*, pp. 59–66.

88   The statement that reading and math scores show little change is supported by David C. Berliner and Bruce J. Biddle, *The Manufactured Crisis: Myths, Fraud, and the Attack on America's Public Schools* (Reading, MA: Addison-Wesley, 1995), p. 26.

90   . . . literacy "that goes beyond basic skills . . .": Rexford Brown, Preface to *Schools of Thought: How the Politics of Literacy Shape Thinking in the Classroom* (San Francisco: Jossey-Bass, 1991), p. xiii.

Chapter 6

92   "Data on the long-term effects . . .": Richard C. Anderson and others, *Becoming a Nation of Readers* (Washington, DC: The National Institute of Education, 1985), p. 37.

93   The material on onsets and rimes is based on Marilyn J. Adams, *Beginning to Read: Thinking and Learning About Print* (Cambridge: MIT Press, 1990).

95   For specifics on how to use shared reading and shared writing to teach and reinforce phonics generalizations, see *Invitations*, pp. 33–38 (shared reading) and 59–68 (shared writing).

96   The board of directors of the Ohio Council of the International Reading Association stated this position on phonics in a Resolution dated September 29, 1995.

100   Regie Routman and Andrea Butler, "Phonics Fuss: Facts, Fiction, Phonemes, and Fun," *School Talk: Ideas for the Classroom from the NCTE Elementary Section* (Urbana, IL: National Council of Teachers of English, November 1995).

100   Don Holdaway, Appendix C: "A Simplified Progression of Word Recognition Skills," *Independence in Reading* (Richmond Hill, Ontario: Scholastic-TAB, and Portsmouth, NH: Heinemann, 1980), pp. 157–62 .

101   The position paper and resolution were published in May 1994 and May 1992, respectively, by the International Reading Association, Newark, DE.

101   The statement about actual reading being the most important factor contributing to reading success is supported by Stephen Krashen's *The Power of Reading: Insights from the Research* (Englewood, CO: Libraries Unlimited, 1993).

101   *Parents, Kids and Books: The Joys of Reading Together*, 1993. Produced by KERA-TV, Dallas, TX, for grades K–3. Available from NCTE, Urbana, IL.

102   "analysis of the words . . ." is from my book *Transitions: From Literature to Literacy* (Portsmouth, NH: Heinemann, 1988), pp. 48–50.

Chapter 7

105   The Frank Smith quotation is from his *Writing and the Writer*, Second Edition (Hillsdale, NJ: Lawrence Erlbaum, 1994), p. 37.

106   All of Lisa Delpit's comments are taken from her book *Other People's Children: Cultural Conflict in the Classroom* (New York: The New Press, 1995), pp. 18–19, 46.

107   The Judith Newman quotation is from her *Interwoven Conversations: Learning and Teaching Through Critical Reflection* (Portsmouth, NH: Heinemann, 1991), p. 14.

109   Some of these ideas and statements about invented spelling originally appeared in my article "The Uses and Abuses of Invented Spelling," *Instructor* (May/June 1993), pp. 36–39.

109   Charles J. Sykes, *Dumbing Down Our Kids: Why America's Children Feel Good About Themselves but Can't Read, Write, or Add* (New York: St. Martin's, 1995), p. 93.

111   "focused, small-group work . . .": Darrell Morris and others, "Teaching Low-Achieving Spellers at Their 'Instructional Level,'" *The Elementary School Journal* (November 1995), p. 176; complete discussion found on pp. 163–77.

111 "Just as we learn . . .": Frank Smith, *Writing and the Writer*, Second Edition (Hillsdale, NJ: Lawrence Erlbaum, 1994), pp. 150–51.

112 Sandra Wilde made this suggestion during a presentation at the annual fall meeting of the National Council of Teachers of English, San Diego, November 1995.

113 *First Steps* is a professional development program created by the Education Department of Western Australia (1994) and available from Heinemann, Portsmouth, NH.

113 However we do it . . .: One of the ways I have become more knowledgeable about teaching spelling is through professional reading. See *The Blue Pages: Resources for Teachers* (Portsmouth, NH: Heinemann, 1994), pp. 83b–86b, for many excellent spelling resources, among them a sampling of the research on spelling.

119 For the research on teaching grammar, see G. Hillocks, Jr., "Synthesis of Research on Teaching Writing," *Educational Leadership* (May 1987), pp. 71–82, and C. Weaver, "Facts: On the Teaching of Grammar," in C. Weaver, L. Gillmeister-Krause, and G. Vento-Zogby, *Creating Support for Effective Literacy Education* (Portsmouth, NH: Heinemann, 1996).

119 *The NAEP 1992 National Writing Trend Assessment for Grades 4, 8, and 11* (Princeton, NJ: Educational Testing Service, July 1994).

120 "noun-verb agreement . . .": Frank Smith, *Writing and the Writer*, Second Edition (Hillsdale, NJ: Lawrence Erlbaum, 1994), p. 203.

120 "the study of traditional school grammar . . .": G. Hillocks, Jr., 1987, p. 74.

121 "h-mail—handwritten and heartwritten": the phrase is children's author Louise Borden's.

Chapter 8

124 The definition is from the *American Heritage Dictionary of the English Language*, Third Edition (Boston: Houghton Mifflin, 1992).

125 "nearly two-thirds . . .": *Interviewing Children About Their Literacy Experiences: Data from NAEP's Integrated Reading Performance Record (IRPR) at Grade 4* (Washington, DC: U.S. Department of Education, Office of Educational Research and Improvement, 1995), p. 56.

126 "much of students' reading . . .": Ibid., p. 43.

126 My comment that illustrations and format are commonly changed is based on D. Reutzel, Ray Larsen, and Nycole S. Larsen, "Look What They've Done to Real Children's Books in the New Basal Readers!" *Language Arts* (November 1995): 495–507.

127 The comments regarding media centers are based on Keith Curry Lance, Lynda Welborn, and Christine Hamilton-Pennell, *The Impact of School Library Media*

Centers on Academic Achievement (Castle Rock, CO: Hi Willow, 1993). The publication is available from Libraries Unlimited, Englewood, Colorado.

127   The comment that access to public libraries affects the amount of reading is supported by Stephen Krashen, *The Power of Reading: Insights from the Research* (Englewood, CO: Libraries Unlimited, 1993), p. 35.

127   The statistic that less than half of all public school libraries were staffed by a professional librarian or media specialist was proffered in *Curriculum Administrator* (January 1996), p. 62.

127   "To merely keep their jobs . . ." and the rest of the statements in this paragraph: Renée Olson, *School Library Journal* (December 1995), p. 27.

128   The statistics regarding children's materials and attendance at children's programs were told to me by Mary Jo Lynch, Director of Research, Office for Research and Statistics at the American Library Association, in a conversation we had in November 1995.

128   Bookstore retail sales are taken from *The Bowker Annual: Library and Book Trade Almanac*, Fourth Edition (New Providence, NJ: R.R. Bowker, 1995).

128   The statement about the growth of educational book clubs and book fairs is based on the *Book Publishing Report* (Wilton, CT: SIMBA Information Inc., November 6, 1995).

128   The statistic that the majority of book purchases were made by households with an annual income of fifty thousand dollars or less is taken from *Publishers Weekly*, October 30, 1995, p. 31.

130   "teachers who are literate . . .": Louisa Cook Moats, "The Missing Foundation in Teacher Education," *American Educator: The Professional Journal of the American Federation of Teachers* (Summer 1995), p. 47.

132   "Most of the candidates . . .": Gloria Ladson-Billings, *The Dreamkeepers: Successful Teachers of African American Children* (San Francisco: Jossey-Bass, 1994), p. 95.

139   The demographic statistics are from Sam Roberts, *Who We Are: A Portrait of America Based on the Latest U.S. Census* (New York: Random House, 1993), pp. 7, 62, 199, 222, 246.

139   The 50-percent-at-risk statistic is supported by Aaron M. Pallas, "Current Dimensions and Future Trends," *Educational Researcher* (June/July 1989), pp. 16–22.

139   "those students who are unlikely . . .": Wendy Hopfenberg and Henry Levin and Associates, *Accelerated Schools Guide* (San Francisco: Jossey-Bass, 1993).

139   John Pikulski, in "Preventing Reading Failure: A Review of Five Effective Programs" (*The Reading Teacher* [September 1994], pp. 30–39), describes five reading programs, including Success for All and Reading Recovery, that have been successful with "at-risk" first graders.

139   "By the middle of the next century . . .": The study referred to is Michael S. Knapp, Patrick M. Shields, and Brenda J. Turnbull, "Academic Challenge in

High-Poverty Classrooms," *Phi Delta Kappan* (June 1995), pp. 770–76. The quotation is from p. 773.

140   The statistic relative to single-adult households is from Daniel Tanner, "A Nation 'Truly' at Risk," *Phi Delta Kappan* (December 1993), pp. 294–95.

141   The term *reading-test reading* was coined by Jeanne Reardon in "Putting Reading Tests in Their Place," *The New Advocate* (Winter 1990), pp. 29–37.

142   "In summary . . .": Barbara B. Gaddy, T. William Hall, and Robert J. Marzano, *School Wars: Resolving Our Conflicts Over Religion and Values* (San Francisco: Jossey-Bass, 1996).

142   "We can estimate . . .": Ibid.

143   "Americans from all . . .": Jean Johnson and others, *Assignment Incomplete: The Unfinished Business of Education Reform, A Report from Public Agenda* (New York: Public Agenda, 1995), p. 11.

143   Lack of discipline as the biggest problem in public perception is supported by Stanley M. Elam and Lowell C. Rose, "The 1995 Phi Delta Kappa/Gallup Poll of the Public's Attitudes Toward the Public Schools," *Phi Delta Kappan* (September 1995), p. 52.

Chapter 9

148   Eve Bunting, *Smoky Night*, illustrated by David Diaz (San Diego, CA: Harcourt Brace, 1994).

149   "Should an award-winning . . .": Deirdre Donahue, "Award-winning Children's Book Merits a Caveat," Books: News and Views, *USA Today*, February 7, 1995.

159   Janet M. Grant, Barbara Heffler, and Kadri Mereweather, *Student-Led Conferences* (Markham, Ontario: Pembroke, 1995). Also available from The Wright Group in Bothell, WA.

164   "Beneath the surface . . .": Gloria Ladson-Billings, *The Dreamkeepers: Successful Teachers of African American Children* (San Francisco: Jossey-Bass, 1994), p. 116.

164   "They had determined . . .": Mike Rose, *Possible Lives: The Promise of Public Education in America* (Boston: Houghton Mifflin, 1995), p. 421.

164   "Kindergarten is the one place . . .": Deborah Meier, *The Power of Their Ideas: Lessons for America from a Small School in Harlem* (Boston: Beacon Press, 1995), pp. 48–49.

165   "What I now know . . .": Lorri Neilsen, *A Stone in My Shoe: Teaching Literacy in Times of Change* (Winnipeg, Manitoba: Peguis, 1994) , pp. 5–6.

Chapter 10

166   "What makes me a good leader . . .": Leon Botstein, quoted in Anthony DePalma, "The Most Happy College President," *The Sunday New York Times Magazine*, October 4, 1992, p. 54; italics mine.

167 "Research is . . .": Charles Kettering, quoted in Ruth S. Hubbard and Brenda M. Power, *The Art of Classroom Inquiry: A Handbook for Teacher-Researchers* (Portsmouth, NH: Heinemann, 1993), pp. xv-xvi.

167 "What separates . . .": Gordon Wells and others, *Changing Schools from Within: Creating Communities of Inquiry* (Toronto: OISE Press, and Portsmouth, NH: Heinemann (1994), p. 101.

169 Vito Perrone, *A Letter to Teachers: Reflections on Schooling and the Art of Teaching* (San Francisco: Jossey-Bass, 1991), pp. xiii–xiv.

170 "If you don't . . .": Mem Fox, *Radical Reflections: Passionate Opinions on Teaching, Learning, and Living* (San Diego, CA: Harcourt Brace, 1993), p. 163.

173 "If you have to ask . . .": Daniel Pennac, *Better Than Life*, translated by David Homel (Toronto: Coach House, 1994), pp. 145–46.

173 "Make time to think . . .": Ricardo Semler, *Maverick: The Success Story Behind the World's Most Unusual Workplace* (Warner Books, 1993), p. 297.

174 "The ability of many . . .": Mike Rose, *Possible Lives: The Promise of Public Education in America* (Boston: Houghton Mifflin, 1995), p. 421.

174 "1. talk with one another . . .": Roland S. Barth, *Improving Schools from Within: Teachers, Parents, and Principals Can Make the Difference* (San Francisco: Jossey-Bass, 1991), pp. 31 and 163.

176 Gloria Ladson-Billings, *The Dreamkeepers: Successful Teachers of African American Children* (San Francisco: Jossey-Bass, 1994).

176 Vivian Gussin Paley, *Kwanzaa and Me: A Teacher's Story* (Cambridge, MA and London: Harvard University Press, 1995)

177 See *Invitations*, pp. 465–472 for procedures for setting up and facilitating a support group.

182 Some excellent teacher resources for literature conversations include *Grand Conversations*, by Ralph Peterson and Maryann Eeds (Richmond Hill, Ontario: Scholastic-TAB, 1990); *Literature Circles*, by Harvey Daniels (York, ME: Stenhouse, 1994); *Literature Circles and Response*, edited by Bonnie Campbell Hill, Nancy J. Johnson, and Katherine L. Schlick Noe (Norwood, MA: Christopher-Gordon, 1995); and *Talking About Books*, edited by Kathy G. Short and Kathryn M. Pierce (Portsmouth, NH: Heinemann, 1990). Also see Chapter 6 in *Invitations*.

182 "If teachers are in the habit . . .": Flannery O'Connor, quoted in Daniel Pennac, *Better Than Life*, translated by David Homel (Toronto: Coach House, 1994), p. 169.

184 "Basically, if you want to become . . .": Natalie Goldberg, *Writing Down the Bones: Freeing the Writer Within* (Boston and London: Shambhala, 1986), pp. 53–54. Another terrific book to get you writing is Georgia Heard, *Writing Toward Home* (Portsmouth, NH: Heinemann, 1995).

185 "Change is not easy . . .": Susan Egging, a Title I special education teacher in Jefferson County School District, Buffalo, Wyoming.

Index

achievement, 127, 156
Adams, Marilyn, 38
administrators. *See also* educators
  partnership with, necessity of, 62–64
  political involvement of. *See* politics of education
  sharing research on, with administrators
    grammar, 120
    phonics, 101
  support of, needed for move to whole language,
    38–40
  supporting alternative assessment, 158–59
  teachers' professional development supported by,
    135–36
African American students
  changing demographics and, 138–39
  quality education and, 139–40
  spelling instruction and, 106
  whole language and, 43
Alief Independent School District, Texas
  community questions about language arts program,
    23–24
  lessons from, 25
anxiety in learning, 107–9
apprenticeships for new teachers, 133, 138
assessment
  alternative, 149–65
  committee process used to develop document for,
    57–58
  in Fairfax County, Virginia, 32
  multiple assessment, implementing, 28
  self-evaluation. *See* self-evaluation
  sharing informal, direct assessments, 103
  in whole language instruction, 48, 50
Atwell, Nancie, 87

back to basics
  controversy, 4, 24, 26, 43
  defined, 77
  realities of "the good old days," 55, 77–78
  reenvisioning, 88–89, 90, 157
  research on "the basics," 68
Bakkila, Leslie, 47, 169–70

basals
  concerns, 18, 124–26
  dealing with, 126, 130
  evaluation of, 125–26
  frequency of use, 124
basic skills. *See also* specific skills
  defined, 105, 106
  "Facts: On Teaching Skills in Context," 106, 199–202
  informing parents about teaching of, 40, 69–70
  teaching skills, methodology for, 105–9
  in whole language instruction, 43, 49
  reenvisioning, 88
Beers, Julie, 72
Bender, Jon, 56
Berlin, Barbara, 131
Better Than Life, 173
Bliss, Marcia, 119
Book Links: Connecting Books, Libraries, and
  Classrooms, 172
book reviews, 181
Boston Globe, The, phonics/whole language article, 10
Botstein, Leon, 166
Brown, Rexford, 89, 90
browsing of books, 181
Bruck, Maggie, 38
Bunting, Eve, 148
Burgess, Holly, 60, 68, 72, 106
Bush, Betty J., 130, 131
Butler, Andrea, 81
Butze, Hallie, 133, 138
"'Buyer Be Wary' Cautions International Reading Asso-
  ciation," 101

California
  educational problems in, 20–22
  English–language arts controversy, 9, 20
  as leader in education, 18–19
  lessons from, 22–23
  literature-based framework, history of, 18–20
  misrepresentation of language arts instruction in,
    11, 37

National Assessment of Educational Progress results
in, 6, 19
school libraries in, 127
task force report, 20
teacher training in, 19, 20, 21–23
Calkins, Lucy, 88, 199
Cambourne, Brian, 80
Cangiano, Nell, 71
centers, literacy, 45
change. See also professional development; staff development; teacher education
acting as a teacher-researcher, 167–69, 185
committee process for, sample. See committee
process
difficulties, 56, 57, 59–60, 63
evaluation practices, 149, 152–65
in-house resistance to, 55, 58–59
involving parents in process of, 23, 25, 28, 34, 40,
61–62, 64–72
lessons from process of, 61–62
parents included at beginning of process, 71
politics of, 29, 54–55
successful innovation, 31–33
teaching of reading, 142–43
Chavez, Cile, 25, 27–30, 34
choice in whole language instruction, 48, 50
choice with intention, 148–49
choosing books to read, 178–79, 180–81
classroom community, 46, 86
class size
in California, 21
reducing, in grade one, 32
collaboration
among teachers, 175–77
in whole language instruction, 46–47, 50
collegiality, 60, 156, 173–75
Colorado, Littleton. See Littleton, Colorado
committee process
being too democratic, 57
change created through, 55–56
ownership for teachers, creating, 56–57
perspectives from sample process, 59–61
resistance, dealing with in-house, 58–59
communicating with parents
about instructional program, 33, 70–71
about phonics, 101–3
about spelling, 117–19
about standardized testing, 142–43
about student self-evaluation, 158, 159, 161
about teaching practices, 70–71
effective communications, suggestions for, 15–16,
30, 34, 64, 68–72
inviting into classroom, 71, 102
research findings, communicating
on grammar, 120–21
on language learning, 68, 69
on phonics, 101
on spelling learning, 118
community of learners, classroom, 46, 53, 87, 175
competition, 46–47
comprehension. See higher-level thinking
conferences
parent, 142
student-led, 153–59
triangular, 153–59
conventions, teaching, 43, 88

Cooper, Linda, 68
core lists of words, 115–16
correctness, whole language instruction and, 44
Crider, Liz, 54
curriculum, negotiated, 47–48, 50

decoding. See phonics
deficit model, 141
Delpit, Lisa, 106
democracy, need to educate children about, 22, 143,
184
demographics, teachers and changing, 139–40
demonstration, 50
Diaz, David, 148
dilemma
defined, 124
other dilemmas, 124-43
direct instruction, not using term, 69
disabled readers, intensive phonics instruction and,
99–100
discipline, 46, 143
discussions of literature, importance of, 85
Distar program, 12, 69
Downs, Hugh, 11
Dreamkeepers, The: Successful Teachers of African American Children, 176
Driscoll, Jack, 13, 15
Dumbing Down Our Kids: Why America's Children Feel
Good About Themselves but Can't Read, Write, or
Add, 109

Eastin, Delaine, 19
Eaton, Harryette, 148
editing. See also writing
final drafts, 116–17
raising expectations through editing process, 113,
114, 118
education
bad news about, public interest in, 4
good news about, suppression of, 4
life long learning, 147
politics of. See politics of education
Educational Leadership, 172
Education Week, 70
educators. See also administrators; teachers
dealing with media, learning to, 13–15
getting message out, 15–16
"Elementary School Practices: Current Research on
Language Learning," 81
Englemann, Zig, 11, 13
English as a second language (ESL)
coordinating ESL and language arts programs, 33
more effective teaching of, need for, 23
population of ESL students, 21, 143
ESL students. See English as a second language
evaluation, 149–65
explicit instruction
in instructional program, 44, 85, 94, 133
use of term, 69

"Facts: On Teaching Skills in Context," 106, 199–202
"Facts: On the Teaching of Phonics," 101, 194–97
Fairfax County, Virginia
community support in, 30–31
successful practices, 31–33

Feinstein, Robyn, 133–34
fiction
    discussions, importance of, 85
    in reading instruction, use of, 82–83
    in whole language instruction, 48
    in writing instruction, 88
First Steps, 113
focus lesson, use of term, 69
Foundations of Literacy, The, 80
Fox, Mem, 170
Freeman, Mark, 79, 171
Frostburg State University, Maryland, whole language
    instruction at, 50–51
funding for education
    in California, 21
    lack of, 4
    libraries and cuts in, 127–28
    student achievement and, 23

Gardner, Howard, 173
Gardner, Susan, 97
Gentry, Richard, 7
"Getting Reform Right: What Works and What
    Doesn't," 56
goal setting, 48
Goldberg, Natalie, 184
Goodman, Ken, 80
Goodman, Yetta, 41
grammar
    in context, facts on teaching grammar, 201
    NCTE position on grammar exercises to teach
        speaking and writing, 187
    research findings, 120, 187
    suggestions for teaching, 120–21
    value of teaching, 119–20
Graves, Don, 88, 91
Grossman, Sherri, 135
grouping, 45, 50. *See also* reading
Groves, Delores, 79
guided silent reading, 85
"Guidelines for the Evaluation of Commercial Reading
    Programs," 101

handwriting
    educating parents about, 123
    parent concerns about, 70
    value of teaching, 121–23
Hayward, Chris, 72, 134–37, 138
higher-level thinking
    in reading instruction, 82, 140
    U.S. students and, 5–6
Hispanic students
    changing demographics and, 139
    quality education and, 140
    spelling instruction and, 106
    whole language and, 43
Holdaway, Don, 80, 100, 138–39
Hooked on Phonics program, 10

independent reading, 180, 188. *See also* choosing books
    to read
integrated curriculum, 70–71, 82–83, 138
interests, cultivating, 169–71
International Reading Association, 5
invented spelling, as loaded term, 69
    research on, 7

in perspective, 109–11
in Reading Recovery, 52
Invitations: Changing as Teachers and Learners K-12, 81,
    131, 137, 181
Iowa Test of Basic Skills (ITBS), 28

jargon-free language, using, 31, 69
Jarvie, Sherri, 68
Jeffus, Barbara, 127, 130
journals
    parents helping with, 72
    phonics instruction and, 95
    in writing instruction, 87

Kenny, Maeve, 13
Kibby, Michael, 82
Kimberly, Rebecca, 142
kindergarten, as metaphor for our schools, 164–65
Kohm, Barbara, 62
Kwanzaa and Me: A Teacher's Story, 176

Ladson-Billings, Gloria, 132, 163, 176
Landers, Ann, 4
language arts course of study, 157–58
Language Arts, 172
language learning
    environmental factors common to early readers,
        79–80
    research on, 80–81
    teaching reading, recommendations for, 82–86
    understanding, by looking at ourselves, 81–82
learning
    how humans learn, 81–82
    language. *See* language learning
learning centers, 45
learning disabled, benefits of phonics to, 100
Letter to Teachers, A, 169
Levin, Diane, 11, 19
Lewis, Shelly, 12, 13
librarians. *See* libraries
libraries
    classroom, importance of well-stocked, 84
    connection to achievement, 127
    inadequate, in California, 21
    preserving our, importance of, 127–28
    promoting quality, 128–30
library media specialist, 129
light reading, value of, 84
limited English proficient (LEP) students. *See* ESL stu-
    dents
literacy
    moving to new, 5–6
    myth of declining, in media, 4, 13–15
    raising the standards of, 142
literacy centers, 45
literacy life, leading the
    importance of, 166
    interests, cultivating, 169–71
    models for teaching, using literate selves as, 177–82
    professional development and learning, taking
        charge of, 171–77
    teacher-researcher, becoming a, 167–69
    writers, envisioning selves as, 182–84
literacy of thoughtfulness, 90
literature
    discussions, importance of, 85

in reading instruction, 82–83
in whole language instruction, 48
in writing instruction, 88
responding to, 180–82
Littleton, Colorado
back-to-basics backlash, 26–27
as educational leader, 25–27
lessons from, 27–30
parental concerns with instructional program, 26

Martin, Loretta, 39, 71, 94, 101, 203
materials
purchasing whole language, 44
teachers sharing, 175–76
Mazzarella, David, 149
Mc Callum, Ann, 33, 72, 130–31
McNally, Karen, 64–65
Mears, Susan, 70–71
media
declining literacy, myth of, 13–15
educators getting message out, 15–16
learning to deal with media, educators, 13–16
phonics and media hype, 10–13
media specialists, value of, 127, 128, 129
Meier, Deborah, 82, 164
mentors. See teachers
minilesson, not using term, 69
minority students
changing demographics and, 139
quality education and, 140
spelling instruction and, 106
whole language and, 43
Moats, Louisa Cook, 130
modeling. See also demonstration
reading discussion, 182
spelling errors and, 112–13
teaching behavior, 136, 138
in whole language instruction, 51, 136, 168–69
writing, 88, 113, 182, 183
Murray, Don, 14, 15–16, 183

narratives, evaluation using student written, 122, 159, 163
National Association of Educational Progress (NAEP)
in California, 6, 19
1992 National Writing Trend Assessment for Grades 4, 8, and 11, The, 119
reading assessment, 6, 88
spelling assessment, 8
National Council of Teachers of English, 5
Nation at Risk, A, 3
negotiated curriculum, 47–48, 50
Negotiating the Curriculum: Educating for the 21st Century, 47
Neilsen, Lorri, 165
New Advocate, The: For Those Involved with Young People and Their Literature, 172
Newman, Judith, 107
newsletters, communicating with parents through, 64–68, 118
newspapers. See also media
bad news in education, selling papers with, 4
getting message in, 15–16
nonfiction
discussions, importance of, 85

O'Connor, Flannery, 182
Ohio
Dept. of Education position on intensive phonics instruction, 96–97
intensive phonics instruction for teachers, push for, 96
onsets, 93
oral language skills, valuing, 106–7
oral reading
miscues, treatment of, 86
in whole language instruction, 83, 85
outcome-based education, as loaded term, 69

Paley, Vivian Gussin, 176
parents
change, involving parents in process of, 23, 25, 28, 34, 40, 61–62, 64–72
communication with. See communicating with parents
curriculum night for, 69
as decision makers, 28
instructional program made explicit to, 70–71
involvement in conferences, 153–59
opening classrooms to, 71–72
parental concerns
in Alief Independent School District, Texas, 24
attempting to understand, 30
in California, 19, 22
in Littleton, Colorado, 26–28
over grammar, 119
over spelling instruction, 109–11
over whole language, 37–38
phonics
helping parents keep in perspective, 92, 100–3
messages received about, 9–10
research information, sharing with parents. See communicating with parents
satisfaction with schools, 4
spelling instruction, anxiety over current, 109–11
volunteers, 72, 129
whole language programs
concerns of parents about, 37–38
parents as part of change to, 40
writing materials for, 33
Parents, Kids and Books (video), 101
Parents as Readers groups, 72
Parker, Dennis, 6
Pennac, Daniel, 173
performance-based assessment, in Littleton, CO, 25–26
Perrone, Vito, 169
Perry, Jeannine, 71
Peterson, Ralph, 46
Philbrook, John, 127
phonemic awareness, 94
phonics. See also parents
assessing, 95
commonsense views about, 93–96
defined, 92
in effective reading programs, 9, 92, 101, 103–4
explicit teaching of, 94–95
"Facts: On the Teaching of Phonics," 101, 194–97
intensive systematic phonics

as beneficial to disabled readers, 99–100
concerns, 96–99, 103
responding to supporters of, 101–3
workshop on, concerns after attending, 97–99
keeping in perspective, 101–4, 190–93
messages received by parents about, 9–10
research on, 92–93, 101, 103–4, 194–96, 199–200
"sounding it out" strategy, 92, 93
sound-symbol relationships, importance of, 93–94
teacher education about, 103, 130, 133
in "the good old days," 77–78
time on phonics vs. time spent reading, 96, 102
as tool, not end in itself, 92, 93, 103–4
and whole language, controversy over, 8–13, 37, 103–4
in whole language programs, 38, 101, 190, 192
writing instruction and, 95, 98
"Phonics Fuss: Facts, Fiction, Phonemes, and Fun," 100
Pinnell, Gay Su, 52–53
political, meaning of, xvi–xvii
politics of education
administrators, forming partnerships with, 62–64
change and. See change
committee process, using. See committee process
getting the message out, 15–16, 129
grammar instruction and the, 120–21
handwriting instruction and the, 120–21
intensive phonics instruction supporters, responding to, 100–3
media and. See media
parental involvement in process of change, 23, 25, 28, 34, 40, 61–62, 64–72
partnerships, forming, 62–72
promoting quality libraries, 128–30
spelling, communicating how we teach, 116, 117–19
teachers unions, working with, 63–64
writing from teachers in public debate, value of, 184–85
Popcorn, Faith, 29
Popcorn Report, The, 29
population changes. See demographics
portfolios, as force in moving to student-led conferencing, 153
Possible Lives, 164, 174
postcards for communicating with parents, use of, 68
Primary Voices, 172
principals. See administrators
product, 45
professional development. See also staff development; teacher education
professional reading, 137, 172–73, 177
spelling, 112–13
take responsibility for, 126, 132, 137, 171–77
proofreading, 121
published series. See basals

reading. See also guided silent reading; oral reading; shared reading
achievement, research on, 4–5
aloud, 83
attitude of one high school student about, 178–79
choice, 83, 84
choosing books, 83, 178–79, 180–81
goals, raising, 5–6
grouping, 45, 85, 86
increasing popularity of, 128

independent, 180, 188
instructional needs of U.S. students, 5–6
language learning and. See language learning
light reading, value of, 84
miscues, treatment of, 86
professional and personal for teachers, 172–73, 177
program, 48, 49, 134, 179–82
recording of books read, real world, 169
self-evaluation, 160, 178–79
strategies for unknown words, 197
teachers analyzing own preferences for use in classroom, 177–82
teaching, research recommendations for, 9, 82–86
in "the good old days," 77–78
time for, providing, 84, 96, 102
time on phonics vs. time spent reading, 96, 102
whole language and phonics, controversy over, 8–13
in whole language instruction, 49
Reading Recovery
in Fairfax County, Virginia, 32
under whole language umbrella, 52–53
"Reading Strategies for Unknown Words," 101
Reading Teacher, The, 172
reading-test reading, 141
reflection, 48
reform. See change
report cards, narrative, by students, 159, 163
research
on grammar instruction, 120
on how children learn to spell, 118
on language learning, 68, 70, 80–81
on phonics, 92–93, 103–4, 194–96, 199–200
on reading achievement, 4–5
sharing with parents. See communicating with parents
teacher-researcher, becoming a, 167–69
responsibility in whole language instruction, 46
revisions, realistic approach to, 88
Rimedio, Peg, 39, 87
rimes, 93
role-playing for new teachers, 138
Rose, Mike, 164, 174
rough drafts, creating expectations for, 113–15

SAT scores, 142
Sandia Report, The, 4
Schaefer, Joan, 69–70
school bashing, 3–8
school boards, getting message to, 16
school-centered decision making, 28
schools
bad news about, public interest in, 4
good news about, suppression of, 4
parents satisfaction with local, 4
Secretary of Labor's Commission on Achieving Necessary Skills (SCANS), 47
self-evaluation
narrative report cards written by students, 122, 159, 163
reading, 160
student-led conferences, 153–59
transition from traditional evaluation, 149, 152
in whole language instruction, 48, 50
Servis, Joan, 44, 68, 122, 159, 168, 171
Sesame Street, 10
shared reading

phonics and, 95
use of, 86
shared writing
editing in, 113, 115
phonics and, 95
use of, 88
Sher, Karen, 60, 171, 175
"Simplified Progression of Word Recognition Skill, A,"
100
Sizer, Theodore, 164, 173
skills. *See also* basic skills
in context, 105–7, 133, 199–202
instruction, 20, 49, 105–9
Slavin, Robert, 173
sloppy copy, 115
Smith, Frank, 80, 88, 105, 107
Smoky Night, 148–51
socialization, 46
"sounding it out" strategy, 92, 93. *See also* phonics
Speer, Barbara, 100
spelling
communicating how we teach spelling, 116, 117–19,
203
in context, facts on teaching spelling, 199–200
core lists of words, developing, 115–16
current state of spelling instruction, 6–9, 109–11,
126
expectations, 113–15, 117
invented spelling, as loaded term, 69. *See also*
invented spelling
misspellings, approach to, 110–11, 116
parental anxiety over instructional practices, 109–11
parents helping with, 72
phonics and, 8
program, 203
strategies, 118–19
successful teaching of, 111–17
Spillane, Robert, 32
Spohn, Laurie, 135, 138
staff development. *See also* professional development;
teacher education
in California, 19, 20, 21–23
in Fairfax County, Virginia, 32, 33
focusing training in reading on primary grades, 32
individuals taking charge of own professional development, 171–77
new teachers, support for, 132–38
whole language program, training needed for move
to, 38–40
standardized testing
dealing with, 92–93, 140–43
putting into perspective for parents, 142–43
standards, as loaded term, 69
Stokes, Bernice, 60
strategies, 49. *See also* reading; spelling
Strickland, Dorothy, 43
Student-Led Conferences, 159
student-led conferences, 153–59
students
encouraging smart students to become teachers,
131–32
higher-level thinking in U.S. students, 5–6
in parent-teacher conferences, 33
self-evaluation
student-led conferences, 153–59

students writing own narrative report cards, 159,
163
trusting, 169
support groups, teachers starting, 176–77
Sweet, Anne P., 103
Sykes, Charles J., 109
"Synthesis of Research on Teaching Writing," 120

Talking Points, 172
tape-recording conferences with children, 102
teacher education. *See also* professional development;
staff development
encouraging smart students to become teachers,
131–32
individuals taking charge of own learning, 171–77
state of, 130–31, 135
teacher-researcher, becoming a, 167–69, 185
teachers. *See also* educators
analyzing own reading preferences for use in classroom, 177–82
assessing the achievable, 108–9
collaboration, 175–77
collegial, being more, 173–75
demographic changes and, 139–40
education of. *See* professional development; staff
development; teacher education
encouraging smart students to become teachers,
131–32
good teachers, qualities of, 163–65
inadequate grounding in whole language, 36–37
literacy life, leading the. *See* literacy life, leading the
mentors, 138, 159, 175
modeling in whole language instruction, 51, 136
new teachers, support for, 132–38
opening classroom to parents, 71–72
ownership, creating, 56–57
philosophical differences with school district, dealing with, 29
political involvement of. *See* politics of education
professional and personal reading for, 172–73
sharing knowledge and materials, 175–76
successful teachers, qualities of, 163–65
support groups, teachers starting, 176–77
teaching practices explained to parents, 70–71
time for own reflection, writing, and action, teachers
making, 184–85
training. *See* professional development; staff development; teacher education
treating as professionals in Fairfax County, Virginia,
31
unions, value of forming partnerships with, 63–64
wisdom of practice, 165
writers as 182–85
Teachers as Readers groups, 72
teachers unions. *See* teachers; unions
teacher training. *See* professional development; staff
development; teacher education
teaching, defined, 107
Teaching PreK–8, 172
television at home
limiting use of, 84, 189
influence of, 14
20/20 television program, 11–13
Texas
Alief Independent School District

community questions about language arts program, 23–24
  lessons from, 25
  prescribed spelling program, return to, 8
Thelen, Judie, 49–51
three-way conferencing, 153–59
time
  reading time, providing, 84, 180
  reexamining traditional use of, 158
  teachers making time for own reflection, writing, and action, 184–85
  time on phonics vs. time spent reading, 96, 102
  whole language, time needed for move to, 38–40
  writing time, making, 87
Title I
  coordinating language arts program with, 33
  programs, 52
"Toward an Educationally Relevant Theory of Literacy Learning: Twenty Years of Inquiry," 80
Transitions, story of, 78
Treadway, Jerry, 131
triangular conferencing, 153–59

unions, value of forming partnerships with, 63–64.
unknown words, reading strategies for, 198
USA Today
  phonics/whole language article, 10
  students writing to editors of, 149, 150, 151

video games at home, limiting use of, 189
videos, getting message out with, 16
Virginia, Fairfax County
  community support in, 30–31
  successful practices, 31–33
Voices from the Middle, 172
volunteers, valuable experiences for, 72, 129

Wallis, Judy, 25, 49, 141
weekly review, 190–91
Weltman, Rosemary, 135–36
whole language
  beliefs about, 42
  change process, 38–40
  defining, 41–42
  dissenting voices within, 35, 51–53
  in effective reading program, 9
  empowerment in whole language classrooms, 147–48
  evaluation in whole language classrooms. See assessment; self-evaluation
  materials, purchasing, 44
  misconceptions. See whole language, misinterpreting
  misinterpreting, 36–37, 42–45, 51
  moving toward, 152
  parental concerns about, 37–38
  parents as part of switch to, 40
  and phonics, controversy over, 8–13
  phonics in, 38
  place of, in educational program, 38
  principles and practices, key, 45–49
  Reading Recovery and, 52–53
  as scapegoat for educational problems, 35
  support groups for teachers, 176–77
  support needed for move to, 38–40
  time needed for move to, 38–40
  university model of instruction, 49–51
Whole Story, The, 80
Wilde, Sandra, 7, 8, 112
"Will Our Schools Ever Get Better?" (Business Week), 4
Wonderfully Exciting Books (WEB)
  encouraging independent reading at home, 188
  log, 168–69
writing. See also communicating with parents; editing; journals; shared writing; spelling
  choice with intention, 148–49
  conventions, teaching, 43, 88
  final copy, expectations for, 116–17
  grammar lessons to teach writing, NCTE position on, 187
  handwriting, 121–23
  language learning. See language learning
  letter, persuasive, 149–51
  modeling, 87, 88, 183
  narrative report cards, 159, 161–64
  need for teacher to write, 183–84
  newsletter to parents, 64–65
  phonics instruction during writing time, 95–96
  raising expectations, 116–19
  record, 88, 118
  revisions, realistic approach to, 88
  rough drafts, creating expectations for, 114–15
  teachers envisioning selves as writers, 183–85
  teaching, recommendations for, 86–88
  in "the good old days," 77–78
  time for, making, 87
  topics, choosing, 87, 88
  in whole language instruction, 49
Writing Down the Bones: Freeing the Writer Within, 184
writing to learn, 183

Yankelovich, Daniel, 29
Young, Danny, 122